INTERNATIONAL RELATIONS
AND HISTORICAL SOCIOLOGY

The last decade saw a revival of interest in historical approaches to the understanding of International Relations. Concurrently, historical sociologists have demonstrated a renewed interest in the idea of the state and attempted to include the notion of an international system in their work. This confluence of interests between International Relations theorists who seek to understand large-scale social processes and historical sociologists who are looking to international forces in order to analyse developments in the state, is deftly addressed and explored in the present volume.

Stephen Hobden provides an original analysis of recent work by key historical sociologists through the prism of International Relations. He investigates the number of issues which overlap between the two disciplines by focusing on three main themes: the ways in which historical sociologists approach International Relations in general and the concept of an international system in particular; recent advances in the concept of the state as developed by Historical Sociology and their implications for International Relations; and the potential for productive dialogue between the two schools of thought.

An important addition to the theoretical literature on International Relations, this volume will also be of interest to students and researchers in the areas of Sociology, Social History and International Political Theory.

Stephen Hobden is Lecturer in the Department of International Politics at the University of Wales, Aberystwyth. His research and teaching interests include International Political Theory, International Politics of Latin America and the United Nations.

ROUTLEDGE ADVANCES IN INTERNATIONAL RELATIONS AND POLITICS

INTERNATIONAL RELATIONS AND HISTORICAL SOCIOLOGY

Breaking down boundaries

Stephen Hobden

London and New York

First published 1998
by Routledge
11 New Fetter Lane, London EC4P 4EE

Simultaneously published in the USA and Canada
by Routledge
29 West 35th Street, New York, NY 10001

Typeset in Garamond by Routledge
Printed and bound in Great Britain by Clays Ltd, St Ives PLC

British Library Cataloguing in Publication Data
A catalogue record for this book is available from the British Library

Library of Congress Cataloging in Publication Data
Hobden, Stephen, 1956–
International relations and historical sociology: breaking down
boundaries/Stephen Hobden.
p. cm. – (Routledge advances in international relations and
politics; 5)
Includes bibliographical references and index.
1. International relations. 2. Historical sociology. I. Title.
II. Series.

JZ1251.H63 1998

327.1'01–dc21

98–18070
CIP

ISBN 0–415–18539–4

CONTENTS

CONTENTS

ACKNOWLEDGEMENTS

Writing this book has been a surprisingly communal and convivial affair that has brought me into contact with a number of people. This page gives me the opportunity to acknowledge the considerable debt that I owe to friends and colleagues.

First of all I want to express my gratitude to the people who, for various reasons, have read and commented on one or another of the complete drafts: Sarah Cohen, John Hobson, Richard Little, Jan Aart Scholte, Steve Smith and the referees from Routledge. Their advice (when I have been sensible enough to follow it) has strengthened the book considerably.

I also want to take this opportunity to thank Steve Smith for all his personal support over the last eight years, and for his tireless efforts to make the Department at Aberystwyth the supportive, challenging and exciting place to work that it is. Some debts are not repayable!

A lot of people have read and commented, directly and indirectly, on drafts of parts of the text. I would like to thank them all, especially Michael Barnett, Rodney Bruce-Hall, John Cameron, Susie Carruthers, Tim Dunne, Jennifer Edkins, Michael Mann, Dominic Marner, Nalini Persram, Véronique Pin-Fat, Justin Rosenberg, Martin Shaw, Theda Skocpol, Charles Tilly, Roger Tooze, Nick Wheeler and Marysia Zalewski. I would also like to express my gratitude to the people who made comments or asked questions at the seminars, panels and workshops where I have tried out some of the ideas.

I would like to thank all my friends and colleagues in the Department of International Politics, University of Wales, Aberystwyth, for their very kind support and encouragement.

I have come into contact with a number of undergraduates over the past five years and I would like to thank them: first for showing an interest in the particular area of International Political Theory into which I had wandered; and second for asking 'Haven't you finished yet?' – which has proved a great incentive to get on with it.

All the staff in the Hugh Owen library also deserve my gratitude for their help, especially those in the Periodicals and Inter-Library Loan departments.

I acknowledge the considerable financial support given to me by the

ACKNOWLEDGEMENTS

University of Wales. The first two years of study were made possible through a University of Wales Scholarship. Since then I have been employed by the Department of International Politics.

Finally, I would like to thank my editors at Routledge, Victoria Smith, Steven Jarman, Andy Soutter and Simon Wilson, for their contribution to getting this book into print.

1

INTRODUCTION

A 'historical turn' in International Relations?

An intense debate between contending approaches to the understanding of world politics has characterised the theoretical scene in International Relations[1] since the late 1980s. Various reasons can be proposed to explain this theoretical ferment: a 'linguistic turn' in many of the social sciences; dissatisfaction with the positivist approaches that have been dominant in the discipline; or a reaction to the rise of social movements concerned with sexism, racism and the environment. A further factor contributing to this intellectual tumult is the scale of the changes that have happened worldwide over the past decade. These have included the end of the Cold War, the collapse of the Soviet Union, the apparent discrediting of Marxism, and the impacts of globalisation. It is hard to argue with the view that 'international theorists are now condemned to live in interesting times' (Smith, S. 1992: 490). The dominant theoretical framework of the discipline, Realism, has been singularly unsuccessful in offering guidance to explain these global developments. As a result there has been a splintering of the discipline. Although many have retained their loyalty to Realism (arguing that, despite its weaknesses, Realism still provides the best explanation of the 'core' issues of international politics, war and peace), others have sought alternatives.

Since the 1980s alternative approaches to International Relations theory have become more vocal. Such approaches have challenged the notion of what constitutes the core of the discipline, and the way in which it should be studied. Some have argued that the study of international politics alone is not sufficient, and must be combined with the study of international economic relations. This has led to a flourishing of the field of International Political Economy. Some have pointed to the gender bias of traditional International Relations theory and have sought to challenge the discipline using the many insights of feminist theorising. Some have sought to employ a revitalised Marxist approach based on the Frankfurt School to produce a Critical Theory of International Relations.

There have been other more direct reactions to the scale of changes occurring on the global scene. One reaction to the environment of uncertainty that prevails following the immutability of the Cold War period has been the

1

rejection, by some theorists, of the view that there can be any foundations to knowledge. Many have become sceptical that grand theory can explain much. Indeed, they argue, it can actually reinforce an existing and unjust world (George 1994: Ch. 3).

For others there has been a turn to History, in particular to those approaches to History that seek to understand large-scale social change. For example, Scholte (1993a) has called for a change of emphasis in International Relations from the study of power politics to the study of social change. Linklater (1990) has outlined a historical and sociological project that will go 'beyond Realism and Marxism'. Booth (1996: 335) has argued that the study of Global-Macro History may lead to 'insights into the meanings of the present and prospects for the future'. Puchala (1995) has welcomed the renewed interest in what he calls the History of International Relations, and Little (1994: 9) has pointed to 'an important convergence of interest in recent years between students of International Relations and students of large-scale historical change.'

Much of this interest in the study of large-scale historical and social change has focused on a group of writers working in a different disciplinary area, but concerned with a similar range of issues. These writers, generally known as historical sociologists, are part of a long tradition of philosophers and historians who have sought to reveal patterns and structures in human history. The recent work by historical sociologists has received recognition in International Relations primarily because of their renewed interest in the development of the state. This work has resulted in a different notion of the state than that employed traditionally in International Relations. Recent work in Historical Sociology has developed Weberian notions of the state, seeing it as a set of institutions that claim precedence over a particular territorial area. Furthermore, a key advance in the recent work of historical sociologists has been the locating of their analysis of the state within an international system. Traditional Sociology has been concerned with social relations within one society (usually within the boundaries of a particular country). More recent work has moved away from regarding societies as discrete units. Sociologists have become increasingly interested in examining the impact that multiple societies have on each other. To do this they have sought to analyse international impacts on social development.

Hence a core feature of recent work in Historical Sociology has been an interest in the notions 'international system' and 'state'. Both of these concepts are central to International Relations. The foundation of much International Relations theory has been the state. States are seen to comprise international systems. Hence, as the quotation from Little indicated, there are overlapping interests between the two disciplines, or, at least, a potential for dialogue. My purpose in this book is to assess the character of this overlap and potential dialogue. Does the possibility exist for a fruitful exchange of ideas between the two disciplines? Alternatively, when the two approaches invoke the notions of international system and state, are they employing radically different concepts? My aim is to explore these points by answering questions concentrated around three main issues:

The international system How is the international system theorised in Historical Sociology? Have there been problems with the way in which historical sociologists have used this concept? Can International Relations theorists gain anything from this approach?

The state Can the approaches to the state developed by historical sociologists be transferred to International Relations theory? More specifically, can it contribute to Neorealism, which has been criticised for its lack of a theory of the state?

The relationship between Historical Sociology and International Relations How can the relationship between Historical Sociology and International Relations be described? Does it provide a 'second agenda', a 'challenge', or, because of its state-centred approach and concentration on war, does it provide grounds for the reinforcement of Realism?

The remainder of this first chapter provides an introduction to these issues.

HISTORICAL SOCIOLOGY AND INTERNATIONAL RELATIONS: SECOND AGENDA, CHALLENGE OR REALISM REINFORCED?

There is considerable dispute over the meaning of the term 'Historical Sociology'. A full definition of 'Historical Sociology', and a discussion of the problems involved in a study of the social world that aims to be both historical and sociological, will be left for the next chapter. For our current purposes, Skocpol's definition of Historical Sociology will be sufficient. She (1984: 4) describes it as 'a continuing, ever-renewed tradition of research devoted to understanding the character and effects of large-scale structures and fundamental processes of change'. The implication from this definition is that Historical Sociology concerns the analysis of social change over a broad perspective. It is distinct from 'traditional' Sociology because of its prime concern with change and historical context. It is distinct from 'traditional' History because of its concern with social structures rather than recounting the stories of individuals and describing events. Alternative disciplinary labels that give an idea of what historical sociologists do are 'Macro-sociology' or 'Structural History'. The first stresses the abstract level of analysis undertaken. The second stresses the dimensions of change and time, and the attempt to historicise social formations.

That there has been an increased interest in Historical Sociology over the last few years can be demonstrated by two factors: a large number of references made to the works of historical sociologists such as Skocpol, Tilly, Mann and Wallerstein in articles and books; and the development of approaches to the study of international relations which are attempting to combine a theoretical approach with a historical framework. References to works by historical sociologists have appeared in articles from across the range of International Relations Journals from *Alternatives* to *International Studies Quarterly*. The element in the work of specific historical sociologists that has generated particular interest in International Relations is their renewed interest in the analysis of the state. Much of the recent work in Historical Sociology has been concerned with 'bringing the state back in'.[2]

The notion of the state is a central concern of International Relations. Indeed for realist approaches it is the foundation of the discipline. However, International Relations theorists have lacked a certain 'curiosity' about how this central element of their discipline is constituted. Despite being a focal point, the state is surprisingly under-theorised. The state is usually conceived as being a territorial area together with everything that is contained within it. For example, when referring to the Spanish state, what is meant is the equivalent of what appears on a map – the land that is enclosed by what is known as the Spanish borders, and everything contained within that territory: the government, the population, the military, and the natural resources. This kind of approach to the state is typified by this definition from Fred Northedge:

> A state . . . is a territorial association of people recognized for purposes of law and diplomacy as a legally equal member of the system of states. It is in reality a means of organizing people for the purpose of their participation in the international system.
>
> (Northedge 1976: 15)

The key term in this definition is 'territorial association of people'. Compared with this view of the state, historical sociologists tend to stress an institutional definition. This entails a much more limited view of the state. For most historical sociologists the state does not denote a territorial and social totality, but rather a limited set of institutions with coercive powers. It is not equal to a particular territory, but makes a claim to control that area. This set of institutions not only has to compete for resources with other groups within a territorial area, but also with other actors in different territorial areas. In other words, the typical International Relations definition of the state is territorially based, while the Historical Sociology definition is based upon institutions. Historical Sociology purports to provide accounts not only of what the state comprises, but also of how states develop and change. The major reviews of the Historical Sociology literature by International Relations scholars have concentrated on this aspect of their work. They have also discussed the implications of such an approach for the study of international relations.

Fred Halliday (1987) has argued that the approach to the state in Historical Sociology provides a 'second agenda' for International Relations. Halliday draws a contrast between traditional realist views of the state as an abstract social/territorial entity and the Historical Sociology approach that sees the state as a centralised grouping of coercive and administrative institutions. For historical sociologists, states, societies and governments are viewed as separate but interconnected social formations. Halliday cites some examples of the differences that might illustrate these two approaches:

> In discussing land, we distinguish between the territory of the state, in its total sense, and the areas of land owned by the state, in its institutional sense. Similarly we distinguish between the population or working population of a state, and the percentage of that population who are directly employed by the state. In revolutions the institutional state is overthrown, but the total state remains.
>
> (*ibid.*: 218–19)

One particular problem with the realist approach is that it prejudges the character of non-state actors. These are seen as subsidiary to the state and constrained within territorial limits. By contrast, the approach to the state in Historical Sociology generates the possibility of a much wider agenda for International Relations. It opens the possibility of discussing the state, both as an actor in competition with other domestic social formations, and in terms of its relations with other states and with other actors in different territories. It also becomes possible to examine the ways in which states manipulate their non-domestic activities as a means of strengthening their position internally. Furthermore, by separating state and society, it becomes easier to theorise how non-state actors operate regarding their international interests. At times they may act counter to the foreign policy of the state. For example, when companies export to countries against which their home government has implemented sanctions. Alternatively, domestic groups who consider that their interests have been threatened may pressurise the state to take action against other states. Historical Sociology, argues Halliday, provides a second agenda for International Relations because by providing a view of the state as a set of institutions, it opens up a much wider set of parameters within which theorising can take place.

Adopting a similar viewpoint to Halliday, Jarvis has suggested that the approach to the state in Historical Sociology provides a challenge which International Relations needs to address. The notion of the state is central to International Relations. 'International Relations is about states and the system of states' (Jarvis 1989: 281). However, realist, interdependency and dependency writers have all depicted the state as a derivative of the international system. Realists see the state primarily in terms of its political and strategic relationships with other states. There is no attempt to analyse the state with regard to its domestic situation. Interdependency writers, conversely, do consider domestic relations. In contrast to realist writers, the state is not viewed as a unitary actor, but as one actor amongst many, having to balance both internal and external concerns. However, although this provides a wider concept of the state than that provided by Realism, Jarvis argues that it is still an under-theorised account. 'This is because while seeming to suggest the operation of a logic of economic interdependency it still uses a theory of the state insufficiently distanced from its conceptual origins in the dynamic of the system of states' (*ibid.*: 282). In other words, the state is still viewed as primarily a product of international relations. With its class-based analysis, Dependency Theory, Jarvis argues, provides a potentially promising research avenue. In this kind of analysis state development is seen as a function of the international economy and class relations. This is an improvement on realist and interdependency approaches, but because it privileges social and economic factors, it still leaves much unexplained in terms of state action (for example, requirements to maintain military security).

In comparison, Jarvis argues, the kinds of approaches to the state being developed by historical sociologists provide a better 'fit' in the theorising of societies, states and geopolitics. This is primarily for two reasons. First, because of the multi-causal logic which historical sociologists apply, no one element in the relationship between states, societies and geopolitics is seen as dominant. International Relations theorists tend to see geopolitical relations between states as the primary factor in state development. In contrast, recent work by historical sociologists sees multiple logics at work. Additionally, the significance of these multiple logics varies historically. At different times one or more of the influences between society, state and geopolitics have been of greater importance than others. Historical Sociology, Jarvis argues, provides a challenge to International Relations because it provides 'a number of convincing accounts, theoretical and historical, of how such a fit might exist; not only as a general account but one sensible to variance in such relationships' (*ibid.*: 283).

Hobson is similarly critical of the 'reductionist' approaches adopted by International Relations scholars. In their own ways, he suggests, both Neorealism and Marxism are 'billiard ball theories of history' (Hobson 1994: 4). For Waltz it is the clash of undifferentiated states that is the source of the international system, whilst for Marx it is class conflict that is the motor for history. In both approaches the state becomes 'a passive bearer of external structures' (*ibid.*). The state is seen as a product of external structures rather than as having significance in its own right:

> There really is no room for power forces other than the structures of
> the mode of production (Marxism) or the international system of

states (Neorealism) to make an impression in the overall development of history. Attempts to bring in additional variables are
immediately dismissed as either 'bourgeois' (Marx) or as 'reductionist' (Waltz).

(*ibid.*)

To redress the reductionism of Neorealism and Marxism, Hobson proposes an
approach to the study of international relations based on six principles derived
from the insights being produced by historical sociologists (Hobson 1998).
Such an approach would include six main elements (Hobson 1994: 5):

1   An account of the state which Hobson describes as 'neo-statist'. This
    includes seeing the state as a causal variable, capable, with other forces,
    of shaping both domestic and international space.
2   A multi-logic approach, which is not reducible to any one factor.
3   A view of space as overlapping, with no clear boundaries between the
    international, national and sub-national.
4   A more developed view of power. Rather than power being considered
    as purely zero-sum, it is possible to analyse power as positive-sum, nega-
    tive-sum, or zero-sum.
5   A view of time as discontinuous, rather than continuous.
6   A view of the autonomy of actors as being always partial rather than
    potential, relative or absolute.

The prime aim is to remedy the neglect shown by Neorealism and Marxism
to the issues of states, power, space and time.

Halliday, Jarvis and Hobson all suggest that Historical Sociology
provides a more developed approach to the state than is available within
International Relations. The notion of state used by realists is too abstract to
be of any use except in the most limited of theorising. As Jarvis (1989: 283)
comments, 'we now expect the discipline . . . to do much more than simply
give an account of the interaction of states in the system of states'. The
approach to the state from Historical Sociology provides a way to extend the
theorising possible in International Relations. This is because it opens the
possibility of theorising much more extensively across the fields of state,
society and geopolitics.

The significance in this difference of emphasis is that the traditional
International Relations definition only permits the analysis of relations
between states. Other international actors are subordinated to the state as a
result of the territorial-based model. What goes on inside the state does not
matter. Agnew (1994) warns that this approach to the state leads
International Relations into a 'territorial trap'. This trap privileges relations
between states internationally over any other actors. Furthermore, it makes
it more difficult to assess the impact of changes within a society on wider

international relations. Historical Sociology opens up the 'state', and allows for the analysis of a much greater number of actors and their interrelations. Historical Sociology sees no dichotomy between domestic and international realms, and this provides part of its attraction for International Relations scholars. Although Waltz argues that internal and external politics should be analysed separately, he did suggest that it might be possible to develop an approach that integrated both realms (Waltz 1986: 340). Historical Sociology could provide just such a means. Historical sociologists view the social world as a totality. There is no dichotomy between a domestic and an international realm. There are not separate sets of social relations active in the international sphere. This therefore opens up a greater possibility for producing an all-encompassing theory rather than separate theories for domestic and international politics.

There is a long tradition of historical sociology approaches in International Relations. In recent years this trend has become even more apparent. Writers such as Rosenberg, Spruyt, Thomson, Hobson, and Ferguson and Mansbach are addressing issues such as state formation, state development and state–system relations. Furthermore, they are employing historical works as a primary source for their research. These writers are developing the agenda that Historical Sociology has been setting, but from within the International Relations discipline. For example, Spruyt is very heavily influenced by Tilly's work, though he seeks to refute Tilly's explanation of state development. Ferguson and Mansbach's work on polities draws on Mann's notions of cross-cutting and overlapping social formations.

Although the work of Historical Sociology has been well received by some writers within International Relations, others have been more sceptical. Some writers argue that it is far too heavily influenced by Realism. Navari is critical of the use of Hintze and Weber in the production of the *Machtstaat* version of the state in the work of historical sociologists such as Skocpol and Wallerstein. Navari (1991: 8) argues that 'Skocpol's theory is a perfectly machiavellian formulation'. This is on account, she claims, of Skocpol's view of the state as a semi-autonomous actor, insulated to a degree from the rest of the society. This degree of autonomy allows 'the rational calculations of advantage, together with the ability to will one's own will and not the will of others' (*ibid.*). Navari claims that Skocpol has replaced domestic constraints on state action with external ones (*ibid.*: 10).

Scholte acknowledges the contribution made by historical sociologists, in that they have argued that societies cannot be viewed as self-contained totalities. Additionally, they have done much to demonstrate the impact of the international system on social developments. However, he argues that the direction some have taken is too state-centric. He argues that reliance on realist views of relations between states has lead the work of historical sociologists such as Michael Mann 'into a cul-de-sac' (Scholte 1993b: 23).

Both Scholte and Navari argue that the influence of Realism on recent

Historical Sociology writings is a reason for being sceptical about the work of Tilly, Skocpol and Mann. Buzan propounds a somewhat different view. He argues that the work of Historical Sociology on the state confirms Realism's claim to a 'timeless wisdom':

> In what amounts to an unintentional thought experiment, several historical sociologists writing macro-historical studies have come to analytical conclusions remarkably similar to a rather crude view of classical Realism. Few of these writers had much awareness of the Realist tradition in International Relations, yet all focus on war as crucial to the evolution of the modern state. . . . The result of their enquiries has been to support a harsh, social darwinistic, interpretation *that shares much with the main assumptions of realism.*
>
> (Buzan 1996: 60, my emphasis)

Buzan is suggesting that, even though historical sociologists have a different set of starting assumptions, in their study of the state and the international system they have ended up with a set of conclusions that are remarkably close to those of Realism. Buzan suggests that the kind of Realism that they have developed is of a rather unrefined type. If this is the case then it would be counter to the view that Historical Sociology has much to offer as an alternative approach to International Relations.

Hence there have been a variety of reactions to the Historical Sociology literature from International Relations. Those International Relations writers who have considered the work of historical sociologists have directed their main attention towards the alternative analysis of the state offered. It has been suggested that this alternative view of the state contributes a 'second agenda' for International Relations, or even a 'challenge'. Hobson argues that an engagement with Historical Sociology will allow an escape from the 'iron cage of reductionism' in International Relations theory. This reductionism results from either the reification of the state in Neorealism or the reification of class in Marxism (Hobson 1994: 23). For some, however, the approach offers little more than a restatement of Realism, and hence has little to offer. One of the aims of this book is to enter into this debate about the value of the Historical Sociology literature. This will be achieved through a discussion of some of the core writers in recent Historical Sociology literature. The next section outlines the main themes to be considered.

THE PURPOSE OF THIS BOOK

Reviews of the Historical Sociology literature by International Relations scholars have concentrated primarily on its analysis of the state. There has been less discussion of a further element of the recent writing in Historical

Sociology: an attempt to locate the analysis of the state within the framework of an international system. A key factor in recent sociological writing has been to move the focus of analysis away from single societies. The intention is to show how social developments are affected both by relations within and between societies. Several historical sociologists refer to an 'international system' or some equivalent, and employ it as a variable for explaining social change. However, so far, little attempt has been made to examine exactly what they mean. The central purpose of this book is to provide just such an analysis, and the core endeavour is to examine how four contemporary historical sociologists conceptualise the international environment in their writings.

The notion of an international system has been a focal point for many International Relations scholars. There have been various attempts to theorise what an international system might comprise, and what impact it might have on the prime actors, namely states. The most significant attempt to produce a systemic theory is that developed by Kenneth Waltz, which has been elevated to the core paradigm of the discipline – Neorealism. There is much that an examination of Waltz's work can reveal about the character of systemic theorising and its strengths and weaknesses. Waltz's systemic theory provides a benchmark against which other approaches can be compared.

Waltz's approach to systems theorising also opens a second line of enquiry. Waltz's work has been criticised for its inability to explain change. Waltz's central argument is that the international system heavily influences the behaviour of states. Different sorts of system will lead to different forms of behaviour from states. For example, Waltz argues that the behaviour of states in a bipolar system will be different from those in a multipolar system. However, Waltz's theory is generally regarded as being static. It offers no explanation of how change within a system (e.g. from bipolar to multipolar) could come about, nor how one type of system (an anarchic one) could be replaced by another (a hierarchic one). Most critics of Waltz account for this inability to explain change by pointing to Waltz's lack of a theory of the state. For Waltz, states are functionally undifferentiated, and for this reason the constitution of the state is not theorised further in his analysis. Various writers have suggested that the inclusion of a theory of the state into Neorealism would provide the capability of explaining change. Hence the second issue to be addressed is whether the theories of the state provided by Historical Sociology could overcome this perceived shortcoming in Neorealism. Historical Sociology provides a theory of the state, as has been noted by various International Relations writers. This approach aims to place state development within an international context. We will examine whether such a means of theorising the state can be combined with the neorealist view of the international system in order to provide Neorealism with a means of explaining change.

Recent writings in Historical Sociology have been concerned with two core concepts of International Relations: the state and the international system. This implies that a dialogue between Historical Sociology and International Relations could prove fruitful. The third aim of the book is therefore to examine the potential relationship between two ways of theorising international relations. Does Historical Sociology provide a challenge to International Relations? Does the multi-logic approach to understanding the social world, employed by writers such as Mann, offer an improvement on the mono-causal accounts advanced by Neorealism and Marxism? Does Historical Sociology in effect swallow International Relations whole through its attempt to theorise the social world as a totality? Alternatively, does the theory of the state offered by Historical Sociology suggest a new agenda for International Relations? Does it provide a means of adding a theory of the state to those approaches in International Relations that lack one? Does such a theory of the state open new avenues for investigation? By contrast, if writers such as Navari, Scholte and Buzan are correct, that the work of writers such as Tilly, Skocpol and Mann does little but reformulate Realism in its treatment of the state and the international system, then perhaps it could be concluded that it has little to offer. The final intention is to consider these positions and to suggest to what extent a dialogue between Historical Sociology and International Relations could prove valuable.

OUTLINE OF THE BOOK

The structure of the book is as follows:

The next chapter, Chapter 2, provides an introduction to Historical Sociology. It will attempt to define Historical Sociology, and to consider what historical sociologists do. To help clarify the definition there will be a discussion of the development of the discipline, and the work of some of the exemplars of this tradition will be outlined. The writers who have recently generated so much interest within International Relations follow on from a very long tradition of writers and thinkers who have sought to understand large-scale social change. This introduction will provide a context for appreciating the more recent work of the writers considered in this book.

Having considered the development of Historical Sociology, we will turn our attention towards International Relations. Chapter 3 examines how the international system, a core concept for the discipline, has been theorised. As Buzan and Little (1994) have suggested, there are many ways that the international system is conceived within International Relations. Not surprisingly, it will be discovered that there have been many different attempts to grapple with this central notion. The chapter will briefly summarise some of these approaches, before turning attention to its main focus, the work of Kenneth Waltz. Waltz's Neorealism develops from a tradition of theorising that can be traced back through the work of writers such as Morgenthau, Kaplan and Rosecrance. Waltz's key move is to abstract the international system from all other social phenomena as a way of analysing the forces at work in the international realm. This has provided him with a theory that is very parsimonious. However, a trade-off of this parsimonious approach is the charge that Neorealism actually explains very little. In particular, there seems no way that Waltz can analyse change in a system (e.g. the end of the Cold War), let alone change of a system (the transition from the feudal period to the modern era of the sovereign state). Several writers have suggested that the weakness of Neorealism lies in its lack of interest in the state. The definition of the state employed by Waltz is like the traditional realist approach, seeing it as a unitary, territorial actor. Some writers have suggested that by extending the analysis of the state Neorealism might provide the basis for a more wide-ranging theory of international politics. This chapter will provide a benchmark example of how the concept of the international system has been theorised in International Relations. It will suggest the strengths and weaknesses of Waltz's approach and will prepare the ground for considering how a theory of the state, derived from Historical Sociology, could be included in Neorealism.

The subsequent four chapters look at the historical sociologists being considered in this book: Theda Skocpol, Charles Tilly, Michael Mann and Immanuel Wallerstein. Each of these chapters employs a similar pattern of analysis. First the broad body of their work will be discussed. Second, there will be a review of the way in which their work has been received. Finally, each chapter will provide an appreciation of the way in which the specific writer approaches the notion of an international system. The intention of each of these chapters is to provide a brief introduction to the work of each of these writers and to supply a more in-depth discussion of the way in which they address the issue of the state and the international environment. These four chapters will provide the basis for answering our core questions.

Skocpol's work provides an accessible way into the type of analysis of the state provided by historical sociologists. A clear theoretical statement at the beginning of her book *States and Social Revolutions* aims to provide a theory of the state and of the international system. Her view of the international system appears to combine political and economic structures. But she is unable to sustain this in her empirical analysis. Here, the international system becomes little more than the occurrence of international war. Her more recent work on the development of the United States' social system does not incorporate an international element – perhaps reflecting her failure to sustain this factor in her previous work.

Tilly's main contribution to the debate is his analysis of the development of the state. Initially he saw a close link between the state and its involvement in war fighting: war made the state and the state made war. His more recent work has become more sophisticated. He has tried to analyse why a particular form of the state has become globally dominant, from the vast array of different social formations that existed 1,000 years ago. Two views of the international system underlie his account of the development of the state: one as an anarchic realm; the other as a web of social practices. So far he has failed to untangle these two accounts or to discuss the relationships between them.

Mann's work is the most ambitious of the four historical sociologists considered. He appears reluctant to use the term 'international system', though he does argue that geopolitical space has been crucial for the development of social formations such as classes, and the state. However, untangling the way that he analyses geopolitical space or the way that it influences social development is complicated by the apparent four different views of the international environment at work in his analysis. These represent different epistemological and ontological assumptions. The attempt to combine them results in a lack of clarity as to how Mann envisages international influences on social development.

Wallerstein's work comes as a complete contrast to the works of the three historical sociologists considered in the previous chapters, and is included for that reason. His work represents the attempt to produce a systemic theory, though produced from a Historical Sociology background. Wallerstein's modern-world system is a more systemic account of international relations than Waltz's Neorealism. However, this comes at a high price: economic determinism and an insubstantial analysis of the state.

The choice of authors examined in this book is clearly selective, and there are a number of other writers whose work could have been discussed. Skocpol, Tilly, Mann and Wallerstein have been selected to give an indication of the type of work being conducted by historical sociologists, and my intention is to be illustrative rather than comprehensive. A feature of these four writers is their very different points of departure. Skocpol is concerned with developing a structural explanation of revolution. Tilly seeks to understand state development over a wide historical canvas. Mann's project is to analyse the workings of social power throughout the course of human history. Wallerstein provides an account of the workings of a global economic system. Despite these varied starting points, these authors do have several points in common:

- All four pay a high level of attention to international factors in their analyses.
- Their writings draw heavily on the work of historians. It is the work of historical sociologists rather than sociologists. In other words, these writers are interested in how social structures and institutions change over time.

- Their work has generated a high level of interest among International Relations theorists.
- All four are contemporary authors. Two of them (Mann and Wallerstein) are in the process of completing large multi-volume works, in which international influences comprise a central role.
- Finally, each has produced a substantial body of work from which an analysis can take place.

The concluding chapter, Chapter 8, will bring the various strands of the discussion together. The chapter will summarise the analysis of the historical sociologists discussed in Chapters 4–7. It will examine some of the problems with the approach to the international system that have been highlighted. It will also evaluate whether International Relations theorists have anything to learn from the approach to international relations that these writers take. It will then assess the possibility of combining the notion of the state from Historical Sociology with the systemic approach of Neorealism. It will discuss what advantages might be gained from such a merger, and appraises the epistemological and ontological issues involved. The chapter will pose the question of whether such a union would provide a theory based on the strengths of the two approaches, or whether it would highlight weaknesses that undermine either or both. Finally, the relationship between Historical Sociology and International Relations will be discussed.

The main conclusions of the book are as follows:

- That there are serious weaknesses in the ways in which historical sociologists have attempted to locate their analyses of states within a framework of an international system.
- Despite this problem, the work of historical sociologists opens up a range of avenues for International Relations theorists to follow, in particular the institutional approach to the state, and the study of historical structures.
- That there are serious problems with trying to combine a neorealist approach to international systems with a theory of the state derived from Historical Sociology. Such an attempt highlights the weaknesses inherent in neorealist theorising.
- That an approach to the study of international systems needs to be developed which matches the depth of the work of historical sociologists on the state. As the term 'international system' holds many connotations, the study of 'global structures' might be a more apt description of this undertaking.

Having outlined the structure of the book, it might be useful to assess some of the difficulties with the type of analysis that is being undertaken here. This book examines the way that theorists in different disciplines have looked at the concepts of international system and state. We will achieve this by examining the writings of International Relations scholars and historical sociologists, and analysing their statements on the international system. This approach does present some theoretical problems.

First, there is the issue of preconceptions. When examining the statements by other writers, how is it possible to overcome already preconceived notions of what constitutes analytical concepts. It is not possible to stand aside from notions already held when looking at other peoples' views. For example, the preconceived view of person A about what it means to be 'working class', might well be different from that of person B. When person B describes their view, person A will interpret it through the lens of their preconceptions. This makes comparisons between these two notions rather difficult.

This is compounded by a second problem – that different disciplines may hold different perspectives. Does the notion of an 'international system' mean different things for a historical sociologist to an International Relations theorist? If the two notions do mean different things, then is it possible to make comparisons? As an example of how the same terminology may be used differently in different disciplines, consider the use of the term 'Realism'. For International Relations scholars this refers to a body of theory that makes certain assumptions: states are the principal actors in international relations; the state is a unitary actor; the state is rational; national security is top of the state's agenda. For philosophers of the social sciences, Realism refers to the view that 'the entities referred to in theories are as real, and as real in the same sense, as are those referred to in experimental laws and reports on observation' (Ryan 1970: 87). This is not to argue that all International Relations theorists hold the same view of what constitutes Realism. Instead the intention is to suggest that there may be definitions of concepts generally held within disciplines that may differ from those in other disciplines, yet hold the same label. Within Historical Sociology there may be a generally held view of what constitutes the international system, and this may differ from a view generally held in International Relations. If this is the case, then a person whose prime experience is in one discipline may have problems when examining concepts used in another.

To a certain extent these are problems that are not resolvable. It is not possible to know what Theda Skocpol means when she uses the term 'international system'. It is only possible to look at how she defines the term, what she seeks to explain through the use of the concept, and how consistent she is in the use of the term.

I have also sought to provide a consistent procedure for evaluating the way the concept of 'international system' has been addressed by these writers. To accomplish this, I draw upon a framework from the work of Hollis and Smith (1990, 1991, 1992, 1994, 1996; Hollis 1994). Hollis and Smith contend that there have been two traditions in the way that the social world has been analysed. The first, which they describe as an 'outsider' account, derives from approaches of the natural sciences dating back to the sixteenth century. The second, an 'insider' account, developed from the nineteenth-century approach to history. The former is an approach that aims at 'explaining', the latter an approach that aims at 'understanding'. These two traditions are notably distinct in terms of epistemology, ontology and methodology.

Explaining, or outsider accounts, originate from the positivist ideas of natural science. These approaches treat the social world in a way similar to a chemist evaluating a chemical reaction. Elements are separated, the causes of the reaction isolated and explanations for the reaction produced. This type of approach has a long history in social science and has been dominant, though not exclusive, in International Relations, particularly in the post-World War Two period. The underlying assumption of this kind of approach is that the methodologies of the natural sciences can be applied to the study of the social world. In other words, that the investigator can remain detached from what is being observed and can make explanatory statements about the causal mechanisms at work.

Insider approaches are based on a totally different method of comprehending the social world. These approaches reject the view that the methods of the natural sciences can be applied to the social world. These differences arise because social actors impute meanings to their actions. Hence the stress in insider approaches is on the meanings actors derive from and apply to social actions. The clearest example of this kind of approach is the Weberian notion of *verstehen*. This literally means 'understanding', or as Weber described his method, 'interpretative understanding' – trying to think oneself into the situations of the people the investigator is interested in. The intention of interpretative understanding is to reveal the meanings that direct the social understanding of individuals. This means that the predictability that underlies natural science methodologies is inappropriate for the study of the social world. Rather it is necessary to seek to uncover the norms and rules which condition human behaviour, and the beliefs individuals hold with regard to the roles that they play.

Hollis and Smith create a matrix from these two traditions of explaining and understanding combined with another area of dispute in the social sciences: the structure–action debate. This debate will be discussed more fully in relation to Waltz's work in Chapter 3. For the moment it is enough to distinguish between analyses that proceed 'bottom-up' or 'top-down': which are holistic or individualistic. In other words, whether it is individual actions that are most important, or the structures or context in which they are made. The former result in individualistic versions whilst the latter produce holistic accounts. The resultant array is as illustrated in Figure 1.1.

Each quadrant represents a different manner in which the social world has been theorised. The top two regions refer to forms of theorising which have

	Explaining	Understanding
Holistic	external structures	collective rules
Individualistic	rational choices	reasoned choices

Figure 1.1 Different approaches to the social sciences

adopted a holistic, top-down approach, concerned with the social world as a whole rather than with individuals. Such approaches see the individual as being constrained by external structures (outsider accounts) or by sets of social rules (insider accounts). The bottom two boxes refer to approaches that concentrate their attention at the individual level. Here, individuals are either analysed as rational actors, or as role-players in the social world. An important point to note is that the two quadrants on the left-hand side of the matrix refer to outsider approaches. These types of approaches imply that the theorist can stand aside from the subject. External structures, for example capitalism, can be described and their causal effects analysed. Such structures have an element of permanency. This means that their impact is consistent and can be predicted. The idea that actors are 'rational' implies that they will react in the same way to similar sets of circumstances. Therefore statistical methods and probability analysis can be utilised. By contrast, the two quadrants on the right-hand side of the matrix imply a completely different form of approach. Here the requirement is to penetrate the web of interactions that constitute the social world and the way in which individuals interpret the world and act accordingly. With this kind of approach it is not possible for the analyst to regard the social world as an external entity. It requires a degree of understanding and empathy with the subject of study.[3]

Hollis and Smith suggest that in the study of international relations such a matrix could be repeated at each of three levels of analysis (Hollis and Smith 1990: 7–9). At each of the three levels the study of different entities would be regarded as providing a holistic or individualistic account. At the highest level the study of the international system provides the holistic account, while states are individual actors. At the next level down the international system is replaced by the state as providing the holistic account. At this second level it is bureaucracies which provide the individualistic account. At the lowest level bureaucracies become the source of a systemic view, while individuals provide the actor-level account. In the current work we are interested in looking at the ways in which writers have theorised international systems, and so our concerns are with the first of these three levels. Our prime concern will be the relationship between the international system and states. However, as will become apparent, the Historical Sociology account is more complicated than that, and will involve other actors.

In their discussion of approaches to theorising the international system, Hollis and Smith concentrate on the explaining side of the matrix. They give the example of Waltz as an example of a holistic approach to the system. For Waltz the international system provides an external structure that can be analysed. At the individualistic level, Hollis and Smith point to the work of game theorists (*ibid.*: Chs 5 and 6). Game theorists provide a rational actor account of states and their interrelations. Approaches to theorising international systems on the right-hand side of the matrix would result in different types of account. At the holistic level, rules and norms would be the centre of attention. The study of international systems with this kind of approach would concentrate on how states, or the people who make foreign policy, are constrained by the existence of international rules and norms. At an individualistic level, analysis would centre on how individuals, especially policy makers, conceive of the international context.

However, as a note of warning, the point of employing this matrix is not to put different writers into boxes. Such an approach involves an over-simplification of different positions. Instead we are looking for a means of understanding different approaches to theorising international systems. We will discover, as we examine different writers, that it is very rare that a consistent line is taken when analysing international systems. The Hollis and Smith framework helps to highlight this inconsistency and to reveal the implications.

There are implications as a result of Hollis and Smith's other contribution to the debate on theorising international relations. Their argument is that there are always two stories to tell. Attempts to theorise the social world that attempt to combine elements of an understanding approach with an explaining approach will always be problematic. This is because the two traditions are examining elements that are not compatible. It is problematic, for example, to add an account of the social world that relies on the analysis of an external structure with a rules-and-norms account. These are different forms of entity and cannot be simply combined. The use of the framework from Hollis and Smith will allow us to consider different epistemological and ontological issues. It will also permit us to think about the problems involved in combining different forms of analysis. The aim is to evaluate approaches to analysing the international system. The intention of using the matrix is to provide a heuristic device rather than a system of classification. The framework provided by Hollis and Smith supplies a starting point for such an undertaking.

QUESTIONS FOR THE CONCLUSION

In order to summarise this introductory chapter, the purpose of the study will be re-stated, and some of the issues that are to be discussed in the conclusion will be outlined.

The aim of this book is to study some recent works of Historical Sociology which have sought to 'bring the state back in' and have analysed its role within an international system. International system and state are concepts that are studied by both Historical Sociology and International Relations. The intention is to examine the possibility of a dialogue between the two disciplines. In particular a range of questions will be addressed, based around three main issues:

International system How is the international system conceived in Historical Sociology? What are the weaknesses of this account? As has been noted in this introductory chapter, Historical Sociology has been criticised for being realist, and this has led some writers to reject the approach entirely. To what extent is this view sustainable? Does Historical Sociology support a realist view of international relations? Alternatively, does the view of the state that is being developed by historical sociologists undermine Realism?

The state Neorealism has been criticised for its inability to explain change. Various writers have suggested that to overcome this deficiency Neorealism requires a theory of the state. Recent writings by historical sociologists address the issue of the state, and of the state within an international system of states. Can Historical Sociology provide a theory of the state that can overcome the problems highlighted in Neorealism?

The relationship between Historical Sociology and International Relations Through its depiction of an international sphere, of social relations beyond the bounds of individual country boundaries, Historical Sociology must have an account of international relations. Does Historical Sociology provide a 'better' account of international relations? What lessons is it possible to draw from the approach to international relations developed by Historical Sociology? What are the implications of the discussion of the way in which historical sociologists have theorised the international system?

We will return to these questions in the concluding chapter, where we will evaluate issues concerning the overlap between International Relations and recent works by historical sociologists. The next chapter provides an introduction to Historical Sociology in more general terms. It locates the writers considered in this book as part of a long-term project in the study of large-scale social change.

2

HISTORY, SOCIOLOGY AND HISTORICAL SOCIOLOGY

INTRODUCTION

The last chapter demonstrated that International Relations scholars have shown an increased interest in the recent writings in Historical Sociology. The main reason for this interest has been the analysis of the state provided by writers such as Theda Skocpol, Michael Mann and Charles Tilly. Writers such as these have developed the notion of the state as a set of institutions that claim control over a particular territory. This is as opposed to the traditional International Relations approach that sees the state as being defined in territorial terms, encompassing all that is contained within a particular set of borders. These more recent writings in Historical Sociology have also included the notion of an international system as a causal variable in their analyses. This makes a break from more traditional Sociology which has seen its area of interest as being within a particular society.

However, the writers who have received recognition within International Relations do not constitute the whole of Historical Sociology. They are part of a much larger and longer tradition of study. The purpose of this chapter is to provide an introduction to Historical Sociology, its development, its concerns, and the position within the subject of the writers who are receiving the attention of International Relations scholars. First it will be necessary to provide a definition of Historical Sociology. To address this question it will be necessary to make an introductory examination of the relationship between History and Sociology, and to consider the debates concerning their association.

My intention is to demonstrate that the writers whom we will be discussing are working in a field that has a very long and rich history. Additionally, my aim is to illustrate that Historical Sociology is a very wide field in itself. I will also argue that a key contribution of the Historical Sociology literature is the inclusion of time in the analysis of social formations. There is a large range of subjects and approaches that are included under the title 'Historical Sociology'. For this reason the term might not provide the best description of the work of the writers to be discussed. Hence some alternative labels will be examined.

My aim is to provide a framework for the subsequent examination of the work of Skocpol, Tilly, Mann and Wallerstein. I will discuss the tradition on which their works draw, and this examination will throw into greater relief the recent move in their writings to analyse the state within an international system.

TOWARDS A DEFINITION OF HISTORICAL SOCIOLOGY

Historical Sociology is a particularly difficult discipline to define. As will become apparent, this is because of the uneasy relationship between History and Sociology. One way of arriving at a definition would be to consider how others, particularly those working in the field, have defined it. Two writers who have produced books on the subject of Historical Sociology have defined it successively as 'a discipline which tries to make sense of the past (and present) by investigating how societies work and change' (Smith, D. 1991: ix); and as 'the attempt to understand the relationship of personal activity and experience on the one hand and social organisation on the other as something that is continuously constructed in time' (Abrams 1982: 16). Another writer working on the subject of Historical Sociology has described it as 'an essential research technique for sociologists to use when attempting to differentiate between what persists and what changes in social relationships over varying amounts of time' (Banks 1989: 540). Turning to one of the key practitioners of the subject, Tilly (1981: 52) has described the problematic of Historical Sociology as being 'to situate social processes in place and time'.

Not surprisingly, these definitions contain different and perhaps conflicting elements that undoubtedly reflect the differing research agendas of the authors concerned. The emphasis on 'large-scale' and 'fundamental processes' in Skocpol's definition, discussed in Chapter 1, underlines her interest in a particularly structural approach. The interests of Tilly, whose work has encompassed both large-scale historical change and an interest in individual action, are reflected in his definition, which concentrates on the potentially less wide-scale 'social processes'. This contrast reflects the wide range of topics that have come beneath the rubric, and perhaps suggests that within Historical Sociology the delineation of some sub-topics might be of use.

Writers who have been working in the field have been interested in a wide range of issues, and hence it could be argued that there is a variety of Historical Sociologies.[1] There is a range of approaches all using the label 'Historical Sociology' to describe their work. There is some work in which the historical element is uppermost, and there are others where the sociological element is uppermost. Some writers have concentrated on very narrow time periods (e.g. Skocpol's work on revolutions) whereas others have taken on the entirety of history itself (e.g. Mann's ongoing project on the sources of social power). Some work has been on very specific areas of social change (e.g. nuclear missile accuracy) whilst other work has been on larger areas of sociological change (e.g. the transition from feudalism to capitalism). What all the works have in common, though, is an examination of particular types of social change within specific historical contexts.

These two elements of change and context return to the two common themes running through the definitions previously offered: the questions of time and of social change. The issue of time comes from the History side of the equation, whilst the issue of change comes from Sociology. In which case Historical Sociology could be regarded as an attempt to put an appreciation of historical contexts into ahistorical Sociology and to include an understanding of sociological forces in the study of atheoretical history. However, such a position would imply that History and Sociology are separate undertakings, a view that is not universally accepted. There are several positions regarding the relationship between History and Sociology. An examination of these views will permit the airing of some of the problems involved in defining Historical Sociology.

First, there is a position of hostility. This position has been held by some historians who argue that their discipline should not borrow from Sociology. This is because the aims of the two disciplines are different. They argue that History is ideographic, concerned with the particular, whilst Sociology is nomothetic, concerned with generalisation.[2] These are mutually incompatible and should be viewed as separate undertakings. There is also the view that the past is the preserve of historians, whilst present-day society is the subject of study for sociologists. This is not a view maintained by all historians. Carr, for example, welcomed the breaking-down of the frontiers between History and Sociology, and rejected this view. He argued that 'the historian is not really interested in the unique, but in what is general in the unique' (Carr 1964: 63). Carr goes on to argue that the historian will use generalisation to test the evidence. In other words, although historians are interested in the explanation of unique events, they will compare such events in order to draw out what is common. The position that History and Sociology are incompatible is now relatively rare, although Goldthorpe (1991) argues that the potential for the use of History in Sociology is strictly limited.

A second, almost equally extreme position is that History and Sociology are identical. Abrams (1982: x) for example, argues that because of their fundamental preoccupations, 'history and sociology are and always have been the same thing'. In other words, it is not possible to study history without an understanding of the sociological processes at work. Nor does a sociological study make sense without an appreciation of the historical context of the issue under study. All History and all Sociology are therefore Historical Sociology. Giddens (1985) has also made this argument. There are problems with this position. Some sociological work appears to pay little attention to historical contexts, whilst many historians claim to be dealing with 'facts' and not 'theories'. A second problem for those who argue that History and

Sociology are the same thing is that the methodologies of the two disciplines are notably different. As Goldthorpe has indicated, sociologists have the potential open to them of generating further evidence to support their inferences, whilst historians are restricted to the traces that already exist (Goldthorpe 1991: 213–14). Goldthorpe has also raised a further issue. He points to the problems of the reliance by historical sociologists on the work of historians as a source for their research. Many historical sociologists, because of the expansiveness of their subjects, and a lack of training in historical methods, make great use of the work of historians as secondary sources. This allows them, Goldthorpe (*ibid.*: 225) argues, to 'enjoy a delightful freedom to play "pick-and-mix" in history's sweetshop'.[3] Goldthorpe's argument that there are methodological differences between the two disciplines certainly suggests that it is hard to see the two undertakings as being identical.

A less extreme position, but one similar to the previous one, is to argue that History and Sociology are converging. Braudel argues that in subject and methodology, History and Sociology are directly comparable and moving closer together. He argues that they are 'the only two *global* sciences' (Braudel 1980: 69, original emphasis).[4] This is because they are ready to inquire into any element of human activity in any location. There are also great similarities, Braudel argues, between the language, tools and materials of the two disciplines. This is also a position that Durkheim took in some of his writings. In the preface to the first volume of *L'Année Sociologique* he called for an increased dialogue between History and Sociology. He expressed his belief that 'these two disciplines naturally tend to veer toward one another, and everything suggests that they will be called upon to fuse into one common study, which re-combines and unifies elements of both' (Durkheim *et al.* 1964: 343).

However, in other writings Durkheim expressed a slightly different view, which leads to the fourth, and for historians at least, perhaps the most contentious view. That is to say that History has a role to play in relation to Sociology as a provider of raw materials. Durkheim argued that the role of History was to play 'in the order of social realities, a role analogous to that of the microscope in the order of physical realities' (quoted in Lukes 1975: 404). History from this viewpoint provides the method of accessing the data for sociological research. For Ginsberg, Professor of Sociology at the London School of Economics in the 1940s and 1950s, it was a matter 'of necessity for the sociologists to derive their data from information provided by historians and anthropologists' (quoted in Banks 1989: 521).[5] The strongest outline of this contention, however, came from Spencer, for whom Sociology stood to works of History 'much as a vast building stands related to the heaps of stones and bricks around it . . . the highest office which the historian can discharge is that of narrating the lives of nations, as to furnish materials for a comparative sociology' (quoted in Goldthorpe 1991: 220).[6]

It is possible to provide an argument that supports any of these four positions. However, the problem with all of them is that they regard both Sociology and History as single entities. There are many approaches to both History and Sociology. As Braudel (1980: 73) observes, 'each historian and each sociologist has his own style'. By implication there will be a variety of relationships between them. Different positions within Sociology are more easily outlined. If Parsonian functionalism is compared to the participant observation practised by Goffman, then clearly the Sociologies involved have different viewpoints, structures and methods. Clearly these two approaches will have a different relationship to, and conception of, History.

Sociology has a variety of relationships with History. In some cases the two disciplines do have a different approach to events, the historian focusing on unique events whilst the sociologist seeks to generalise from events to theory. It is primarily a question of emphasis. Few historians would claim not to have some theoretical background to their work,[7] whilst most sociologists do make use of historical materials. There has been a certain convergence between the two subjects, particularly as History has gradually moved away from a position of expounding an objective truth as exemplified by Ranke. Finally, sociologists do make use of materials provided by historians, and it will be seen that the writers to be considered in subsequent chapters fall particularly into this camp. Even so, it is certain that none of the writers to be considered would endorse the position argued by Spencer, that sociologists are the architects, designing the theory, whilst historians are the hod-carriers, providing the information.

At a deeper level, it is possible to argue for a more profound link between History and Sociology, and this is a link that has particular significance for International Relations students. The link is the inclusion of the element of time in the analysis of social relations. Social relations do not stand apart from time. All social interactions are affected by what has gone before, and in the understanding of the present the past cannot be escaped. Braudel argued that he did not believe that it was possible to avoid history (Braudel 1980: 79). As Bryant notes, the attempt to isolate any social science from history is abstracting from a crucial causal element:

> The 'past' is thus never really 'past' but continuously constitutive of
> the 'present', as a cumulatively and selectively reproduced ensemble
> of practices and ideas that 'channel' and impart directionality to
> ongoing human agency. The present, in other words, is what the past
> – as received and creatively interpreted by the present – has made it.
> (Bryant 1994: 11)[8]

The implication from considering the links between History and Sociology is that it is problematic to analyse social formations without taking historical processes into account. The implication for International Relations is that core variables of the discipline, such as the state and the international system, cannot be understood without a consideration of their historical development.

Having made some introductory remarks about the relationship between History and Sociology, it might now be appropriate to consider the development of Historical Sociology. Through a consideration of the evolution of Historical Sociology, some of the points made above will become clearer.

A VERY SHORT HISTORY OF HISTORICAL SOCIOLOGY

Several writers have produced discussions on the development of Historical Sociology. Smith suggests that its history can be looked upon as two long waves, with the subject currently situated on the crest of its second wave. The first wave dates from the middle of the eighteenth century until the nineteenth century, and encompassed such classical writers as Montesquieu, Hume, de Tocqueville, Marx and Weber. For Smith the end of the first wave came at the start of the 1920s with the rise of totalitarian dictatorships of both left and right. These regimes 'which "knew" the future and invented the past rejected Historical Sociology' (Smith, D. 1991: 2). By contrast, Abrams (1982) takes a less contextual point of view and concentrates more on the themes that Historical Sociology has addressed. His work contains valuable summaries of the works of Marx, Durkheim and Weber. However, the book was written in the late 1970s and early 1980s. It is less detailed on the writers of Smith's second wave in whom we are primarily intersted in this book. Writing from her own personal experience, Skocpol (1987: 19) argues that the social context of the 1960s encouraged US scholars to rebel 'against the twin orthodoxies . . . of "grand theory" and "abstracted empiricism" that dominated Sociology until the late 1960s'. Tilly has produced a book outlining the work of several writers, though he concentrates on those of the latter half of the twentieth century. He aims to show how they have sought to overcome the 'eight pernicious postulates' inherited from a misreading of nineteenth-century social theorists (Tilly 1984: 11). Abbott (1991) provides an institutional analysis of the development of the subject in the United States, whilst Hall has traced the growth of the discipline in Britain, where he suggests that 'they do things differently' (Hall 1989).

The summary that follows will draw on all these sources, but will begin by arguing that the same interests that motivate today's historical sociologists were being written about prior to the nineteenth century.

The romantic historians

As Easton (1990: 646) has suggested, 'at one time all knowledge about human, social and physical nature was viewed as one', and there was not, for example, a division between History and Sociology. It is only within the last century that there has been a growth in fragmentation and specialisation amongst the social sciences. As Burke (1980: 15) points out, 'in the eighteenth century there was no dispute between sociologists and historians for a simple and obvious reason: sociology did not exist as a separate discipline'. Although a relative newcomer to the social science scene, the concerns of Sociology predate its presence as a separate discipline. Similarly, the concerns of historical sociologists predate the existence of both Sociology and Historical Sociology as specific undertakings. This is particularly the case in the work of those writers whom Collingwood (1961: Part 3) calls the 'romantic' historians.[9] These historians are also known as the philosophical historians, in the sense that they sought a theory of history.[10] The romantic historians regarded the history of humankind as a single process of development stretching from a 'savagery' of antiquity to a perfectly rational and civilised society of the future. It was this conception of a process of development that they sought to comprehend. Although contemporary historical sociologists are critical of such evolutionist notions in earlier works, and reject the idea of a teleology of history, the search for a theory of history links their work to the 'romantic' historians.

Herder, for example, saw a very close relationship between the natural world and the human world. He envisaged the teleological development of history as a series of matrices, one forming inside the other, so that the solar system was formed out of the universe, the earth out of the solar system, within the earth certain rock and crystal formations occurred, and so on. The unfolding of these matrices was an evolutionary process. The unfolding of each was not an end in itself, but the preparation for the next phase. However, the human race was to be the culmination of the process, once it had completed all its phases of development up to the rational society.

Herder had been a pupil of Kant, who read the first volume of Herder's work when he was sixty. It inspired him to produce his own work on the philosophy of history: 'An idea for a universal history from the cosmopolitan point of view'. Kant takes a less teleological point of view than does Herder. He argues that although it is difficult or impossible to detect the laws of history, it might be useful to pursue the idea that the history of the human race has followed a course of development.

Since men in their endeavours behave, on the whole, not just instinctively, like the brute, nor yet like rational citizens of the world according to some agreed-on plan, no history of man conceived according to a plan seems to be possible. . . . Since the philosopher cannot presuppose any conscious individual purpose among men in their great drama, there is no expedient for him except to try to see if he can discover a natural purpose in this idiotic course of things human. In keeping with this purpose, it might be possible to have a history with a definite natural plan for creatures who have no plan of their own.

(Kant 1988: 415–16)

Not only might the construction of such a plan be possible, it might even contribute to the unfolding of the scheme. Kant's argument is that in order to produce a 'universal history' it is necessary to carry out historical scholarship together with the application of a philosophical mind. For Kant, human development took the form of increasing rationality. The human race has the special facility of being able to benefit from previously gained knowledge. So, for example, if one wanted to learn about the geometry of triangles there is no need to work it all out from scratch. It would be possible to refer to the work of Pythagoras. Kant sought to understand this process of increasing rationality. His answer was that the evil in human nature drove the increase in rationality. This evil led to a conflict in human relations, between a social motive that sought harmony, and an anti-social motive that led to a desire for some members of society to domineer over others. This conflict provided the motivation for changes in society. This may seem a pessimistic outlook, but Kant's point is that if history is a process of increasing rationality, then it is not possible for the human race to have begun by being rational.

Schiller developed Kant's work. He shared Kant's views about the relationship between the philosophical mind and historical scholarship. Collingwood notes that he draws a contrast between the:

Daily bread scholar (the professional researcher with his dry-as-dust attitude towards the bare facts which are the dry bones of history . . . whose ambition is to become as narrow a specialist as possible and go on knowing more and more about less and less) and the philosophical historian who takes all history for his province and makes it his business to see the connexions between the facts and detect the large-scale rhythms of the historical process.

(Collingwood 1961: 105)

However, there are two very important points in Schiller's work that distinguish it from Kant's. First, and most crucially, he asserted that the goal of universal history was not to predict a future of rationality, but was a means to understand the present. Second, he extended the analysis from Kant's concern with political development to also include art, religion, economics and further areas of human endeavour.

Collingwood argues that the culmination of the romantic period is found in the work of Hegel, whose work was a summary and reinterpretation of the writings of his predecessors (Collingwood 1961: 113). Hegel also called for the development of a philosophy of history, but this was to be more than

27

a philosophical reflection on history. History was not to be a collection of facts, but an understanding of why those facts occurred in the way that they did. This philosophical history would be a universal history in the sense that it would encompass all human development from savagery through to civilisation. For Hegel, the main ingredient to be analysed would be the development of freedom, which for Hegel was exemplified by the modern state. Hence for Hegel the main purpose of philosophical history was to understand how the modern state came into being. The driving force of Hegel's history was, as for Kant, the concept of reason, but this was developed into the notion of the 'cunning of reason'. Human beings can only be perceived as being both rational and passionate, never purely one or the other, and for Hegel passion was the acting force in history, even though it was controlled by reason.

The intention of this brief foray into eighteenth- and nineteenth-century thinking has not been to provide an in-depth analysis of its works. The intention is to suggest that the idea of a theory of history has a long pedigree. At the point which most discussions of Historical Sociology begin, a flourishing and progressive research programme was already underway. Clearly there are differences between the work of the romantic historians and that of present-day historical sociologists. However, their interests are broadly similar, that is to say an attempt to derive an understanding of patterns of history that transcends the level of individual events.

In the late nineteenth century three writers, Marx, Durkheim and Weber, developed this research agenda. These three are considered as being amongst the founders of Sociology. The next section demonstrates that, from the beginning, Sociology contained a strong historical element.

History in early Sociology

Abrams points to Marx's two long essays analysing the 1848 French Revolution as being amongst the classic texts of Historical Sociology. As with most writing by historical sociologists, these essays were an attempt to make sense of contemporary events through an understanding of their historical context. Marx worked at two levels of analysis in these pieces: at the level of political action; and by considering the social structure as a whole. As Abrams notes:

> The argument moves constantly and with breathtaking agility from one level to the other; detailing a sequence of events, then placing it in the context of some structured balance of social forces; interpreting the balance of social forces and then tracing a new sequence of events through which that balance expressed itself.
>
> (Abrams 1982: 50–1)

That Marx had a theory of history is clear from the opening lines of the *Manifesto of the Communist Party*: 'The history of all hitherto existing society is the history of class struggles' (Marx and Engels 1977: 35). Marx argued that a change in the historical epoch occurs through the development of superior forces of production by a new social group. These developments occur within the framework of the previous era. Up to the existing capitalist epoch, Marx argued, there had been three previous eras: primitive communism, ancient society and feudal society. In capitalist society the class division was between capitalists, who own the means of production, and proletariat, who provide wage labour. In each class society the subordinate, majority class supplies the labour power required for production. It is the conflict between the classes that provides the motor of history.

Although Marx asserted that there had been four historical epochs, the majority of his analysis concerned the transition between feudalism and capitalism, and what he anticipated would be the transition to communism. The transition to capitalism occurred because of the struggle between merchants and industrialists on the one hand and the feudal aristocracy on the other. The former group led the development of capitalist forces of production during the feudal era. The manifest superiority of the capitalist mode of production led to a rapid transformation of the structure of society. This involved the replacement of the feudal organisation of society by one based on the relationship between the factory owner and the wage labourer.

In capitalist society the two protagonists would be the capitalist and wage-labouring classes. The contradictions inherent in capitalism and the increasing pauperisation of the labour force would lead the subordinate class to overthrow capitalism and usher in a classless society where all property would be communally owned. As the driving force of history had been the struggle between the classes, the arrival of this classless society would mean the end of history.

By contrast, Durkheim did not have a theory of history as such, but believed that members of society created a meaning of history for themselves (LaCapra 1972: 201). Central to Durkheim's work is the notion of social integration, the forces that hold society together. In *The Division of Labour in Society*, he examined this with specific reference to the transition from feudal to capitalist society. The core idea involved is that of solidarity. Durkheim claimed that in less industrially developed countries the strong feelings that people have of being a member of a group produced solidarity. The division of labour is so rudimentary that the same set of rules governs the activities of all members of the society. Solidarity is *mechanical*, because nobody has to wonder about whether something is right or wrong, because everybody thinks in the same way. In more developed societies the complex division of labour makes such mechanical solidarity impossible. Solidarity in industrial society is based on difference, not on uniformity. The only way that societies can maintain cohesion is through *organic* solidarity. The individuals in a more socially differentiated society have greater interdependence. Durkheim equated this form of solidarity to the workings of a complex biological organism where the organs – heart, liver, lungs – are functionally interdependent. None can survive without the proper functioning of the other, and the smooth operation of the whole is conditional on a correct balance amongst the individual parts. Hence for Durkheim the process of increased specialisation caused by an increased division of labour provides the dynamic for history.

As already noted, Durkheim saw a close relationship between History and Sociology, though his exact position did seem to change from time to time. In his prefaces to the early editions of *L'Année Sociologique* he called for closer links between the two subjects, and exhorted historians to make greater use of sociological theory in their work (Thompson 1982: 17). This approach was taken up by the founders of the *Annales* school in France, Bloch and Febvre, and subsequently by another French historian, Braudel, whose work on the Mediterranean will be considered shortly.

The third of the founders of Sociology to be considered here, Weber, started off as a historian and ended up as a sociologist. However, his contempt for disciplinary boundaries is indicated by his comment, upon his appointment to the Chair of Sociology at Munich University, that he was now a sociologist 'according to my appointment papers' (quoted in Roth, G. 1976: 306).

Weber is a large influence on the writings of historical sociologists such as Skocpol, Tilly and Mann for his analysis of the state,[11] but he also produced several works that combined historical and sociological analyses. The most famous of these more historically based works is *The Protestant Ethic and the Spirit of Capitalism*. In this work he sought to analyse how a particular type of religious ethic came to influence economic behaviour. Weber argued that this cultural basis for capitalism, the values of the Protestant middle class, was found exclusively in western society. Weber carried out a comparative analysis between western and non-western societies. He argued that the missing factor that explained the rise of capitalism in Europe, and its failure to appear anywhere else, was the work ethic inherent in the Protestant faith.

Roth, in a discussion of Weber's methodology, suggests that he used three levels of analysis: the sociological, the historical and the situational. Roth argues that the sociological level concerned the 'type or model construction and rules of past experience', whilst the historical level sought a 'causal explanation of past events', and the situational level outlined the 'general social and political situation' (Roth, G. 1976: 310). At the sociological level lies a battery of models, such as bureaucracy, industrialisation, the development of capitalism, which seek to provide the means for understanding long-term structural change. This level provides the ability to explain the causal factors of historical change at the second, historical level. Finally, the situational level allows for the extrapolation of current trends through an examination of 'the contemporary play of forces' (*ibid.*: 311).

The role of history was central to the early sociological works. The three scholars considered here contributed to the ongoing research agenda set by the romantic historians. However, following their writings there was a decline in the output of work that represented a philosophical approach to history. This, in Smith's terminology, marks the end of the first wave of Historical Sociology. The question to be addressed in the next section is why this flourishing programme produced so little in the first half of the twentieth century.

The dominance of archives and Anthropology

As already mentioned, Smith accounts for the decline in the writing of large-scale Historical Sociology at the turn of the twentieth century to the actions of totalitarian governments. However, he offers little to substantiate this claim. It is true that all the writers considered so far were of German and French origin, and that in the 1930s and 1940s both Germany and France came under the control of the Nazi regime. The Nazis killed Bloch, and Braudel spent the war years in a German POW camp. Even so, until his arrest Bloch continued teaching at the University of Strasbourg-in-exile at Clermont-Ferrand, and Braudel wrote the first draft of his major work on the Mediterranean whilst detained (Bosworth 1993: Ch. 5). Whilst there might be some truth in Smith's contention, this would not explain the paucity of writing in the years before the rise of Nazi Germany.

Munz has also noted this relative scarcity in the writing of Historical Sociology in the early part of the twentieth century. He accounts for it with the arrival of an individual-based methodology in the middle of the nineteenth century (Munz 1991). This methodology was based on the proposal of the idea in History and Anthropology that 'every human being as well as every social system or constellation is a unique *individual* and that therefore neither human beings nor social systems can be understood in terms of general laws or regularities' (*ibid.*: 257, original emphasis). According to Munz, this discovery was evaluated in two ways, one correctly and one incorrectly. Darwin argued that the differences between individuals led to competition amongst them, and that this competition provided the driving force of evolution. Hence a connection did exist between the individual and the non-individual (the species). By contrast, in the work of many nineteenth-century historians – and Munz cites Ranke in particular – the conclusion drawn was that 'every single event, every human being, and every social system was unique and would have to be understood entirely on its own terms, without the help of generalizations' (*ibid.*). In other words, his view was that all individuals and events could only be considered singularly. It was not possible to infer a causal relationship between events. Furthermore, it was not possible to conceive of social structures, let alone analyse them.

31

The triumph of this viewpoint was aided by two other occurrences. The first was the opening of the archives of the great powers. This permitted the production of historical works based solely on the careful evaluation of archival material. The second element was the illustration by Malinowski that Anthropology could be conducted without reference to the history of the society under investigation, through the practice of participant observation. As with the archives, this generated a deluge of research possibilities, though not for projects involving an element of historical background. Munz argues that 'the proper business of historical inquiry was buried by a twin wave of archival scholarship and anthropological functionalism' (*ibid.*: 258).

A further factor that should be taken into account, however, is the specialisation that has increasingly typified disciplines within both the natural and the social sciences. This process dates from the early years of this century and became increasingly prominent in the years immediately following the Second World War. Areas of academic study became increasingly divided into discrete areas of enquiry. Within the social sciences, 'society' became the sole preserve of the sociologist, the past was reserved for historians, and the economy was claimed by economists. The view was that each subject could be studied in isolation, without reference to the others. Any attempt to cross these disciplinary boundaries was discouraged and regarded with suspicion.

Despite the changes in historical methodology, the belief in the requirement of the study of the individual, and the restrictions of working in the times of authoritarian rule, research into the grand themes of history did not cease altogether. At the forefront of this approach during this period was undoubtedly the French *Annales* school, and in particular the work of its first post-war editor, Fernand Braudel.

Braudel and the Mediterranean

Braudel is most famous for his work on the Mediterranean during the sixteenth century (Braudel 1975). Of particular note in this work is his approach to the analysis of time. In his analysis of the Mediterranean region Braudel made a three-way division of time. This was between the short term, the middle term and the long term (or, as it is usually and more lyrically known, *la longue durée*). Braudel's intention was:

> To write a new kind of history, *total history*, written in three different registers, on three different levels, perhaps best described as three different conceptions of time, the writer's aim being to bring together in all their multiplicity the different measures of time past, to acquaint the reader with their coexistence.
>
> (Braudel 1975: 1238, orginal emphasis)

A problem for Braudel, as he conceded, was that this choice of three levels in itself was arbitrary. He noted that 'there are not merely two or three measures of time, there are dozens' (*ibid.*). The particular three that he chose would appear to bear some relation to the three levels of analysis employed by Weber, as previously discussed. For Braudel, the short term is concerned with events, which he described as 'the ephemera of history; they pass across its stage like fireflies, hardly glimpsed before they settle back into darkness and as often as not into oblivion' (*ibid.*: 901). This was for Braudel the least interesting level, and comprised the last third of the work. Somewhat disdainfully, he notes that Ranke would find much that was familiar in this section 'both in subject matter and treatment' (*ibid.*).

The middle term was concerned with social history, and it is probably at this level that Braudel's work is closest to the writers considered later in this book. He described this level as being 'concerned with social structures, that is with mechanisms that withstand the march of time; it is also concerned with the development of those structures' (*ibid.*: 353). The types of topic that Braudel was interested in at this level include the development of capitalism, population, communications, the interrelations of civilisations and war.

Clearly for Braudel the most significant and interesting is the long term, although some readers of his work might be tempted to describe this as the very long term indeed. At this level Braudel is concerned with the environment, though not in isolation: the particular emphasis that he applies is the geographical impacts on human history. In this first section of his work Braudel considers the impact of the mountains of the region, then the Mediterranean Sea itself. He assesses the effects that these geographical features have had on the human development of the region.

Moore, dictatorship and democracy

Moore is another writer whose influence on contemporary historical sociologists has been considerable. This is particularly the case with his work on dictatorship and democracy (Moore 1967). The intention of this work was to examine the roles of different social groups during the transformation from agrarian to modern industrialised societies. The specific aim was to trace the conditions that led in some countries to the emergence of democracy, and in others to the rise of dictatorships, whether of the left or right.

Moore proposed that there were three main routes to the modern world, with the example of India providing a possible fourth. The first route led to a western-style democracy through a bourgeois revolution. This might be typified as a capitalist revolution from below. The prime example of this path is Britain. In this instance a sufficiently strong bourgeoisie existed which was able to overthrow the existing feudal order. The feudal system was replaced by a new social order that was able to attack the constraints to capitalism through the mechanism of a democratic system.

The second route was also based on capitalism, though combined with reactionary forces. This might be termed as the capitalist revolution from above. In this instance Moore had in mind the rise of dictatorships in Germany and Japan. The revolution came from above because the weakness of the bourgeoisie precluded the possibility of a revolution in the British or French style. Elements from within the bourgeoisie were forced to make alliances with dissident groups in the old ruling classes in order to force through the necessary transformations to create a modern society.

The third route, communist revolution, occurred in countries which Moore terms 'agrarian bureaucracies'. These bureaucracies acted as a restraint on the development of forces pushing for industrial and commercial development. Examples of this route would be Russia and China. In both these examples the bourgeoisie was insufficiently organised to produce its own revolution. Additionally, the prospect of forming sustainable alliances with the old order was also impossible. In this model it was the huge peasantry who 'provided the main destructive revolutionary force that overthrew the old order and propelled these countries into the modern era' (*ibid.*: xiii).

Moore's book is considered to be one of the major contributions to understanding the troubled history of the twentieth century. Despite this it has come under considerable and sustained attack. It is of particular importance for our concerns because of the influence that Moore's work has had on subsequent writers. This is particularly because of Moore's use of the comparative method, perhaps refined to an even higher degree by Skocpol. Skocpol was a student of Moore, and his influence is particularly evident in her work. Her book on revolutions is a development of Moore's thesis. This is especially the case regarding the way that she developed the inclusion of international factors.

The works of Braudel and Moore are the highlights of a range of works that mark the restitution of the long-term research project that has been outlined in this chapter. Their writings also provided much inspiration for later writers. But just as there was a range of factors that brought a period of decline to the project, there were several influences that led to its renewal.

The return of Historical Sociology

Smith has divided this process of resurgence in Historical Sociology in the post-war era into three phases: the first from the mid-1950s until the mid-1960s; the second from the mid-1960s until the mid-1970s; and the third from the mid-1970s onwards (Smith, D. 1991: 4–7). According to Smith, the first phase was a reaction to Cold-War concerns. The writers in this period were strongly affected by the belief in the triumph of democracy over totalitarianism and the value of all other aspects of the 'American way'. Writers typical of this phase include Talcott Parsons and T. H. Marshall.

The second phase marked a reaction to the turbulent years of the 1960s:

the Vietnam war protests; the fight for civil rights; the rise of the women's movement. During this period there was a resurgence in Marxist forms of class analysis, and this found its way into the writings of historical sociologists trying to make sense of the myriad changes. Key figures of this period include E. P. Thompson and the earlier writings of Charles Tilly and Theda Skocpol. Abbott (1991: 203) notes that the prime target during this period was Parsonian functionalism. Historical Sociology provided the best line of attack on functionalism's main weakness, its difficulties with the explanation of social change.[12]

Although not mentioned by Smith, it would seem likely that the emergence of the Dependency school of thought had an impact on the writers emerging during the 1960s. This is a point raised by Evans and Stephens (1988). They highlight the work of Cardoso and Faletto as being particularly influential. Cardoso and Faletto describe their approach as 'historical structural'. By this they meant that that they 'tried to analyze the historical evolution of the major Latin American countries in a way that would reveal the central structural determinants of that evolution' (*ibid.*: 718). Their analysis concentrates on the interrelationships of domestic social classes with external classes and actors. Different combinations of these actors would result in different forms of dependency. There was not one form of dependent relationship between developed and developing countries. The form that the relationship took would vary, dependent on the character of internal and external actors.

Writers of the third phase, which continues up to the present day, are largely reacting to the enormous changes in the global power structure: the breakdown of the bipolar system; the collapse of state-centred communism; the failure of models of development to alleviate poverty in the countries of the South. These global developments are reflected in the increasing interest in geopolitical levels of analysis in the work of historical sociologists such as Michael Mann. Other writers typical of this phase include Perry Anderson and Immanuel Wallerstein.

Into the 1990s – towards a structural History?

The writers to be considered in depth in this study have all been producing work during the 1970s, 1980s and 1990s. The distinguishing features of their work are that they have all been considering the features of the state, and they have all included in their analyses a concept of the international system.

The writers whom we will be considering are all concerned with large-scale social change. This area of investigation is very specific within the field of Historical Sociology. Abbott makes a distinction between two main strands of Historical Sociology, which he labels as HS1 and HS2. He describes HS1 as being characterised by Comparative Sociology. By contrast, HS2 comprises 'students of past social groups – families, occupations and the like' (Abbott 1991: 212). The work of Skocpol, Tilly, Mann and Wallerstein is perhaps closest to HS1. Skocpol's work is the most developed form of this comparative approach. However this distinction between HS1 and HS2 is not entirely correct. As will be seen, Mann's work, which certainly would not fit into HS2, is not purely a comparative work either.

The main feature that characterises the writers to be discussed subsequently is their interest in structure. As such, their work should be distinguished from that of, for example, Erikson, who studied deviance amongst a seventeenth-century Puritan community in Massachusetts Bay (Erikson 1966). Erikson was concerned with using the historical records of the community to investigate the relevance of sociological theories of deviance. This approach provides a good example of Abbott's HS2. This work is in a different realm to that which is under consideration here, though both can be described as Historical Sociology.

For that reason it might be worth considering the use of a more appropriate term to describe the large-scale historical-sociological endeavours with which this work is concerned. Various possibilities spring to mind. First there is, of course, the term used by Kant: 'universal history'. Then, of course, there is philosophical history, or even theoretical history. Skocpol (1988a) has used the term 'macroscopic sociology', presumably drawing on a distinction between micro- and macro Sociology in the same sense as micro- and macroeconomics. However, none of these terms draws on the combination of history and structure, which seems to be the distinguishing feature of these writers. For this reason the term used by Braudel (1975: 1241) might seem the most appropriate, namely 'structural history'. This term is also close to 'historical structural' as used by Cardoso and Faletto. These terms provide the sense of an examination of the past with the emphasis on the pervasive, the continuous, the ongoing, rather than at the level of actions and events.

CONCLUSION

Tilly (1990: 685) has remarked that 'all reliable knowledge of human affairs rests on events that are already history'. The problem is how knowledge of these events is to be gained and understood. The writers discussed in this chapter and to be examined in Chapters 4–7 have two things in common. They would all agree that it is not possible to understand present-day social formations without an analysis of their history. No element of the social world is static. They are all in a state of flux, and this process of change is one that needs to be examined. They have all also located their analyses at a level above that of specific events. They are studying the past, but not using traditional historical methods. They are not 'historians', assuming that part of the qualification for the job is a person who examines primary sources.

What they are attempting to do is study the past in an attempt to determine certain patterns to history. This is not to say that many historians are not also doing this, but it is a question of emphasis. Tilly also notes that historians, when choosing their approach, place themselves closer to an analysis based on individual experience and narrative as opposed to large-scale processes and explanation (*ibid.*: 695). The writers to be considered here would place themselves nearer to the study of large-scale processes and explanation. The point is how analyses at different levels are to be combined.

This chapter has attempted to define what Historical Sociology is and to discuss how its approach is based on a relationship between History and Sociology. It has been suggested that, as there are different forms of History and Sociology, this relationship is not a consistent one. Additionally, there has been a variety of Historical Sociologies, with different writers taking an interest in different themes. In the 1980s and 1990s there has been a resurgence of writing that takes the major themes of history as its starting point. The kinds of questions that these writers are addressing are: how did we get here; where are we going; are there long-term structures that determine the character of events, and can these be the subject of analysis? Given the momentous changes in the global system in the latter half of the twentieth century, and with the approaching millennium in mind, the attraction of such questions is not surprising. However, this research agenda has not emerged from thin air. This chapter has attempted to locate its position in an ongoing research programme. This is a programme that has had its high and low points, but which is now undergoing something of a renaissance.

One factor that is important in the work currently being undertaken and which has not been a feature previously, is the attempt to incorporate the international system into the analysis. The way in which this issue has been approached will be discussed in Chapters 4–7. However, before this is undertaken, the next chapter will outline one of the central approaches to the concept of the international system in International Relations.

3

KENNETH WALTZ AND THE CONCEPT OF SYSTEM IN INTERNATIONAL RELATIONS

INTRODUCTION

In the introductory chapter we noted that there had been an increased interest in the inclusion of an international system as a variable in the work of recent historical sociologists. Chapter 2 examined how the work of writers such as Skocpol, Tilly, Mann and Wallerstein fits into a long tradition of theorising about World History and the Philosophy of History. The key point that distinguishes their work from previous writers is that they conceive of the state as an actor within an international system. In the following four chapters we will consider their work, with particular reference to their approaches to the state and the international system. In this chapter we will examine the ways in which the concept of an international system has been utilised in International Relations. In particular we will examine Waltz's Neorealism and highlight the lack of a theory of the state as a particular weakness. In the final chapter we will examine whether the possibility exists of combining Historical Sociology and Neorealism to provide the latter with a theory of the state. We will also discuss whether International Relations theorists have anything to learn from the approach to the theorising of international systems in Historical Sociology.

The idea of an international system has been a central theme of International Relations. The implication of adopting a systems approach to the analysis of international relations is that individual agents are seen to act within an international context that influences their options and shapes their perceptions. In methodological terms it implies that international relations can be studied at a different level than that of the interactions between actors. Additionally it implies that the study of such a level offers benefits for understanding the social world. However, within International Relations the notion of an international system has been surrounded by considerable and ongoing controversy. This revolves around three main issues:

- What constitutes an international system?
- Who, or what, are the actors?

- What are the relationships between an international system and the actors?

Various theorists have sought to analyse such a system, what it comprises and how it is conceived to influence behaviour, particularly that of states. My purpose in this chapter is to examine the dominant view of an international system in International Relations, namely that provided by Neorealism. This will be accomplished by looking specifically at the work of Neorealism's main architect, Kenneth Waltz. It will be argued that the major intellectual move that Waltz made was to abstract the notion of an international system from other social forces. This enabled him to generate a parsimonious theory. However, this advance was purchased at considerable cost. As was suggested in Chapter 1, a particular problem is the lack of a theory of the state. Without a theory of the state, Neorealism finds it hard to explain change. This is because, as Waltz (1986: 343) has noted, 'changes in, and transformations of, systems originate not in the structure of a system but in its parts'. Therefore to provide an analysis of change it is necessary to provide a discussion of the units, which for Waltz are the states. This argument will be pursued at greater length later in this chapter.

Although Kenneth Waltz's work is central to any discussion of an international system in International Relations, he was not the first theorist to attempt to provide such an analysis. In order to place his work in context, we shall begin with a brief discussion of some of the previous accounts. This will include an examination of the works of Morgenthau, Kaplan and Rosecrance as well as a consideration of the 'English school'. These accounts will convey various ways in which the concept of an international system has been employed in International Relations. Waltz's systemic theory will then be discussed, along with the debates that it has engendered. Regardless of the criticisms made of his theory, much of the theorising in International Relations in the 1980s and 1990s is a development of, or a reaction to, his work.

EARLY SYSTEMS THEORY

Ideas about the character of international systems have a long pedigree, dating back to the balance of power ideas that underlie the Treaty of Westphalia. However, as Little (1978: 183) argues, developments in the natural sciences which favoured a holistic approach to understanding natural phenomena, and the impact of behaviouralist approaches in the social sciences were key factors in the development of systems approaches in International Relations. The works to be considered here are drawn from those written in the post-World War Two period and are within a realist framework.

Although Morgenthau did not claim to be making a systemic analysis, he had the view of an automatic tendency towards equilibrium within an international system. At the centre of his analysis lie 'objective laws that have their roots in human nature' (Morgenthau 1960: 4). Primary amongst these objective laws is the concept of 'interest defined in terms of power' (*ibid.*: 5). It is the supposed constancy and objectivity of this concept that allows Morgenthau to claim the label 'scientific' for his version of political Realism. It also permits him to construct a theory of the balance of power.

He assumes that statesmen (and for Morgenthau it always is statesmen) think and act in terms of interest defined as power, and this permits the possibility that their actions can be anticipated. According to Morgenthau all statesmen act to increase the power at their disposal. Because all the individual actors act in the same way there is an automatic tendency towards a balance. As he remarks:

> The international balance of power is only a particular manifestation of a general social principle to which all societies composed of a number of autonomous units owe the autonomy of their component parts. . . . The balance of power and policies aiming at its preservation are not only inevitable but are an essential stabilising factor in a society of sovereign nations. . . . The instability of the international balance of power is due not to the faultiness of the principle but to the particular conditions under which the principle must operate in a society of sovereign nations.
>
> (Morgenthau 1960: 167)

Hence Morgenthau depicts the system as a balance created through the actions of individuals in states. These actors are consciously pursuing power in itself, but their actions lead to the creation of a balance of power mechanism. The system is the creation of these activities and is 'inevitable'. Its source is the inescapable character of the 'perennial forces that have shaped the past as they will the future' (*ibid.*: 10). The system in itself has no conditioning effects on the actors, but emerges as a result of their policies to maximise power.

Kaplan undertook a more methodical attempt to produce a systems analysis. He states in the introduction to his work on systems theory that 'this book represents an attempt to analyse international politics systematically and theoretically' (Kaplan 1957: xi). Here Kaplan appears to be employing a methodological definition of system. This immediately poses the question: was Kaplan's intention to analyse the international system as an independent variable? Alternatively, was his intention to produce an organised analysis of the processes of international politics? Was he attempting to produce an analysis of the system, or an ordered account of the units?

Kaplan, like many other systems analysts, was heavily influenced by a combination of functional sociology and general systems theory, as can be seen from much of his terminology (Weltman 1973: 4, 75). He produced his systems work in the mid-1950s, the heyday of Parsonian sociology. Kaplan made a distinction between his concept of a system and the elements, or units. His term for system was 'system of action', which he described as follows:

> A set of variables so related, in contradistinction to its environment, that describable behavioral regularities characterize the internal relationships of the variables to each other and the external relationships of the set of individual variables to combinations of external variables.
>
> (Kaplan 1957: 4)

There appears to be some confusion concerning the ontological status Kaplan accords his system. At one point he writes that 'the system consists of the variables under investigation. It has no absolute status', it is an 'analytical entity' (1957: 12, 18). Elsewhere he suggests that it 'has an identity over time' (*ibid.*: 4).

The status of the international system becomes more uncertain later on when Kaplan goes on to describe the relationship between the system and the units:

> International action is action taking place between international actors. International actors will be taken as elements of the international system. . . . It is important to examine both what happens to the international system as changes occur inside the systems of the international actors and to examine how the behavior of the international actors is modified as the international system undergoes change.
>
> (Kaplan 1957: 20)

This implies that a two-way process of interaction takes place. Changes within the actors lead to a change in the system, and a change in the system results in changes to the behaviour of the actors. This would appear to contradict the previous point. Previously the international system was merely an 'analytical entity', now, changes in the 'analytical entity' result in modifications to the behaviour of the actors. This would imply that the system was more than an analytical entity.

The condition of the system could be described through the use of a set of variables (Kaplan 1957: 9–12). For Kaplan these were:

- The essential rules, which describe the general relationships between the actors or which assign particular roles within the system to an actor.
- The transformation rules, which define what constitutes a change to the system.
- The actor classificatory rules, which categorise the characteristics of the actors depending on their position within the system.

41

- The capability variables, which determine the ability of individual actors to pursue their own interests, depending on the type of action and the circumstances.
- The information variables, which outline the aspirations, needs and capabilities of the actors in the system.

Through an analysis of these variables Kaplan claimed that it would be possible to define the state of the system. Kaplan (1957: 21) then went on to outline six different international systems, 'or, with possibly greater accuracy, six states of equilibrium of one ultrastable international system'. He labelled the six possible systems as: balance of power, loose bipolar, tight bipolar, universal, hierarchical, and unit veto. According to Kaplan other systems were possible, though in practice only the first two had historical counterparts. The others were 'heuristic models'.

Kaplan's next move was to examine the processes by which systems are maintained or changed. He pointed to three different kinds of process: regulatory, integrative and disintegrative. Regulatory processes refer to those that seek to maintain the system as a reaction to changes in its circumstances. The introduction of international laws might be an example. Integrative processes refer to changes in the relations between the actors within the system. For example, two or more actors coming together to form an alliance. Such actions may preserve the system or transform it, depending on the transformation rules. Disintegrative processes refer to those that have a tendency to cause system change even though these might be brought about by powers seeking to introduce stability into the system. Through the introduction of these processes Kaplan was able to introduce the very valuable notion of how one system is transformed into another.

Rosecrance (1963) has also attempted to produce a 'systematic' approach to International Relations. He argued that there were two fundamental approaches to International Relations, based either on the use of general explanatory concepts, or on detailed empirical analysis. The former approach tended to seek explanations through a single concept, for example 'power'. Here the attempt was made to uncover what was common to relations between states through the use of a concept. The latter approach sought to demonstrate the unique. 'One explained the common features in all international events; the other explained the uniqueness of a given international event' (Rosecrance 1963: 3). There were disadvantages to the use of both approaches, and each had to forgo a certain element in their analysis. Those approaches which aimed to analyse what was general in international relations had a tendency to be weaker in analysing specific events. On the other hand those that concentrated on the analysis of unique incidents failed to produce general propositions which could result in a unifying concept for the analysis of international relations.[1]

It was Rosecrance's intention to use an approach that would seek to overcome these shortcomings. He aimed to employ the empirical content of a historical approach while at the same time utilising the unifying concept of an international system. His approach sought to divide historical periods of international relations into systems 'each enduring for a limited period of time and demarcated by significant changes in diplomatic style' (1963: 5). As with Kaplan's approach, Rosecrance viewed the concept of a system as a descriptive device. The change from one system to another would be defined by a change in the practice of diplomatic relations. He noted (*ibid.*: 6) that 'in this sense international relations might be conceived in terms of separate "systems", each operating over a short period'.

Having outlined various historical eras, Rosecrance proceeded to investigate each era in some depth, discussing the historical context and the form of the diplomatic processes in action. This historical study provided the material for a more detailed analysis of the character of the different systems.

As with Kaplan's work, Rosecrance appears to have been very heavily influenced by Parsonian functional analysis, and his work makes extensive use of diagrams displaying the various influences upon the different international systems. This approach enabled Rosecrance to analyse international systems in terms of: inputs, or sources of disruption or disturbance; regulators which change as a result of the disturbing influences; and environmental constraints which translate the effects of the disruptions upon the regulators into the final element, the outcomes. Rosecrance makes the analogy to systems analysis as follows:

> In this application (and more than analogous application cannot yet be attempted) the actors provide the source of disturbance; regulatory mechanisms are found in formal or informal processes (the alliance system, balance of power mechanisms, a Concert of Europe, etc.); the environment or nature helps to translate disturbances and states of the regulator into outcomes.
>
> (Rosecrance 1963: 224)

To summarise Rosecrance's position, it can be seen that he has used system in two ways. First, he has used it as a term to describe the distribution of resources during different historical periods. For these historical periods he utilises terms such as stable/unstable, and unipolar/bipolar/multipolar. In a second form he has used the language of systems analysis to outline what led to the overthrow of the stability of a particular system. He analysed how regulators and the environment affected inputs, in the form of disruptions, to produce outcomes. It should be noted that the system has no analytical status of its own. Its influence is in one direction only. As Rosecrance (1963: 220) observes, 'changes in the components make for changes in the international system'.

The work of the 'English school' provides something of a contrast to the

American writers just considered. These writers can be regarded as an independent group because they have concentrated on a particular facet of the international system, the issue of how order is maintained. In fact they have chosen to use the term 'society' to describe the features of the relations between states.[2] The work of two of them, Hedley Bull and Adam Watson, will be considered.

In a sense the character of Bull's position can be derived from the title of his most significant work: *The Anarchical Society: A Study of Order in World Politics*. The riddle is in the title. How is it possible for a society to develop in a situation of anarchy? How can there be order in world politics? The choice of Bull's title suggests that he held the view that order does exist in world politics. For Bull, this order emerged through the development of what he described as an international society.

Bull went on to elaborate the distinction between an international system and an international society:

> A system of states (or international system) is formed when two or more states have sufficient contact between them, and have sufficient impact on one another's decisions to cause them to behave – at least in some measure – as parts of a whole.
>
> (Bull 1977: 9–10)

He makes a comparison between his definition and that employed by Kaplan. Although not dissimilar, Bull viewed Kaplan's work as an attempt to use system analysis as an explanatory and predictive tool, whilst he employed the term international system 'simply to identify a *particular kind of international constellation*' (1977: 12, my emphasis). By contrast:

> A society of states (or international society) exists when a group of states, conscious of certain common interests and common values, form a society in the sense that they conceive themselves to be bound by a common set of rules in their relations with one another, and share in the workings of common institutions.
>
> (Bull 1977: 13)

For Bull, the distinction between international system and society is marked by the acceptance of common rules that govern behaviour, and the operation and membership of common institutions. The common rules have to be accepted because of the lack of a governing body to enforce the rules. The international system is anarchical, and Bull employs the word in the sense of absence of centralised rule (1977: 46), but this does not exclude the possibility of the formation of a society.

Bull argues that the move towards an international society is only one of several elements at work in the international system. There are three different views of international politics. These are derived from the Hobbesian, Kantian and Grotian traditions. Bull (1977: 46) contends that the modern international system reflects all three views: 'the element of war and struggle for power among states, the element of transnational solidarity and conflict, cutting across the divisions among states, and the element of co-operation and regulated intercourse among states'. Although order does exist in the international system, it is not the only element, nor necessarily the dominant one. It is always 'precarious and imperfect'.

To summarise Bull's position, the international system has no distinct existence. Instead it is a picture at one particular time of the shape of relations between states. It is not something that has an analytical existence of its own. A system exists when states become aware of each other and have to take the actions of others into account when considering their own behaviour. However, for Bull, the study of international politics is concerned with more than this. States can have common interests and this can lead to the formation of rules or norms of behaviour. These rules and norms condition states' actions. Order, based on these norms, can exist in the international system.

A central problem with Bull's account is his attempt to combine all three traditions of international politics into one account. Is it possible that these three traditions can be merged happily together? Do they contain analytical elements that can be combined? How is it possible to tell which reflects best the form of international politics at any one time? This issue is central to the understanding of Bull's notion of the international system. The extent to which relations between states are typified by cooperation indicates to what degree the system can be perceived as a society. When relations are more violent, relations are less like a society and more systemic. The problem is to decide where Bull intends his specification to lie. The assumption made here is that it lies more towards the society end of the spectrum, with states' activities influenced by the norms and rules generated in their interactions.

Watson (1992) developed Bull's approach by considering how international society has evolved historically. His study involved an examination of the various systems that led to the creation of the European nation-state system. The significant thing about Watson's study is that he developed the idea of society to include a spectrum of various forms to describe the relationships between the members of the system:

> When a number of diverse communities of people, or political entities, are sufficiently involved with one another for us to describe them as forming a *system* of some kind . . . the organisation of the system will fall somewhere along a notional *spectrum* between absolute independence and absolute empire.
>
> (Watson 1992: 13, original emphasis)

Note that in Watson's formulation of a system – 'political entities sufficiently involved with one another' – there is an immediate implication that there will be a degree of organisation, hence a society. Watson (1992: 14) suggested that there would be four broad categories of relationship: independence, hegemony, dominion, and empire. The Greek city-states would be an example of independent states, as would medieval Europe. The control exerted by the Roman Empire would conform to the opposite end of the spectrum. Watson took his analysis of international systems a stage further. He suggested that a pendulum effect exists whereby state systems oscillate between one extreme position and the other: between complete independence and empire. The swing between the control exerted by the Roman Empire and the relative independence of medieval Europe would be an example. The factors which determine the position of the pendulum include the distribution of resources, the legitimacy generated for the contemporary organisation of the system, and a gravitational pull away from the high points of complete independence or empire. 'Thus the most stable point along the curve is not some invariable formula, but is the point of optimum mix and legitimacy and advantage, modified by the pull on our pendulum away from the extremes' (ibid.: 131).

In Watson's analysis the degree of international coherence is much more prominent than in Bull's approach, and this would account for the conflating of the terms 'system' and 'society'. This leads him to make a rejection of the realist approach in favour of one that stresses the idea of a system managed by the norms generated by the interactions between actors (1992: 126). He (ibid.: 120) maintains that 'whenever a number of states or authorities were held together by a web of economic and strategic interests and pressures, they evolved some set of rules and conventions to regulate their intercourse'.

Watson's work can be seen as an important development of Bull's society approach, and very much within an 'English' tradition. He plays down the anarchical element of Bull's 'Anarchical Society' and places more emphasis on the tendency of interacting states to generate rules to mediate their interactions.

Before proceeding to a consideration of Waltz's Neorealism, we shall briefly summarise the position so far, and compare and contrast the 'English' and 'American' positions.

The basis of Morgenthau's approach was the drive to enhance power. Morgenthau believed that this drive was inherent in all individuals. This desire drove the action of statesmen, and through their behaviour automatically resulted in a balance of power. Hence Morgenthau's concern is with the actions of individuals.

The other writers considered have concentrated on states and their interactions. The two Americans were very heavily influenced by functional sociology, and their writings are full of systems-type language. Kaplan produced a list of six possible system types (although he claimed that only two of these had ever existed) and produced an analysis based on these. Rosecrance worked the other way round, starting with a historical analysis and then deriving a system to correspond to each era. Not surprisingly, these two writers end up at different points. Kaplan has a much stronger conception of an international system, defined as a set of variables. For Rosecrance the system is rather more a way of describing an arrangement of particular powers during a specific historical epoch.

The English school writers have also placed their analysis at a state level, but by contrast have concentrated their attention on the ways in which states create a society to regulate their dealings. For Bull this society was a very fragmentary thing, very easily overthrown by other pressures existing in the international system. For him, states create rules to ease the pressures of surviving in the international system. Watson accords less significance to the role of anarchy in the international system. He concentrates more on how international society has matured. He argues that there is a tendency for international society to swing between empires and independent states.[3] For the English school it is necessary to make a distinction between system and society. A system occurs through the interactions of states. Although these states may coexist without the generation of rules (Bull), in general their interactions engender norms by which their interrelations are governed. The presence of these norms indicates the existence of an international society.

Our attention now turns to one writer who most specifically has attempted to produce a holistic explanation of international relations.

KENNETH WALTZ: A STRUCTURAL APPROACH

Although situated broadly within a realist tradition,[4] Waltz's work on the international system seeks to overturn all that went before it. He claims to have produced the first genuine systemic theory. He argues that all previous attempts to produce a systemic theory within International Relations were unsuccessful because they were reductionist. But the extent to which Waltz has been successful in producing a systemic account has in turn been questioned, as we will see later.

A further issue has been the extent to which systemic theory provides an advance on traditional Realism. Waltz's work has had a profound effect on the discipline of International Relations. It has also caused deep controversy, with the resultant debate still healthy more than fifteen years after the publication of his major work. No International Relations work since 1979 which discusses the international system can afford to ignore Waltz, and one of his most important contributions has been to inspire a much greater interest in the idea of theorising an international system.

The intention of this chapter is to take a broad view of Waltz's writing on the international system, and perhaps more importantly to outline some of the main debates that it has generated. Our approach to discussing Waltz's work will be as follows. First we will examine his work as a whole. This will concentrate on the development of the idea of an international system. We will then evaluate the issues that have arisen. These debates will extend from those who seek to modify his work to those who completely reject it. As a part of this debate, we will examine one exercise in modifying Waltz's work. This discussion of the criticisms of Waltz will concentrate on the view that his theory is unable to explain change, primarily because of a lack of a theory of the state. We will then examine further the question of Waltz's approach to theorising the state.

Man, the State, and War

Waltz's discussion of international systems begins with his first major work, *Man, the State, and War*, published in 1959. In this book Waltz sought to derive the causes of war. He argued that three levels of analysis had been employed to explain war:

1 Those theories which sought explanations of war at the level of the individual (for example, Morgenthau's views on human nature).
2 Those theories that place the explanation at the level of the state (for example, the Marxist view that capitalist states cause war).
3 Theories which seek to explain war at a systemic level.

The theories of the first and second levels (or 'images', as Waltz labels them) are insufficient, not because they are unable to explain specific wars, but because they are unable to explain why wars in general occur (Waltz 1959: Chs 2–5). It is only through the study of the international system that the reason why warfare has been a constant factor in human history can be derived.

Waltz draws heavily on Rousseau for his understanding of the international system, and specifically Rousseau's use of the fable of the stag hunt. Summarised briefly, the story tells how one individual defects from the group aim of trapping a stag when the possibility arises of catching a rabbit for themselves. As a result of this individual defection, the stag escapes. The moral of the story is that individual interests will triumph over group interests. The conclusion that Rousseau draws is not that the defecting individual is immoral or irrational, but that their actions can be best explained by their circumstances.

This situation can be extended to the international system, Waltz argues. The international system is typified by the condition of anarchy, meaning that there is no overruling authority to discipline any states that defect. Although cooperation may be possible, there is always the likelihood that a state may defect in pursuit of its own short-term interests. In a situation where there is no higher authority to appeal to, states have to be self-help. In a situation of conflict, states can rely on no other state, or agency, to come to their assistance. They need to be constantly aware that other states may defect from any collaborative activities. In this self-help anarchic system there is always a potential that disputes may become violent:

> War occurs because there is nothing to prevent it. Among states as among men there is no automatic adjustment of interests. In the absence of a supreme authority, there is then constant possibility that conflicts will be settled by force.
>
> (Waltz 1959: 188)

Waltz argues that the inclusion of an analysis of the third image makes up for the deficiencies in the other images. At times individuals have caused wars, whilst at other times particular types of states have done so, but neither is responsible for all types of war. This can only be understood through an investigation of the relationship between the three different levels. Waltz makes a distinction between what he calls 'efficient' and 'permissive' causes of war. Efficient causes refer to those that can be related to particular interests, for example a war over a particular piece of territory. Permissive causes are the circumstances that allow war to happen. With relation to the international system, this refers to the condition of anarchy. Permissive and efficient causes can be closely interrelated:

> State A may fear that if it does not cut state B down a peg now it may be unable to do so ten years from now. State A becomes the aggressor in the present because it fears what state B may be able to do in the future. The efficient cause of such a war is derived from the cause we have labelled permissive.
>
> (Waltz 1959: 234)

In other words, the fear generated through insecurity, brought about by the anarchy in the international system, can be just as much a cause of war as more straightforward reasons, such as the desire to control resources. States have to be self-help. If attacked they can, ultimately, only rely on their own resources for defence. The fear of what a rival state may do in the future can prompt aggressive action in the present.

In his first major work, Waltz's view of the international system can be seen as a set of circumstances. The prime feature of these circumstances is the lack of a controlling authority, which means that all states have to be responsible for their own security. As distinct from the works already considered, the international system has now become a subject of analysis in its own right, though in this early work the concept still remains rather vague. The international system does not explain war in itself. Instead it demonstrates how the causes of war at the individual and state level are not restrained at an international level.

Theory of International Politics

Over twenty years after the publication of *Man, the State, and War*, Waltz produced his full-blown systemic theory. *Theory of International Politics* ranks as one of the most influential books in the discipline of International Relations. It was also responsible for the launch of a paradigm, known by some as Neorealism, and by others as Structural Realism.[5] In his second major contribution to International Relations theory, the international system itself came to the forefront as the object of analysis, and Waltz aimed to provide a description of the system itself and of its effects on international relations.

The book can be seen as four closely interrelated parts. First there is a discussion of the role of theory in the social sciences. This discussion is crucial for what is to follow. What follows is a critique of existing theories of international relations, especially those that have labelled themselves as systems theories. Waltz argues that all existing International Relations theory, even that claiming to be systemic, is reductionist. He claims that he will produce a theory that will overcome this problem and be truly systemic. The extent to which he has been successful in this endeavour is one of the central debates that this work has generated. The next part of the book outlines the theory, and the final part attempts to apply the theory, using historical cases as a means of testing.

Waltz commences by attempting to make a definition of what laws and theories are. Laws appear to be reasonably uncontentious, and Waltz (1979: 1) settles for the following definition: 'laws establish relationships between variables, variables being concepts that can take different values'. Laws can come with different statuses. A law is absolute if there has never been found a variation in the relationship 'if *a* then *b*'. If it is a highly constant law then it can be expressed in the form 'if *a* then *b* with probability *x*'.

The question of the definition of theory is more problematic. One definition of theory is that it is a collection of laws related to a specific phenomenon. Waltz rejects this view, which he associates with those social scientists who attempt to build theories through the careful collection of information. This is a reference, presumably, to the behaviouralist school. The problem is that there is an infinite amount of data available for collection. Anyone attempting to collect it all would simply be overwhelmed and have no time for the creation of theory.

At times Waltz argues that reality is a social construction. 'Reality emerges from our selection and organization of materials that are available in infinite quantity' (1979: 5). This leads to the definition of theory which Waltz proposes: that theory acts as a guide to the infinite data that are available.

'Rather than being mere collections of laws, theories are statements that explain them. Theories are qualitatively different from laws. Laws identify invariant or probable associations. Theories show why those associations obtain' (*ibid.*).

There is a further crucial distinction between laws and the definition of theory that Waltz is employing. Of laws it is possible to ask 'are they true?'. Laws contain a purported relationship between two variables. It is possible to observe this relationship, and potentially to refute it. Theories are made up of descriptive terms and theoretical notions or assumptions. Of these it is only possible to ask 'how useful are they at explaining the laws?'. According to Waltz, a theory is more remote from reality than the laws it seeks to explain. He (1979: 6–7) notes that: 'a theory, though related to the world about which explanations are wanted, always remains distinct from that world. "Reality" will be congruent neither with a theory nor with a model that may represent it'. Note that Waltz has now introduced a third important term, a model. For Waltz (*ibid.*: 7) a model 'pictures reality while simplifying it, say, through omission or through a reduction of scale'. Naturally, a model should have some relationship to reality: as Waltz notes, a model aeroplane should have some resemblance to a real aeroplane. However, in general terms, a model gains greater explanatory value the further it moves from reality:

> Explanatory power . . . is gained by moving away from 'reality', not by staying close to it. A full description would be of least explanatory power; an elegant theory of most. The latter would be at an extreme remove from reality. . . . Departing from reality is not necessarily good, but unless one can do so in some clever way, one can only describe and not explain.
>
> (Waltz 1979: 7)

There would seem to be various elements in theory building for Waltz:

- An infinite quantity of data.
- A socially constructed reality constituted of those elements selected by theory.
- Theory which seeks to explain laws.
- Laws which represent consistent relationships between variables from the selected 'reality'.
- Waltz also adds the notion of models that represent a further abstraction from 'reality'.

There is plenty of room for confusion here. Initially this would seem to be caused by the introduction of the term 'model', which plays no further part in Waltz's exposition. From a subsequent description of what theory is, it

51

would appear that Waltz conflates all the concepts that he has previously introduced, as well as introducing a further one:

> A theory is a picture, mentally formed, of a bounded realm or domain of activity. A theory is a depiction of the organization of a domain and of the connections among its parts. The infinite materials of any realm can be organized in endlessly different ways. A theory indicates that some factors are more important than others and specifies relations among them. In reality, everything is related to everything else, and one domain cannot be separated from others. Theory isolates one realm from all others in order to deal with it intellectually.
>
> (Waltz 1979: 8)

This requires some simplification. Waltz's changing conception of 'reality' causes the main problem. Note that earlier in his text this word was enclosed in quotation marks, presumably denoting that this is a term of disputed definition. In the above extract the word stands on its own. Waltz has presented a double usage of theory that has then got mixed up. First, theory creates 'reality' through a selection from the infinite volume of information. Second, theory enables the depiction of a bounded realm, abstracted from reality. His bold attempt to define laws and theories is undermined by this double confusion. What is reality? In what sense is Waltz using the term theory? His position is made more difficult by his ensuing discussion of theory testing. Initially he outlines a straightforward positivist method of theory testing (1979: 13–16). Later in the text the position is modified. A theory need not be rejected if it fails a test, depending on its usefulness. He notes that 'in the end, one sticks with a theory that reveals most, even if its validity is suspect' (*ibid.*: 124).

The key move that Waltz is seeking to articulate in his opening comments on theory is the power that can be gained from a theory that abstracts from 'reality'. 'Reality' is too complex to be encompassed in one theory. A theory that tried to explain everything would be as useful as a map that was the same size as the territory that it represented (i.e. no use at all!). The theory that moves the furthest from reality is the most elegant and powerful.[6] This is because such a theory requires only the minimum number of important variables, and thereby concentrates on the most important elements.

Having opened with a discussion of his approach to theory, Waltz proceeds to discuss the reason why all previous attempts to produce a systemic approach to International Relations have been reductionist. By reductionist he (1979: 18) referred to those 'theories of international politics that concentrate causes at the individual or national level'. This is as opposed to systemic theories, which 'conceive of causes operating at the international level *as well*' (*ibid.*, my emphasis).

Waltz argues that reductionist theories regard the whole (the international system) as merely the sum of the parts (interactions between individual states). He finds this problematic because 'internationally, different states have produced similar as well as different outcomes. The same causes sometimes lead to different effects, and the same effects sometimes follow from different causes' (1979: 37). Waltz argues that this variety of outcomes means that a theory based at the national level will not be sufficient. Reductionist theories, and even supposedly systems theories, had been frustrated by their failure to account for the similarity and repetition in international outcomes despite the 'wide variations in the attributes and the interactions of the agents that supposedly cause them' (*ibid.*: 67). There must be other causes at work, which Waltz attributes to systemic forces. In order to provide a full-blown theory of international politics these effects must be taken into account. He remarks (*ibid.*: 39) that a reductionist approach will be insufficient, and a systemic approach is required in the study of international relations because 'outcomes are affected not only by the properties and interconnections of variables, but also by the way they are organized'.

Hence for Waltz, reductionism refers to those types of theory that attempt to explain wholes through an explanation of the parts: in other words an atomistic approach. However, it is worth noting that this is only one definition of reductionism, and that in the social sciences the label 'reductionist' has also been applied to those theories which reduce their explanations to a single cause. The most commonly cited example of this is Marxism. Critics suggest that Marxism is reductionist because of its reliance on economic factors as the prime motor of human history.[7]

After an examination of other international theorists, from Lenin to Kaplan, Waltz turns to a discussion of how a systemic theory should be constructed. Waltz (1979: 79) defines a system as being 'composed of a structure and of interacting units'. He then proceeds to define what is required in the definition of the structure:

> Definitions of structure must leave aside, or abstract from, the characteristics of units, their behaviour, and their interactions. Why must those obviously important matters be omitted? They must be omitted so that we can distinguish between variables at the level of the units and variables at the level of the system.
>
> (Waltz 1979: 79)

Here Waltz restates his intention to produce a theory based on abstraction. By abstracting other social phenomena, Waltz aims to isolate the forces active in the international system. By proceeding in this fashion the problem of reductionism will be avoided.

Waltz argues that there are three parts to the definition of structure: the ordering principles, the character of the units, and the distribution of capabilities.

As will be seen below, there is a very close connection between these three components. He claims that for his theory to be systemic, all of these must be defined without reference to individual units.

For the ordering principle this is straightforward. In the international system the ordering principle is anarchy. This is as compared with the domestic political system, where the ordering principle is hierarchical. What Waltz means by anarchy is the absence of government, and this leads him to assume that a state's prime aim will be to survive.[8]

The second feature of the definition is slightly more problematic: that of the character of the units. Waltz spends little time on this criterion. Due to the anarchy of the international system, all states have to fulfil the same functions: they are 'functionally undifferentiated'. The key term here is sovereignty. It means for Waltz (1979: 96) that a state 'decides for itself how it will cope with internal and external problems'. In the anarchical condition of the international system all states can only, in the end, rely on themselves for their survival. They have to be 'self-help'. There is no outside agency to which they can appeal for assistance and be certain of support. As all states have to fulfil the same functions, this means that the character of the units can be dropped from the definition of structure. This does not mean, however, that all states are equal. Quite to the contrary, some states are more able to fulfil these functions than are others. This leads directly to the third component.

The third component, the distribution of capabilities, is potentially more problematic for Waltz. Is this not, almost by definition, a reference to the national level? Waltz argues that this is not the case. He is interested in the distribution of power across the system, not the capabilities of individual states. 'Although capabilities are attributes of units, the distribution of capabilities across units is not. The distribution of capabilities is not a unit attribute, but rather a system-wide concept' (1979: 98). It is power relative to other states that is important, not the absolute level of power of the individual state.

The distribution of power is obviously a very important factor in the form of the system at any one time. The previous two components are comparatively stable. Any change in those would mean a complete change to the system, and the only change that Waltz can envision is from the anarchical order to a hierarchical one through the emergence of a world government. This would involve a change of system. Changes in the distribution of power result in changes in the system. Waltz is here concerned with the great powers, and for him the important distinction is between whether the system is bipolar (two great powers) or multipolar (more than two). He argues that there is virtue in a smaller number of great powers, and much of the rest of the book is devoted to defending this proposition, along with a sustained attack on the position of the interdependence writers (1979: Chs 7–9).

Waltz's account of Neorealism constituted a major development in the theorising of international systems. His aim was to produce a theory abstracted from social reality. This theory would contain a minimum amount of variables, but would have a large explanatory power. His work was a major attempt to produce a theory of international politics based on such principles of abstraction. We now turn to some of the reactions that this work has provoked.

Debates over Neorealism

One of the most positive impacts of Waltz's work has been the level of debate that it has generated. The discussion will be examined from three angles. First, the work of those who have argued that the theory Waltz has produced is too abstract will be discussed. These writers suggest that the incorporation of further elements is required. A brief digression will then be included to examine one attempt to overcome some of the problems in Neorealism. This will be followed by a brief foray into the structure–agent debate that has emerged in reaction to Neorealism. Finally, the views of those who would reject the entire enterprise will be considered. The key criticisms with regard to our discussion are concerned with Waltz's failure to develop his second level of structure, an analysis of the state.

Keohane is one writer who has been sympathetic to the neorealist project. He notes (1986: 190–1) that it 'helps us to understand world politics as in part a systemic phenomenon, and provides us with a logically coherent theory that establishes the context for state action'. However, it does have a central problem. This concerns the use of the concepts of power and interests. Keohane argues that these make poor variables from which to derive predictions. It is necessary to modify the theory to overcome its weaknesses, without changing it to such an extent that its strengths are lost.

In order to do this Keohane (1986: 191) proposes 'a multidimensional approach to world politics that incorporates several analytical frameworks or research programs'. One of these research programmes would involve the development of the neorealist approach. In addition, work needs to be carried out on bridging the gap between the domestic and international environments. This would require research programmes encompassing domestic politics, decision making and information processing.

Keohane argues that the context of state action needs to be extended. It is also necessary to take into account the institutional context of action. He argues that there are influences that reduce the significance of anarchy and, as a result, the requirement for states to be self-help. He points to the work of Axelrod, whose game-theory analysis indicates that patterns of cooperation can emerge when actors expect that their interactions will continue into the indefinite future. One important factor that reduces state uncertainty is the availability of information, and hence Keohane argues that this should be incorporated into a systemic analysis. He notes that 'actors behave differently in information-rich environments than in information-poor ones where uncertainty prevails' (1986: 197).

Keohane's views are largely supportive, though he sees Waltz's approach as being part of a larger project and not sufficient in itself to provide an all-encompassing theory of international politics.

Ruggie has launched a more serious attack. At the centre of his critique is the view that Neorealism is unable to account for change. He asserts that 'it provides no means by which to account for, or even to describe the most important contextual change in international politics in this millennium: the shift from the medieval to the modern international system' (1986: 141). The source of this error is two omissions in Waltz's analysis: a dimension of change, and a determinant of change.

The former of these two omissions derives from Waltz's dropping of the second level of definition of structure, the character of the units. It will be recalled that Waltz argued that this level could be disregarded because in an anarchical system all the units have to fulfil the same function. Ruggie argues that this is an error. He suggests that Waltz's definition of the term 'differentiation' is incorrect. Waltz had stressed the element of difference in his interpretation. 'Functionally undifferentiated' for Waltz means that all states have to fulfil the same basic functions. There is no difference in the functions undertaken by states. By contrast Ruggie argues that the definition should emphasise separateness. For Ruggie it is the grounds on which the units are constituted as separate entities.

The significance of this distinction is made plain in Ruggie's comparison of the medieval and the modern international systems. He characterises the medieval system as being heteronomous. The prime feature of this system was that it was inherently international, with little distinction between internal and external realms. There were overlapping and reciprocal relations between the various classes and a ruling class characterised by its high level of mobility. The legitimation of this system occurred through common bodies of law and through religion and custom.

In contrast, Ruggie regards the modern system as being characterised by the emergence of sovereign states. The prime cause of this has been the rise of the idea of private property that has fostered the notion of exclusion. This has allowed the development of notionally bounded territories ruled by public authorities. Ruggie notes:

> The modern system is distinguished from the medieval not by 'sameness' or 'differences' of units, but by *the principles on the basis of which the constituent units are separated* from one another. If anarchy tells us *that* the political system is a segmental realm differentiation tells us *on what basis* the segmentation is determined. The second component of structure, therefore, does not drop out; it stays in, and serves as an exceedingly important source of structural variation.
>
> (Ruggie 1986: 142, original emphasis)

By extending the analysis at the second level of structure, Ruggie has suggested that it will be possible to include a dimension of change. It is also necessary to consider the determinant of change. Here Ruggie turns to Durkheim's notion of dynamic density. This refers to 'the quantity, velocity and diversity of transactions that go on within society' (Ruggie 1986: 148). Changes in dynamic density will result in changes in society. Durkheim used this notion to explain the transformation from mechanical to organic societies. Ruggie maintains that the same concept could be used to understand transformations in the international system, and that Waltz's disregard of this concept marks a serious flaw in his theory.

Not surprisingly, Waltz has defended his position. He seems to be extremely wary of adding other elements into his system for fear of losing its parsimony. On these points he sticks very closely to his view of the role of theory. He states that:

> To achieve 'closeness of fit' would negate theory. A theory cannot fit the facts or correspond with the events it seeks to explain. . . . A theory can be written only by leaving out most matters that are of practical interest. To believe that listing the omissions of a theory constitutes a valid criticism is to misconstrue the theoretical enterprise.
>
> (Waltz 1991: 31)

In other words, Waltz adheres to his position, as stated in the first chapter of *Theory of International Politics*, that a theory gains most by the extent to which it can abstract from social phenomena. His intention is not to explain everything, but to explain the most from the least amount of theory.

With more specific reference to Ruggie's comments, Waltz claims that the dimension and determinants of change that Ruggie seeks to incorporate into the theory are unit-level causes and hence should not be included in the definition of structure, and he cites Durkheim to support him on this point. He notes that:

> Durkheim did not confound the internal condition of states with their external environment. Durkheim did not think of dynamic density as part of a unit-level condition that may burst the bonds of the old system and break its structure apart.
>
> (Waltz 1986: 328)[9]

Waltz denies that he overlooks the possibility of change emanating at the system level. Causal effects can operate both from the system to the units and the other way round.

Buzan, Jones and Little: an alternative reworking of Waltz

At this point it might be worth considering one of the most profound attempts to restructure Waltz's Neorealism. This has been carried out by a group of British-based scholars. Buzan, Jones and Little's work builds on Neorealism, but attempts to incorporate the major criticisms, specifically those of Keohane and Ruggie, as discussed above. As such it involves a reworking and extension of Waltz rather than a rejection.

Their prime criticism of Waltz is that he defined his structure too narrowly, and confused structure with system. As a result he 'appropriated the whole content of the system level for his own narrow definition of structure' and 'forced down to the unit level all other attempts to conceptualise the international system in general terms' (Buzan *et al.* 1993: 24–5). Waltz has uncompromisingly rejected any attempt to move factors from the unit level into the structure, such as economic forces. Buzan *et al.* suggest that this has opened his work to two prime lines of criticism. First that it is too narrow; it excludes other structural forces and elements that are important in explaining outcomes. Second that it is too static; that its emphasis on continuity is misplaced. Consider, for example, Ruggie's discussion of the changes in the constitution of the state between the medieval and modern eras.

Buzan *et al.* take a four-pronged approach in their modifications to Waltz's theory. First they apply a sectoral approach to the international system. Waltz attempted to restrict his analysis to the political sector. Buzan *et al.* open up this system level to include economic, societal, strategic factors in addition to the political level. This opens the analysis to several difficulties with regard to combining the sectors, as the authors acknowledge. However, they attempt to resolve this difficulty by making a horizontal division of the system between levels of analysis, and a vertical division between the sectors. This two-way division would allow for a different structure in each sector.

> This scheme enables us to consider levels of analysis either in terms of the international system as a whole (by dissolving the sectoral distinctions) or in terms of specific sectoral subdivisions (by defining the levels in terms that are bounded by one or more sectoral subdivisions, e.g. international political system, or international political economy).
>
> (Buzan *et al.* 1993: 33)

The second part of their modification involves a deeper analysis of the second level of Waltz's structure, the character of the units. As already mentioned, Waltz discards this level as he argues that in an anarchical system all the units have to fulfil this function. Buzan *et al.* attempt to bring this level back in, through a discussion of how it is related to the first level of structure, the ordering system. They argue that the possibility of change at this level should be permitted, in other words, allowing the possibility of a change between functionally differentiated and functionally undifferentiated units. Although the logic of anarchy means that the tendency will exist for the units to be pushed towards fulfilling similar functions, the existence of functionally similar units under anarchy as a transitional feature of the international system is considered possible (Buzan *et al.* 1993: 37–46). The medieval system of states would be the prime example of such a transitional phase.

The third element of their modification is to clarify the notion of power at the third level of structure, which Waltz had called the distribution of capabilities. Waltz had combined all the notions of capabilities into the one concept of power, which Buzan *et al.* claim provides insufficient flexibility. They argue that the concept of power should be disaggregated into military capability, economic capability, political cohesion and ideology. Clearly these attributes would vary and interact with each other over differing time periods. They argue that:

> These can be envisaged as a set of vectors (lines of force) operating within a field. Sometimes their influence would be mutually rein-forcing, as when economic, military, and ideological patterns all coincide – as they did briefly after the Second World War. When that happens strong structural pressure on the behavior of units is created. Sometimes the different vectors would work at odds, perhaps cancelling each other out, or at least creating weaker, more diffuse structural forces, as in the international system of the early 1990s.
>
> (Buzan *et al.* 1993: 64)

Buzan *et al.* argue that such a disaggregation of power would allow consider-ably more flexibility in the development of hypotheses and the possibility of analysing a much wider range of conditions in the international system, as well as the possibility of producing comparative analyses.

The final feature of their modifications of Waltz's idea of structure is the inclusion of what they term interaction capacity. This can be equated to Durkheim's concept of dynamic density. Waltz, of course, argued that any interactions between the units could not be systematised. Buzan *et al.* argue otherwise. They suggest that there are two features of interaction that cannot be confined to the unit level: technological capabilities, and shared norms and organisations. They argue that these two features are systemic because they occur throughout the system, and more importantly 'because they profoundly condition the significance of structure and the meaning of the term system itself' (1993: 72).

Buzan *et al.* argue that the interaction capacity can have differing levels, which will have an impact on the features of the international system. At very low levels it might not even be possible to say that a system exists.

At very high levels they suggest that the effects of interaction may override the structural effects, with the possibility that the units may become functionally differentiated. They suggest that currently the level of interaction capacity is somewhere in the middle.

These four elements (division of the international system, opening of the second level of structure, disaggregation of power and inclusion of interaction capacity) constitute the amendments that Buzan *et al.* propose to Waltz's definition of structure. These are not minor adjustments, and it is likely that Waltz would find them unacceptable, particularly as they reduce the parsimony of his approach. The two questions that would seem most pertinent are whether these proposed changes leave anything of a system that could be described as Waltzian, and whether the reduction in parsimony has a trade-off in increased explanatory capability.

In fact quite a lot of Waltz's system does remain. His basic definition of structure endures, in other words ordering principle, character of units and distribution of capabilities. However, the second and third levels become sites of deeper analytical possibilities. More problematic is the view that Waltz's political system becomes one amongst several sectors comprising a complete system, and more crucially the inclusion of interaction capacity as a systems-level effect, which has the potential of counteracting structural effects. These amendments could hardly be looked upon as extensions, since they appear contradictory to Waltz's original intention.

As for the benefits in terms of explanatory power, these will have to await the further development of this project. So far, Buzan, Jones and Little have applied their framework to a discussion of the rise and fall of the Roman Empire, but apart from this, applications of their Structural Realism will require further investigations.[10]

Waltz and the agent–structure debate

A second area of discussion of Waltz's work centres around issues concerned with the agent–structure debate. This debate is central to the social sciences, and International Relations is no exception. Dessler provides a concise introduction:

> It emerges from two uncontentious truths about social life: first, that human agency is the only moving force behind the actions, events and outcomes of the social world; and second, that human agency can be realized only in concrete historical circumstances that condition the possibilities for action and influence its course.
>
> (Dessler 1989: 443)

That agents act within a context places a limitation on explanations of action. Which should we consider as being more important, the act or the context? Dessler goes on to state that the agent–structure problem refers to the difficulty of developing a theory that successfully meets both demands. This is a difficult and contentious area, as it is far from certain that such a theory can be produced. However Dessler does modify his position slightly in a footnote:

> Not every specific explanation, of course, need give a complete anal-
> ysis of both agential powers and the conditions in which those
> powers are deployed. But the explanations must make room for such
> completion; or, more accurately, the conceptual scheme or framework
> underpinning specific explanations must recognize and make appro-
> priate allowance for the workings of both agency and structure, even
> if each specific explanation does not exploit this allowance.
>
> (Dessler 1989: 443–4, note 12)

This debate is of particular relevance to Waltz's work because of his claim that all previous theories of international relations were reductionist, whilst he was the first scholar to have produced a truly systemic theory. Hence it is of some significance when his work in turn comes to be accused of reduc-tionism. This argument can be approached in two different ways, both of which will be outlined below. The first debate considers which, for Waltz, came first, the state or the system. The second is concerned with ontological issues in Waltz's definition of the international system.

The first version of the debate revolves around the issue of primacy. In the article cited above Dessler goes on to make a comparison between Waltz's Neorealism and Scientific Realism. Crucial in this distinction is which comes first, the system or the units (structure or agents). In Neorealism the system is brought into being through the unintended action of the units. To illustrate this point, Waltz makes an analogy to microeconomic theory. 'No state intends to participate in the formation of a structure by which it and others will be constrained. International-political systems, like economic markets, are individualist in origin, spontaneously generated, and unintended' (Waltz 1979: 91). In other words, for Waltz, states come first. The international system comes into existence as a result of the interactions between states.

The crucial point for Dessler (1989: 450) is that, in Neorealism, the structure is 'a by-product rather than a product of interaction'. By contrast, Scientific Realism, and here Dessler draws heavily on the work of Bhaskar, presupposes a structure. No social activity can occur without the pre-exis-tence of structure: no structure – no action. However, the relationship is more complicated, as action can bring about changes in the structure.

> All social action presupposes social structure, and vice versa. An
> actor can act socially only because there exists a social structure to
> draw on, and it is only through the actions of agents that structure
> is reproduced and potentially transformed.
>
> (Dessler 1989: 452)

61

Hence Dessler's view is that, in Waltz's formulation, the system is secondary and unintentional. This would clearly coincide with Waltz's view. Does this imply that Waltz's approach is reductionist? As suggested above, this is a matter of definition. Returning to Waltz's own definition, it is clear that, in his own terms, whether the international system is primary or secondary is irrelevant. What is important is that system effects are taken into account and that structure can be defined without reference to unit-level characteristics. However, what is also clear from Waltz's own account is that the system is a secondary feature.

This leads straight into the second line of argument. Wendt argues that because of Waltz's individualistic ontology, it is not possible to describe his theory as holistic:

> The distribution of capabilities is a function of state attributes, the lack of functional differentiation is a function of the fact that modern states all have the attribute of sovereignty, and even the fact that the states system is a competitive system in which power politics rules is a function of the fact that states are egoistic about their security. The sovereign, egoistic state endowed with certain capabilities, in other words, is the ontologically given unit by the aggregation of which the structure of Waltz's state system is constituted. This is a thoroughly individualist ontology.
>
> (Wendt 1991: 389)

This is a more powerful argument for reductionism in Waltz. The implication of the above extract is that Waltz's international system is solely the sum of the units and that he has failed to derive an independent international system. Is such a view sustainable? It will be suggested here that this is not the case. It has already been conceded above that in Waltz's formulation, the international system is secondary, so to accept Wendt's view that Waltz's ontology is thoroughly individualist is not a problem. Wendt, however, misses a step in Waltz's formulation. Although the system comes into being through the unintended actions of the units, 'once formed, a market becomes a force in itself, and a force that the constitutive acting singly or in small numbers cannot control' (Waltz 1989: 90). The implication of this is that once the system is created it has an existence of its own which can be analysed as a separate entity. As Hollis and Smith note in their contribution to this debate, 'it is no obstacle to treating a system as an entity with causal powers that it emerged from an original set of units and their relations' (Hollis and Smith 1991: 401).

The debate is, to a certain degree, unresolvable. The two lines of attack have been that in Waltz's theory the states are primary (i.e. they exist before the system) and that his ontology is individualistic. Waltz can retort that these points are insufficient. He has been able to define structure without resorting to unit-level descriptions. How the system came about is irrelevant. His argument is that once in the system has come into existence, he has provided a means for its analysis. In this debate different definitions of reductionism are being used and hence it is impossible to come to a final resolution. We will return to questions of reductionism in the conclusion.

Critical and post-structuralist critiques of Neorealism

The third and final debate that we will consider is that with the critical and postmodernist theorists, represented here by Cox and Ashley. These two writers have made a profound and concerted attack on the principles and intentions of Waltz's work.

Cox's criticisms revolve around the question of what theory is and what purposes it fulfils. Waltz's views on theory have already been presented, and can be summarised as stating that the purpose of theory is to simplify reality in order to understand and explain certain parts of it. In such a formulation, theory would appear to be objective. It can stand apart from what is considered to be reality. Cox's views on theory are not so straightforward. For Cox, 'theory is always *for* someone and *for* some purpose' (Cox 1986: 207, original emphasis). In other words, theory, for Cox, is never objective. Its purposes and its biases reflect the requirements of the theorist at a particular point in time and place in society. He accuses Waltz of providing a theory that serves the requirements of the superpowers attempting to manage a bipolar international system. He remarks that 'there is an unmistakably Panglossian quality to a theory published in the late 1970s which concludes that a bipolar system is the best of all possible worlds. The historical moment has left its indelible mark upon this purportedly universalist science' (*ibid.*: 248).

Cox suggests that there are two types of theory: problem-solving and critical. The first has a simple function, to resolve problems created by social forces as they are perceived to be. In problem-solving theory the world is taken as it is, and there is no intention to explore the possibility that things could be different. This, Cox suggests, provides its great strength. It is able to produce a bounded realm of few variables that can be analysed in great detail.

The latter type of theory is more complex:

> The other is more reflective upon the process of theorizing itself: to become clearly aware of the perspective which gives rise to theorizing, and its relation to other perspectives (to achieve a perspective on perspectives); and to open up the possibility of choosing a different valid perspective from which the problematic becomes one of creating an alternate world.
>
> (Cox 1986: 208)

Critical theory does not take the world as it is, but asks how the world came to be as it is. 'Critical theory, unlike problem-solving theory, does not take institutions and social power relations for granted but calls them into question by concerning itself with their origins and how and whether they might be in the process of changing' (Cox 1986: 208). It is this element of change that marks one of the major differences between problem-solving and critical theory. It is also a major strength of critical theory and, Cox suggests, a source of weakness in problem-solving theory. This is for two reasons. First, although problem-solving theory derives much of its power of explanation from its acceptance of things as they are, this position reveals its ideological basis. It seeks to resolve the problems of the world as it is currently constituted, and therefore by implication accepts that constitution. Cox's argument is that Waltz aims to advance the benefits of the bipolar system and provide a legitimation for US policies that promote that aim. Second, its inherent ahistorical position is mistaken. Social and political institutions are not fixed. They are in a constant state of flux which problem-solving theory has neither the will nor the ability to analyse.

Ashley (1986) makes some similar points in his critique of Neorealism. He points to errors in the three main commitments of Neorealism: statism, utilitarianism and positivism. Ashley points to the centrality of the state in the neorealist formulation. This generates two problems. First, it means that Neorealism is unable to conceptualise global collectivist notions such as transnational class interests and international capitalism. Its analysis can only include the aggregations of relations composed of state-bounded entities. Second this state-centric view undermines Neorealism's claim to structuralism. This is another version of the first agent–structure debate discussed above. Is a structuralist explanation of international politics possible when the units are considered as being ontologically prior to the system? Ashley notes that 'Neorealism is statist before it is structuralist' (1986: 272). His analysis here calls very closely on that propounded by Ruggie, and points to the impossibility for Waltz to include in his analysis an understanding of how the international system was a generating factor of the sovereign state.

Ashley also criticises Neorealism for its utilitarianism. For Ashley, 'utilitarianism is characterized by its individualist and rationalist premises' (1986: 274). Ashley suggests that this individualist base fails to provide a foundation on which a structuralist explanation can be built. In fact it is in contradiction to a structuralist explanation because the self-interested action of individual rational actors will counteract the creation of a system.

Additionally, Ashley is critical of Neorealism's positivism. This criticism is closely related to Cox's point about problem-solving theory discussed above. Ashley suggests that positivist theory presupposes a particular kind of theory with particular types of elements. He outlines this point as follows:

Even before the first self-consciously theoretical word passes anyone's lips, a theoretical picture worth a thousand words is already etched in the minds of positivist speakers and hearers. . . . This picture, a kind of scheme, orders and limits expectations about what explicit theoretical discourse can do and say. In particular, it commits scientific discourse to an 'actor model' of social reality – a model within which science itself is incapable of questioning the historical *constitution* of social actors, cannot question their ends, but can only advise them as the efficiency of means.

(Ashley 1986: 285, original emphasis)

In other words, Ashley is arguing that Neorealism's commitment to positivism is a limiting factor on the type of theory that can be produced. It fails to comprehend change and seeks only to improve the effectiveness of existing social structures.

To summarise the positions of Cox and Ashley, both criticise Neorealism for what they consider to be the type of theory it is. They suggest its self-portrayal as an objective science is a smokescreen to hide its ideological commitment to the state system and the US's position in a bipolar world. At the same time this type of theory is unable to conceptualise the possibility of historical change in institutions and social constructions. Ashley makes additional points emphasising the centrality of a statist viewpoint in Neorealism. These can be seen as fitting within the agent–structure debate discussed above.

Waltz, not surprisingly, rebuffs these views. He accepts Cox's distinction between problem-solving and critical theory, but finds no problem with his decision to produce the former. He notes that 'Ashley and Cox would transcend the world as it is; meanwhile we have to live in it' (Waltz 1986: 338). He also addresses the issue of the state-centric approach of Neorealism. Simplification is necessary to produce theory. The characterisation of the state as a unitary rational actor was a justifiable and necessary step in the production of theory.

The criticisms of Waltz's work considered in this section have focused primarily on three issues: the issue of the lack of a theory of change, as argued by Cox, Keohane, and Ruggie; the question of the definition of the state, as argued by Ashley; and the relationship between the structure and agents or system and state, as discussed by Dessler and by Wendt. All three of these issues relate to the way that Waltz has handled the notion of the state in his work. The next section develops this issue further.

Neorealism and the state

I now want to concentrate on one particular issue: the implications of the approach taken by Waltz to the idea of the state. I will argue that Waltz, quite intentionally, does not provide a detailed theory of the state. To do so would reduce the parsimony of his theoretical approach, and, based on his definition, open his work to a charge of reductionism. It would be reductionist, in Waltz's terms, because it would introduce analysis at the unit level.

However, the elegance and parsimony of Neorealism is achieved at the expense of a theory of change. Neorealism aims to explain how states are likely to act in certain systems, not how change can occur within or between systems.[11] There is no mechanism by which change can be analysed or explained within Neorealism. Ruggie argues that Neorealism cannot explain a change of system: the switch from the medieval international system to the modern post-Westphalian system. It cannot even explain a change in the system: from the Cold War bipolar system to the post-Cold War unipolar[12] system. The most that Neorealism seems to be able to suggest is how the major states will interact in either bipolar or multipolar systems. As Hollis and Smith comment, 'Waltz's system is not actually capable of explaining much' (1990: 115).[13]

Nevertheless, this does not mean that Waltz has nothing to say about the state. Even though the character of the units drops out as an element of Waltz's definition of structure, this does not mean that there is not an implicit theory of the state in Neorealism. His argument that states are functionally undifferentiated suggests that he has some notion of what a state comprises. However, such a theory might only extend to the functions that a state carries out. Buzan *et al.* (1993: 119) for example, suggest that there is an 'embryonic theory of the state' contained within Neorealism.

Despite the possibility of Neorealism containing an 'embryonic theory' of the state, Waltz provides no formal definition. But it is possible to note certain characteristics of the state through the development of his work. In *Man, the State, and War*, Waltz (1959: 175) argues that the state is 'an abstraction', though 'it is convenient to think of states as the acting units'. In terms of relations between states, 'the state appears to other states as a unit' (*ibid.*: 178). These comments imply that Waltz draws heavily on the traditional realist view of the state as a territorial container, with all the implications that such a definition implies, as discussed above in Chapter 1. There can be many differences between states, but for Waltz there is more that unites the category of 'state' than divides it. He notes that 'states vary widely in size, wealth, power and form' (1979: 96). The factor that unites the states is the common functions that they have to fulfil. 'Each state duplicates the activities of other states at least to a considerable extent' (*ibid.*). Different states may be less capable of fulfilling these functions, but the functions that they undertake will be the same.

A further characteristic of the state that can be derived from Waltz's work is that it precedes the system. For Waltz, the system is a product of state interactions. The state is primary, and it is through the interactions of states that the international system came into existence. The international system is a product of the states, not the other way around. However, once created, the international system has an impact on state behaviour. It constrains the actions of states, and acts as an agent of socialisation. Having to be self-reliant forces states to keep up with their rivals. If a state falls behind it is likely to be overwhelmed. The international system imposes a requirement on states to act in certain ways. Even though the states came first, their subsequent behaviour is influenced by the international system. 'The close juxtaposition of states promotes their sameness through the disadvantages that arise from a failure to conform to successful practises' (Waltz 1979: 128).

Although Waltz does not make a definition of his concept of the state, there seems to be no reason why his view should not be taken as seeing the state as a territorial container, in the traditional realist approach. According to Waltz, states view each other as coherent units. These units reflect the decision making within the borders of the state. The international system can have the effect of socialising the units. However, because Waltz views states as being functionally undifferentiated, this amounts to the socialising process being restricted to decision making rather than influencing the form of the state itself. Competition engendered by the international system forces states to emulate the practices of their rivals if they are to survive. However, Waltz's theory does not allow for the possibility that the form of the state itself may change. In other words, the approach to the state is ahistoric.

To criticise Waltz solely on these grounds is somewhat disingenuous, as he has made it clear throughout his exposition that he intends to produce a theory that abstracts away from many important issues, the state being one of them. The issue is to what extent the resultant theory is *useful* as a means of understanding world politics. That is to say, to what extent can the theory provide a coherent account of the social world? Clearly, given the dominance of Neorealism in the International Relations discipline, many analysts do indeed find it very useful. However, with the changes brought about by the end of the Cold War, it is questionable whether this is tenable. Kratochwil (1993) has argued that there has been an 'embarrassment of changes'. In particular, a change in the international system (from bipolar to unipolar) occurred without a massive redistribution of capabilities, and, thankfully, without a hegemonic war. Both of these predictions are derived from neorealist theory. Furthermore, the impetus to international change was internally generated within the countries of Eastern Europe and the former Soviet Union. Neorealism as it stands is unable to provide an explanation of these events. Given that the end of the Cold War resulted in a change in the international system, the very thing that Neorealism claims as its centre of analysis, this seems to be a particular problem.

The introduction of a theory of the state would undermine Waltz's aim of producing an elegant and parsimonious theory, because it would introduce factors at the unit level. However, in some elements it is clear from his work that he envisions international processes as being two-way, between system and units and vice-versa.[14] For example, he argues that 'structural change begins in a system's units' (1993: 49). Given this position, it does not seem unreasonable to inquire about the possibility of how these unit-level processes might be explored. However, his theoretical construction, which excludes an analysis of the state, excludes the possibility of pursuing such an analysis.

One possibility, as suggested by James, might be to include a rational choice-based theory of state behaviour (James, P. 1995). The aim would be to retain Neorealism's structural explanation for the persistence of international warfare, while strengthening it through the addition of a theory of state decision making as a response to systemic constraints. James (*ibid.*: 202) makes the point that if Neorealism is to be extended it should be through the incorporation of theory 'integrated with structural realism's basic principles'. Rational choice theory would provide just such a theory, he argues.

But I intend to pursue a different possibility. Rational choice theory might provide one way of elaborating Neorealism. However, such a theoretical enterprise would be limited in three ways. First, it would not furnish a theory of the state that could incorporate state development. The view of the state would remain static, and all states would be considered as being constituted in the same way. Second, the combination of rational choice theory with Neorealism would not provide an avenue for investigating change to the international system generated by domestic forces. Finally, such an approach would not provide the possibility of including an analysis of states' relations with non-state actors.

In order to achieve these objectives it is necessary to reconceptualise the notion of the state. This would involve a move away from the idea of the state merely as a territorial container, and as a historical given. As suggested in Chapter 1, Historical Sociology provides a different way of thinking about the state. Rather than being the embodiment of a particular territory, the state becomes a set of institutions that claim to have control over a particular spatial area. These institutions are in competition both with other states in the international sphere and with other social groupings, domestic and cross-border. Crucially, Historical Sociology encompasses the notion that states have changed over time. Furthermore, in the most recent writings by historical sociologists the development of the state is analysed in the context of an international system. In the following chapters we will examine how, in different ways, four historical sociologists accomplish this.

CONCLUSION

The central aim of this chapter has been to examine Neorealism, in particular the work of Kenneth Waltz, as the dominant approach to the analysis of international systems. Waltz's work is part of an ongoing tradition of attempts by International Relations scholars to produce a systems approach for the discipline. However, Waltz rejects as reductionist all previous attempts to produce a systems approach. To overcome this problem Waltz aimed to produce a theory that did not make reference to the character of the units, his intention being to isolate those forces active at the international level. His intention was to produce an abstract approach that could explain the maximum from a minimum of theory.

The dominance of approaches based on Neorealism suggests that Waltz has achieved what he set out to do. However, ever since *Theory of International Politics* was published, other theorists have sought to take it a step further. Some of these proposals have been considered in this chapter. The most ambitious of these attempts is contained in the work of Buzan, Jones and Little. The key motive of these modifications is to overcome the inability of Neorealism to explain change, as noted by Ruggie, Cox, and Ashley: either from one system to another, or within a system. One suggestion to overcome this problem, as raised by Ruggie and by Keohane, is that the analysis of the state should be extended.

What stems from these criticisms is the view that the possibility of analysing change could be included in Neorealism through the inclusion of a theory of the state. This raises the question of which theory of the state is to be used, and how it is to be incorporated into Waltz's formulation. Chapter 1 argued that there had been a great deal of interest from International Relations scholars in the work of historical sociologists such as Mann, Skocpol, Tilly and Wallerstein. A lot of this interest resulted from their particular analysis of the state. Chapter 1 also pointed out that a significant feature of their work was the conceptualisation of the state within an international system, so that state development was influenced not only by the state's relationships with its domestic population, but also by its relationships with other states and other international actors. The work of these writers is discussed in the following chapters, concentrating on their analysis of the state, and outlining how they include a concept of international system in their work. The final chapter will return to the discussion of Neorealism, and evaluate whether a theory of the state provided by these writers could be incorporated into Waltz's theory and thus furnish it with the capacity to explain change.

4

THEDA SKOCPOL

INTRODUCTION

In Chapter 2 we examined the features of Historical Sociology and located the work of writers such as Skocpol, Tilly, Mann and Wallerstein in a continuing line of historical thought. This tradition can be dated back to the romantic historians of the eighteenth century. Having traced the development of this line of thought, attention turned to the concept of the international system in International Relations, with particular reference to the work of Kenneth Waltz. In Chapter 3 I argued that although Waltz's structural approach to the study of international relations was widely celebrated, it suffered from a major fault: the lack of a theory of change. This chapter and the subsequent three will examine in turn the work of four key writers in contemporary Historical Sociology. The significant factor in each of these writers chosen for discussion is that they have attempted to produce an account of the state situated within an international system. Each chapter will examine their work in depth and discuss their approach to analysing the international system and the state. We begin with a discussion of the work of Theda Skocpol.

Skocpol is primarily known for her work on revolutions. Skocpol's first major work, *States and Social Revolutions*, published in 1979, is considered to be one of the most significant works of Historical Sociology of the current era. It is this work on the 'classic' revolutions in France, Russia and China that has generated the most interest amongst International Relations scholars.

Although her treatise introduced no new empirical material, Skocpol advanced the study of revolutions in several major ways. First, she developed a structural, non-voluntarist approach to the study of revolution, reducing the role of individuals, and stressing the significance of impersonal social forces. Furthermore, she placed the state at the centre of her analysis. On the one hand she examined the crisis of the state from above and below, a crisis which she saw as being present in the three revolutions that she considered. On the other, she outlined the processes of centralisation and rationalisation that she claimed were features of each of the post-revolutionary regimes. Moreover, she applied a comparative historical approach with considerable rigour. Such an approach is not new, and Skocpol's inspiration can be found in Moore's work. However, through a careful application of John Stuart Mill's system of logic, she took the methodology to a new level. Finally, she introduced the idea of an international system as an important element in her analysis. Skocpol viewed the role of an international system not only as an influence on the occurrence of specific revolutions, but also as a considerable determinant of their outcomes.

This chapter will examine how Skocpol views the international system and how it interacts at state level in influencing events. I will argue that although Skocpol embarks with a theoretically strong view of the international system, when she applies this to her empirical material she reduces her concept to the occurrence of warfare between states. In her analysis of the French, Russian and Chinese revolutions this is not a problem in itself. It would seem reasonable to assert that international conflict was an important factor in the undermining of the old regimes and in explaining the centralising characteristics of their revolutionary replacements. However, to reduce the international system to the occurrence of warfare is limiting. It will be suggested that this accounts for the dropping of the system level of analysis from her subsequent works on Third World revolutions and social policy in the United States.

The organisation of this chapter will be as follows. First, a brief survey of Skocpol's work will be given, with a brief assessment of some of the criticisms that it has inspired. Attention will then concentrate on her conception of the international system. Her critical reviews of works by Moore and Wallerstein will be considered. This will be followed by an examination of her own theoretical position, including a discussion of how she applied her approach to the empirical material. This will include a discussion of her failure to apply her theoretical position in a coherent fashion and her omission of international contexts in her ensuing work.

OVERVIEW OF SKOCPOL'S WORK

States and social revolutions

In her first book, Skocpol examined the causes and outcomes of three 'classical' social revolutions: France in 1789, Russia from 1917 to the 1930s, and China from 1911 to 1949. Skocpol (1979: 4) defines social revolutions as 'rapid, basic transformations of a society's state and class structures ... accompanied and in part carried through by class-based revolts from below'. Her argument can be summarised as follows: these three revolutions occurred when weakened state structures were subjected to increased economic and military pressure from abroad, combined with agrarian social-political structures that allowed for peasant revolt; similarly, the outcomes of the revolutions can be understood through an examination of the structural pressures faced by the incoming revolutionary governments.

Her analysis begins with a discussion of previous theories of revolution. She points to three existing types of theory: aggregate-psychological theories which examine individuals' psychological motivations for joining revolutionary movements; systems/value consensus theories which, influenced by a Parsonian approach, view revolutions as a functional reaction to severe disequilibria in society; and political conflict theories that place the struggle between rival groups in society at the centre of their analysis. Skocpol finds value in all these approaches, but argues that none can provide an overall explanation. To provide a fuller explanation it would be important to include three important elements in the analysis.

First, a non-voluntarist, structural perspective on the causes and outcomes of revolution would be needed. A structural approach is essential to account for how

> In historical revolutions, differently situated and motivated groups have become participants in complex unfoldings of multiple conflicts. These conflicts have been powerfully shaped and limited by existing socioeconomic and international conditions.
>
> (Skocpol 1979: 17)

In other words, a voluntarist approach (i.e. one in which an individual or group is seen as 'making' a revolution) will be incomplete because of the varieties of different groups and circumstances that have comprised revolutionary situations. To privilege one group or one individual will not give a complete picture of the causes of a revolution. This is a particularly important point when comparing revolutions. The motivations of the participants in the French Revolution were different from those of the actors in the Russian Revolution. Even so, it is possible to draw parallels between the structural pressures affecting the causes and outcomes of these two revolutions. Regarding ideology, she argues that structural forces acted to deflect revolutionary leaders away from their original intentions. She notes that:

> Ideologically oriented leaderships in revolutionary crises have been greatly limited by existing structural conditions and severely buffeted by the rapidly changing currents of revolutions. Thus they have typically ended up accomplishing very different tasks and furthering the consolidation of quite different kinds of new regimes from those they originally (and perhaps ever) ideologically intended.
>
> (Skocpol 1979: 171)

By implication there is little value in studying ideology, because of the difference between intention and outcome. Hence a better understanding of revolution can be gained through a consideration of the role of structural forces in the run-up and aftermath of revolutionary situations.[1]

The second element that Skocpol argues has been missing from previous research has been the failure to consider international and world-historical contexts. Prior investigations had concentrated exclusively on conflict within national societies. Skocpol considered it important to consider transnational relationships which 'have contributed to the emergence of all social-revolutionary crises and have invariably helped to shape revolutionary struggles and outcomes' (1979: 19). These transnational relations take various forms. First, it is necessary to consider economic development. Differing rates of economic development place increased strains on the countries that are left behind. Second, there is the question of direct conflict between states. Involvement in international wars places strains on states as they have to mobilise their populations, divert investment and make claims on their citizens. Finally, it is necessary to take into account world-historical time. Clearly the events of the French Revolution had an impact upon and acted as a model for subsequent revolutions.

The third criticism that Skocpol makes of earlier research on revolutions is the failure to analyse the state properly. Marxist analyses, for example, see the state primarily as an agent of the dominant class. Skocpol sees the state as being more of an autonomous body. This organisation is in competition with other groups in society for the control of resources. Her definition of the state is as 'a set of administrative, policing, and military organizations headed, and more or less well coordinated by, an executive authority' (1979: 29). The state has two basic functions: to maintain order domestically and to compete with other states. Hence again it is necessary to consider the international context. The state has a dual role: one foot in the domestic situation and one in the international. Therefore it is necessary to investigate not only the relations between states and domestic social classes, but also among states in an international system. Additionally, a state, through its external activities, may gain power that can be used domestically. As Skocpol observes, 'a state's involvement in an international network of states is a basis for potential autonomy of action over and against groups and economic arrangements within its jurisdiction – even including the dominant class and existing relations of production' (ibid.: 31).

As an illustration of states gaining more autonomy based on international involvement, Skocpol gives the example of states at war needing to implement programmes of socio-economic reform. Such reforms potentially undermine ruling-class interests. In such circumstances states act contrary to social groups whose interests they might be expected to protect.

Skocpol's analysis attempts to make use of these three elements to provide a deeper insight into the character of social revolution. She divides her analysis into two parts. First she looks at the causes of social revolutions in each of her three examples. Then she turns to examine the outcomes in each case. She applies a comparative methodology, contrasting and comparing the three examples to reveal causes that are common in each instance. Her analysis also draws on examples from failed or partial revolutions (e.g. England, Germany) to see what factors were present or missing from those instances.

In France, Russia and China the revolutions emerged primarily through a political crisis centred on the old regimes. These regimes, trapped in economic and/or military competition with surrounding states, were unable to modernise rapidly enough to cope with the opposition. In China, for example, the Ching dynasty was unable to compete, either militarily or economically, with European, American and other Asian powers. A series of humiliating defeats and concessions led to the implementation of a series of reforms, but these measures only served to further undermine the old regime, which was finally toppled in 1911.

Along with the crisis of the old regime, in each case Skocpol points to the importance of rural insurrections. The rural population taking advantage of the crisis in the old regimes led these insurrections. She quotes Moore's phrase that 'the peasants . . . provided the dynamite to bring down the old building' (Skocpol 1979: 112). She argues that the weakening of the state organisation coupled with peasant revolt provided 'the sufficient distinctive causes of social-revolutionary situations commencing in France 1789, Russia 1917, and China 1911' (ibid.: 154).

Turning to the question of outcomes of the revolutions, Skocpol finds the existence of similar structural factors shaping the character of the outcome of the revolutionary process:

> Social-revolutionary outcomes have been shaped and limited by the existing socioeconomic structures and international circumstances within which revolutionary leaders have struggled to rebuild, consolidate, and use state power.
>
> (Skocpol 1979: 280)

The prime feature of the states emerging from the revolutionary situation was that they were more centralised and rationalised than the pre-revolutionary ones. In addition, these states were particularly successful at the mass mobilisation of their populations (Skocpol 1979: 189; 1988b; 1989: 6). A prime characteristic of these more rationalised states was their enhanced capacity to cope with the internal political situation as well as the international. Napoleon's reforms to the state enabled his French armies to conquer much of Europe. Changes in the Russian state paved the way for the process of rapid industrialisation and the eventual defeat of Nazi Germany. In China the levels of social control under the communist system were much higher than under the imperial system, and on the international scene China became able to determine its own political path.

Skocpol's model of social revolutions therefore attempts to build on her criticism of existing theories of revolution. She uses a structural non-voluntarist approach as opposed to one that stresses revolution making, and emphasises international factors that not only promote revolutionary situations but also have an impact upon the outcome of revolutions. Finally, her view of the state is as a much more autonomous actor, not simply the agent of one particular group in society.

To what extent is Skocpol able to provide a general model of revolution? She (1979: 288) points out that she is not making universal claims, but that the causes and outcomes of revolutions 'vary according to the historical and international circumstances of the countries involved'. However, it is clear that she is trying to suggest a wider application of her theory when she points to the similarities between other revolutions of the second half of the twentieth century (e.g. Cuba, Ethiopia, Mozambique) and those in France, Russia and China. All happened in predominantly agrarian societies in which an administrative-military breakdown occurred, and in each case there were widespread peasant revolts and mobilisation. However, most twentieth-century revolutions have taken place in dependent countries, and hence it is necessary to trace the legacy of colonialism and the impact of shifts in the international political and economic systems.

Even while her work on revolutions was being written and prepared for publication, a revolutionary situation was emerging that would provide a major surprise to analysts everywhere. In Iran an urban-based revolution overthrew a well organised state armed with a frighteningly effective repressive apparatus. In this instance there was no military defeat to provide an internal crisis, and the benefits of oil revenues were being employed for modernisation at least as rapidly as in other countries in the region. Finally, this would appear to be a revolution that was made – by the Islamic religious leaders, headed by Ayatollah Khomeini. This was a very different sort of revolution, and to what extent could the structuralist framework expounded by Skocpol be applied? She set out to explore this issue in an article written three years after the revolution (Skocpol 1982).

In her analysis of the Iranian Revolution, Skocpol stresses the significance of the Iranian bazaar as a focus of socio-economic life in the urban centres. This provided the locus for the organisation of the urban rebellions and, combined with the militant message of Shi'a Islam, became central to the coordination and maintenance of the rebellion. Skocpol argues that, although the revolution was 'made', a structural explanation is possible:

It was made through a set of cultural and organisational forms thoroughly socially embedded in the urban communal enclaves that became the centers of popular resistance to the Shah. Even when a revolution is to a significant degree 'made,' that is because a culture conducive to challenges to authority, as well as politically relevant networks of popular communication, are already historically woven into the fabric of social life.

(Skocpol 1982: 275)

It should be noted, however, that in her analysis of the events leading up to the Iranian Revolution Skocpol makes no reference to the international political system. However, events since the revolution would seem to be more in keeping with the other revolutions that Skocpol analysed. The proponents of a centralised Islamic state, with a religious constitution, have claimed victory over those more liberal elements who sought to decentralise the state. In the international situation, Iraq's attempted invasion of Iran acted to strengthen the position of the Iranian government in the face of an external threat. Otherwise, as Skocpol notes, the international situation was comparatively kind to the new revolutionary government. Neither of the contemporary superpowers were prepared to intervene in the situation for fear of drawing a reprisal from the other. Additionally, Iran's position as a major oil exporter provided the funds to maintain the new state (Skocpol 1982: 279).

Critiques of states and social revolutions

Skocpol's main critics have concentrated on the structural approach that makes her work so distinctive. Lehmann, for example, finds value in the structural approach for understanding the origins of revolutions, but not in explaining their outcomes. He argues that:

Where the old regime elites fail in the face of a myriad of pressures, the new elites succeed in the face of even heavier odds: war and famine among them. The former is easily understood in structural terms, the latter is not.

(Lehmann 1980: 624)

But this particular criticism does not to stand up to much scrutiny. It is certainly true that the new regimes faced even worse situations than the ones they replaced. However, a prime feature of the state in the post-revolutionary situation was its higher degree of centralisation and rationalisation. Skocpol argues that this increased rationalisation and centralisation provided sufficient gains in efficiency for the new regimes to surmount the problems that they confronted.

In a similar vein, Himmelstein and Kimmel (1981) argue that Skocpol has taken the structural approach too far. They argue that it is necessary to consider the factors that mediate between structural conditions and outcomes, specifically human consciousness and action. They suggest that Skocpol 'simply assumes that the appropriate actors are always there, waiting to perform the role required by structural conditions – peasants ever ready to make massive uprisings and marginal elites ever able to consolidate power' (*ibid.*: 1153). This is another variant of the agent–structure debate as discussed in the previous chapter. Skocpol aims to keep her account at the structural level, whilst Himmelstein and Kimmel are seeking to draw the analysis down to a more individualistic level. As we have already seen, the agent–structure argument is very difficult to resolve.

By contrast, Sewell (1985) criticises Skocpol for her failure to consider the importance of ideology in her analysis. He argues that ideology is an autonomous force, and that it should be viewed in structural terms. Sewell's critique drew a response from Skocpol in which she outlined further her description of structures. She (1985: 86) suggests that perhaps 'noninten-tionalist at the macroscopic level' might have been a better way to have described her approach. By this she meant that no particular group in the revolutionary process was capable of causing the crisis or determining the outcome. Instead the focus was 'on "structures", or patterned relationships beyond the manipulative control of any single group or individual. . . . Yet, of course, social structures – such as landlord–peasant relationships, or ties that bind monarchs and administrative officials – are not themselves actors' (Skocpol 1985: 87). With regard to ideology, she views it as systems of ideas deployed by political actors either engaged in political conflict or having to justify the uses of state power (*ibid.*: 91). Additionally there exist 'cultural idioms'. These are 'longer term' and more 'anonymous'. Their existence is drawn upon by political actors in the construction of their ideologies. Here Skocpol gives as an example Stalin's use of Marxism as a means of justifying his actions. She argues that it is necessary to examine both of these forms of ideology for the creation of a more historically based analysis, as these indi-cate the culturally determined choices that actors confront (*ibid.*: 94).

Other critics have questioned the concepts that Skocpol employs. Motyl (1992), for example, criticises the concepts that Skocpol uses as being too ambiguous and vague. He suggests that Skocpol is able to obtain the results she desires from her research through the way in which she has defined her variables. From a similar angle, Badie (1992: 323) warns of the danger of creating 'illusions of universality'. He questions her assumption that there is sufficient similarity between the French, Russian and Chinese states and their relations with their respective agrarian elites for her to draw the encompassing conclusions that she does. He argues that:

> It constitutes a threefold denial of the principles of Historical Sociology: by postulating a universal idea of the state (what did the Tsing Emperor have in common with the King of France?), a universal idea of an agrarian elite, and a universal idea of the link between politics and society.
>
> (Badie 1992: 323)

These universalising tendencies do exist in Skocpol's work. However, they will exist in any attempt at the comparative method. Without some simplification of concepts, the possibility of carrying out a comparative analysis would be extremely difficult, if not impossible.

Davidheiser (1992) has also criticised Skocpol's application of the concept of the state. She argues that Skocpol has failed to provide a means of measuring and comparing the relative strength of states. Instead she has concentrated on the coercive abilities of states whilst ignoring their abilities to intervene in their subject societies in other ways: for example, through their direction of the economy. She suggests that, without some means of determining state strength, Skocpol's argument becomes almost circular: 'revolution is the collapse of the old state; it occurs where the state is weak and collapses' (Davidheiser 1992: 464).

Davidheiser proposes a methodology for the measurement of state strength. She suggests three components: the depth of penetration of the state, its ability to implement policy; the extent of penetration of the state, the scope of transformation that the state is able to execute; and the permeability of the state, its openness to societal interests. Carrying out an analysis of Russia in the pre-1917 era she suggests, contrary to Skocpol, that the Russian state was strong rather than weak. Before the revolution the Russian state was successfully pursuing a policy of industrialisation (penetration), which affected the entire country, including the majority agricultural sector (depth). At the same time the Russian state had very low permeability, 'workers and peasants had no access to the state' (Davidheiser 1992: 467). Her analysis leads her to suggest that, contrary to Skocpol, revolutions are more likely in strong states than weak ones.

Although it is possible to agree with Davidheiser that Skocpol has failed to provide a method for measuring state strength and has confined her discussion of the state to its coercive functions, it is suggested here that she has stretched her conclusions too far. Davidheiser has failed to extend her analysis to the other two states that Skocpol considers, China and France. It is uncertain whether she would obtain similar results. Also, she appears to make the opposite error to that which she accuses Skocpol of making: instead of concentrating exclusively on the state's coercive capabilities, she has ignored them altogether.

Skocpol's critics have argued that her structural approach leaves no room for the analysis of agency, and that she fails to include a discussion of ideology. Moreover, her comparative approach has been criticised. To what extent are the social formations that she examines directly comparable? In particular, is it possible to compare the state in revolutionary France, Russia and China? None of the critics of Skocpol's work have done much to dent her confidence in her work, as can be seen from the introductory and concluding chapters of her book of collected essays on revolution (Skocpol 1994a, 1994b). However, through the 1980s Skocpol's interests have moved from being primarily concerned with revolution to a consideration of welfare policy.

States and social policy

In her work on social welfare Skocpol has been interested in explaining why welfare policies vary from one country to another. As with her work on revolutions, she is very critical of existing approaches to the study of welfare policies. In an article co-authored with Orloff, she noted of existing theories that:

> All understand the development of the modern welfare state as an inherently progressive phenomenon . . . appearing and growing in recognizable stages in all national societies as a necessary and irreversible concomitant of fundamental social processes such as urbanization, industrialization and demographic change – or else capitalist development and the emergence of the industrial working class.
>
> (Orloff and Skocpol 1984: 730)

The solution to this problem is to adopt a methodology similar to that taken in the study of revolutions: a structural approach. In addition, as with her work on revolutions, the state plays a central role. There are two ways in which states affect policy: they may act autonomously, pursuing policies which are not directly reducible to the interest of any major social class; and through the organisational structures that the state possesses to influence the wants and wishes of other groups in society. In this model, then, the emphasis is on the autonomy of the state to pursue its own programme and to affect the agenda in the wider society.

Skocpol's (1992a) most recent work has concentrated on the foundation of social policy in the United States of America. It attempts to explain why, despite the progressive policy of providing pensions for civil war veterans, the US has never developed a welfare state similar to certain European states. In contrast to her work on revolutions, the analysis remains largely rooted within one country, and there is little consideration of the geopolitical environment. Her only reference is to the impact of war on state formation. She (1992a: 44) remarks that 'wars have never had the same centralizing effects for the US state as they have had for many European states'. The implication is that a less centralised state has greater difficulty in imposing its policies and has less structural ability to condition the wants of society as a whole. However, this is only a starting point for the analysis. It is also necessary to consider how 'political struggles and their policy outcomes have been conditioned by the institutional leverage that various social groups have gained, or failed to gain within the US polity' (1992a; 1992b: 574). Hence the degree of centralisation will be a factor in indicating the relative strength of the state compared to other social actors.

This model is essentially one of conflict. Policy outcomes (in the current analysis the question of welfare issues) are determined as the result of the struggle between various social actors. This as opposed to 'natural' progression models such as those that concentrate on the logic of industrialisation, the victory of liberal values, or the gaining of welfare benefits through working class strength. Any progressive model would in any case have problems explaining the current dismantling of the British welfare state, so Skocpol's model would appear to have much to recommend it.

Skocpol's work has concentrated on two main areas: revolution, and the provision of social welfare. In the first of these topics she made extensive use of a notion of the international system as a central part of her analysis. In her more recent work this element has become much less significant. This survey of her work provides a context in which to examine her approach to the international system and the role of the state.

THEDA SKOCPOL AND THE CONCEPT OF INTERNATIONAL SYSTEM

Having provided a summary of Skocpol's work it is now possible to examine in greater detail her views on the international system. As a starting point her evaluation of other Historical Sociology writings will be examined. A brief consideration of these critiques will assist in the understanding of Skocpol's views of the international system.

Critiques of Moore and Wallerstein

During the 1970s Skocpol (1973, 1977) produced two major works of criticism on the work of other historical sociologists. Central to both of these criticisms was the concept of the international system. She criticised Moore for not including the international system in his work, and Wallerstein for including only an economic international system in his analysis, and not considering any political aspect.

Skocpol makes four criticisms of Moore's work. The first three are problems with the definitions of key variables that Moore employs: the strength of the bourgeois impulse; the difference between types of agriculture; and the use of the terms class-struggle and class-coalition for describing political conflict and social transformation. The concern here is with her fourth point of criticism, namely the concentration on intra-societal processes of change.

Skocpol argues that all the variables that Moore employs refer to structures and processes within society. However, these intra-societal variables are not sufficient for him to complete his analysis. He is forced recurrently to resort to 'external conditions'. For example, to explain England's ability to avoid reactionary capitalist development he cites: being an island, which permitted England to compete militarily without the need to maintain an army at home; and being the first industrial nation which permitted the practice of the 'imperialism of free trade'. Skocpol (1973: 30) argues that such *ad hoc* considerations should not be included on an 'as needed' basis, but should form part of 'a theory which recognizes that large-scale social change within societies is always in large part caused by forces operating among them, through their economic and political interaction'. In other words, instead of drawing on these contexts as add-ons to his theory, a consideration of the international environment should constitute part of his approach. Such an approach, she argues, should take into consideration that a large impulse for national modernisation comes from competition between state organisations. The inclusion of these aspects would have greatly strengthened Moore's approach.

Turning to Wallerstein's work, Skocpol makes two major criticisms. First, she argues that he reduces the international system to the existence of market opportunities and the differences in technological production potentials. That is to say, his conception of the international system is purely economic and does not include political factors. Her second criticism is that he reduces the role of the state to the interests of a dominant class (Skocpol 1977: 1078–9). To back up her critique, Skocpol cites problems for Wallerstein's approach in explaining the differences between the transition from feudalism to capitalism in Eastern and Western Europe and in the emergence of monarchical regimes. For the former it is necessary to include an analysis of the comparative strength of agrarian classes in different societies, whilst for the latter a consideration of interstate competition is required. Hence, to understand the emergence of capitalism both a top-down and a bottom-up analysis are needed.

Skocpol suggests that the view of capitalism that would emerge from such an analysis

> will probably pertain to intersecting structures (e.g. class structures, trade networks, state structures, and geopolitical systems) involving varying and autonomous logics and different, though overlapping, historical times, rather than a single, all-encompassing system that comes into being in one stage and then remains constant in its essential patterns until capitalism as a whole meets its demise.
>
> (Skocpol 1977: 1087–8)

To summarise, Skocpol considered that both Moore and Wallerstein had omitted important factors in their analyses. In order to explain the transition to modernised societies, Moore was forced on many occasions to introduce factors external to the societies he was analysing. Skocpol suggested that his approach would have been strengthened if he had included such factors in a theoretical way. By contrast she criticised Wallerstein for privileging the international economic system to the exclusion of all other factors.

We will now turn to a consideration of the extent to which Skocpol has been successful in overcoming the problems that she found in the works of Moore and Wallerstein.

Revolution and the international system

Skocpol's theoretical approach to the international system emerges from a critique of modernisation theories. Such theories, an example commonly cited being Marx's historical materialism, view the development of a society as an internal dynamic.[2] Skocpol argues that this view of societies developing autonomously is unrealistic. Instead, it is necessary to take into account that each society is surrounded by others, and that developments in one will have an impact on those in another. She argues that 'from the start international relations have intersected with preexisting class and political structures to promote and shape divergent as well as similar changes in various countries' (1979: 20). She suggests that two transnational contexts are relevant. First, there are two types of structure, the world capitalist economy and the international states system. Returning to her criticism of Wallerstein, whose method she reproaches for being excessively economistic, she argues that the important factor about these two structures is that, although they are interdependent, neither is reducible to the other (*ibid.*: 22). Furthermore, there is the context of 'world time', the potential for subsequent actors to draw upon the economic and political breakthroughs of previous generations.

Skocpol (1979: 20) views the structure of the world economic system as being based on the flows of 'goods, migrants and investment capital'. These interactions predated the breakthrough to England's industrial and agricultural capital development, and were highly influential upon it. As a result of their absorption into the world economic system, the pre-existing economic and class relations of countries previously on the periphery were either reinforced or modified. Skocpol appears to reject a determining role to the world economic system, but rather views it as an influencing factor:

> We need not necessarily accept arguments that national economic developments are actually determined by the overall structure and market dynamics of a 'world capitalist system'. We can, however, certainly note that historically developing transnational economic relations have always strongly (and differentially) influenced national economic developments.
>
> (Skocpol 1979: 20)

Coexisting alongside this international economic structure is a second structure, 'an international system of competing states' (1979: 20). Skocpol suggests that it is this international political structure that differentiated Europe from other areas of the globe. Although at varying times different states have sought mastery of Europe in its entirety, none have managed to establish their hegemony on a permanent basis. Hence interstate relations in Europe has always been dictated by this competitive element. This competitive political system spurred the modernisation of the continent primarily through the requirement that states either keep in the race or be extinguished. Skocpol (*ibid.*: 21) notes that 'recurrent warfare within the system of states prompted European monarchs and statesmen to centralize, regiment, and technologically upgrade armies and fiscal administrations'.[3] Central to this approach is the role of the state and its position at the intersection of national and international politics.

A central question at this point concerns the relationship between these two structures. As mentioned above, Skocpol regards the two as interdependent, but this does not indicate whether one is more important than the other. She does remark that the 'European world-economy was unique in that it developed within a system of competing states' (1979: 47). This suggests that she views the political structure as primary.

The second context of transnational relations is world-historical time. There are two important aspects involved here. First, changes that have occurred between one time period and another; and second, transmissions, or rather the availability of information or models to later actors. For example, the context and possibilities for the Russian and Chinese revolutions were markedly different from those of the French Revolution. For one thing, important changes in the forms of production introduced by the Industrial Revolution presented the new Russian and Chinese regimes with much greater productive capabilities. For another, the paths of development of these revolutions were greatly influenced by the availability of a pre-existing model (Skocpol 1979: 23, 173, 286; 1989: 69). But the lessons of such a model were not available only to revolutionary regimes. Countries facing potential revolutionary situations were forewarned of the potentials of revolution, and were able to move to counter these possibilities either by increasing levels of repression, or by attempting to buy off opposition groups.

Skocpol (1988b: 152, 162; 1989: 23) argues that a two-way relationship exists between international contexts and domestic events. Domestic events are constrained and influenced by the international, whilst internal changes can have important ramifications on external structures. These influences and constraints act in a number of ways: through an influence on state and class structures; through the results of competition in the international economic and political structures; and through the transformation of political and economic structures caused by domestic changes in state organisation.

A source of confusion that arises from Skocpol's theoretical approach to the international system arises from her use of the term 'system'. She employs this chiefly to describe the arena in which states compete militarily. To describe the entirety of international relations, her favourite term is 'international context', which includes the political, economic and world-historical aspects of her approach. Within International Relations the term is also used to describe a variety of views of what constitutes the international system, so this is not a problem unique to Skocpol, though it can make comparisons between competing views more difficult. However, through the use of the term 'context' she implies that all the elements of her analysis have an impact on societal developments. Hence it would seem appropriate to use the term 'system' to encompass all these factors.

In order to summarise Skocpol's view of the international system it might be worthwhile to compare her approach – or elements of her approach – to that of other writers.

The economic aspect of her method would seem to draw heavily on Wallerstein, though reducing the determinacy of his perspective. Her implication is that there is one international economic system, which from its original base in Europe expanded to incorporate the entire world.

Skocpol does not push her theoretical analysis of the international political system very far. However, there are some similarities between her view of the international political system and Waltz's view of structures, as described in Chapter 3. The prime similarity would seem to be the process of socialisation. States are forced to imitate the strategies of their most successful rivals or face the risk of extinction. However, there are some major distinctions between the views of Skocpol and Waltz, particularly their view of the state, and the relationship between the domestic and the external. In Skocpol's formulation there is considerable interaction. In Waltz's there is none.

Skocpol's work bears a closer relation to the Structural Realism of Buzan, Jones and Little, considered in the previous chapter. Like them, she includes more than one sector in her analysis, though she includes only two – economic and political – compared to their four – economic, societal, strategic and political. There would also seem to be a limited similarity between her view of world-historical time and their concept of interaction capacity. The closest link would appear to be to Buzan *et al.*'s view of technological capability as a system-wide feature, which would equate to Skocpol's view about change having an important impact on subsequent actors.

Skocpol's discussion of the international system is a central feature of the theoretical chapter at the start of *States and Social Revolutions*. She presents an elaborated discussion of what she considers to constitute the international system. Following the theoretical chapter at the start of *States and Social Revolutions*, Skocpol goes on to provide a detailed empirical examination of her three case studies. The next section considers to what extent she has been successful in applying her concept of the international system to the revolutions in France, Russia and China.

The application of theory in states and social revolutions

Skocpol has developed a theoretical position on the international system, which she sees as a combination of two structures: an economic system and an interstate competitive system. Added to these structures is the notion of world-historical time, whereby subsequent actors are influenced by what has occurred in the past. This section looks at how successful she has been in employing this theoretical position to the analysis of revolutions in *States and Social Revolutions*. As was observed in the summary section above, Skocpol's analysis of revolutions can be divided into two parts: the forces creating the revolutionary situation, and the influences on the post-revolutionary states.

France

In the run-up to the revolutionary crisis for the old regime, Skocpol portrays France as being in economic and strategic competition with England. In both respects France was in a disadvantageous position. On the economic front Skocpol (1989: 55) argues that the relative backwardness of French agriculture was a restraining feature on the development of industry. During the eighteenth century France was gradually falling behind, compared to England, in the growth of industrial production. These problems with modernisation of the economy were compounded on the military front. In the mid-eighteenth century France was involved in two major wars, which placed great strains on the country's finances, with no visible gains. Skocpol argues that France's problems were primarily strategic. England, being a maritime nation, could put most of its resources into the maintenance of its navy and did not need to maintain a large standing army. France's other major competitors, Prussia and Austria, essentially land-based powers, had little need of a large navy. France was both a maritime and a land power. As a result, France required both a large standing army and a large navy (*ibid.*: 60). These problems were compounded by the comparative inefficiencies in the French fiscal system for raising the required taxation to pay for these armed forces (*ibid.*: 60, 61). France's involvement in the American War of Independence pushed the system to breaking point. 'To finance the war to deprive England of its American colonies, royal treasurers . . . finally exhausted their capacity to raise new loans, even as they sharply increased royal expenditures and indebtedness to astronomical heights' (*ibid.*: 63). Although France was successful in this war, the impact on the state's finances was such that a general crisis of confidence in the ruling class emerged. This was the forerunner of the revolutionary crisis.

In the aftermath of the revolution, warfare was also a significant factor in the shaping of the new state. Skocpol argues that after a liberal phase of the revolution between 1789 and 1791, the act of declaring war on Austria marked the movement towards a period of terror and the rationalisation of the state.

The pressures upon the French revolutionary leaders after 1791 to mobilise for wars on the continent, even as they fought counter-revolutionaries at home, must be reckoned as a set of conditions comparable in importance to the effects of the social-revolutionary conjuncture of 1789 in determining the centralising nature of the outcomes of the French revolution.

(Skocpol 1989: 186)

Skocpol's analysis of the French Revolution therefore revolves around the effects that warfare had upon both the old and new regimes. The implication is that the costs imposed by involvement in the American War of Independence imposed a stress on the old regime from which it could not recover. The impact of the counter-revolutionary wars for the post-revolutionary regimes was to lead to a centralisation and rationalisation of the new regime.

Russia

The Russian economy at the turn of the twentieth century was not stagnant, especially when compared to that of France in the pre-revolutionary period. Even so, Skocpol argues that the structures of the Russian agrarian economy acted as a brake on the development of industrialisation compared to the rest of Europe (1989: 82–3). Ignominious defeat in the Crimean War led to the imposition from above of a policy of rapid industrialisation. Skocpol argues that these policies were largely successful, but that the European economic downturn of the late 1890s had a much greater impact in Russia than elsewhere in Europe. This economic crisis, combined with the disastrous war against Japan, set the scene for the 1905 revolution. Skocpol (*ibid.*: 95) argues that the Tsar was able to renege on his commitments and roll back this revolution. He achieved this by concluding the war with Japan and returning the troops to break strikes and suppress rebellions. If the Russian army did not have much success in its war against Japan, its performance against the German army in the First World War was abysmal. The relative industrial backwardness of Russia, and the problems with the transport network, aggravated this. Skocpol argues that the attempts by the Russian state to maintain control only weakened its position. When the Petrograd uprising occurred in February 1917, the revolutionaries were pushing at an already opened door (*ibid.*: 98).

Following the October 1917 Revolution, which displaced the Kerensky government, the victorious Bolsheviks were faced with a myriad problems. Foremost of these was the continuing war with Germany. This was not resolved until the spring of 1918, when a negotiated surrender was signed. The war with Germany was, however, replaced with an even larger problem: the protracted civil war. This was fought against units of the army loyal to the old regime, backed by units of the great powers. To counter this threat it was necessary to mobilise a large, centrally controlled military, composed primarily of agricultural workers. Skocpol (1989: 224) argues that this army fulfilled two tasks for the Communist regime. It defeated the counter-revolutionary forces and provided a secure basis for the centralised Communist rule.

Again, Skocpol places the impact of war at the centre of her analysis. The nemesis for the Russian imperial state took the form of the First World War, as compared to the American War of Independence for the French old regime. In a similar fashion, involvement in the counter-revolutionary wars after 1917 had the effect of centralising the fledgling state.

China

As with the examples of Russia and France given above, Skocpol (1989: 68–9) argues that the agrarian structures of pre-revolutionary China acted as a constraint to industrialisation. Skocpol's account of the Chinese revolution places central attention, however, on the enormous pressures that the old regime came under as a result of foreign intrusions on its territory. The first major incursion of this kind was the First Opium War of 1839–42. During the First Opium War, in its quest for free-trading relations to replace the 'Canton System' of regulated trade, Britain inflicted heavy defeats on China. The British success was followed by similar ventures by the other great powers in a quest to 'open' China. As a result of the many concessions the Chinese state was forced to give following a series of defeats, 'China's sheer existence as a sovereign country was profoundly threatened' (*ibid.*: 73). For China the worst humiliation came as a result of the defeat by Japan in 1895, a country historically considered by the Chinese to be inferior (*ibid.*: 77). As with the Russian defeat at the hands of the Japanese, this failure led to the implementation of a series of reforms intended to modernise the education system, industry and the military. However, as with the Russian example, these reforms merely acted to undermine the position of the old regime (*ibid.*: 78). As a result of this weakening of state structures, imperial rule was overthrown in 1911.

Warfare plays a much smaller role in Skocpol's discussion of the development of the post-revolutionary Chinese state. Her analysis concentrates on the relationship with the Soviet Union and the emergence of a tripolar world. Skocpol argues that the development of the Chinese nuclear capability marked a major point in the development of the revolution. Not only did it permit the break from Russia, but it also allowed economic and industrial development to proceed at a slower pace than had been required in Russia. This was because the possession of a nuclear capability enabled China to maintain less technically advanced armed forces. Hence a large industrial base was not required to keep the military supplied (as had been the case in Russia). Additionally, following the split from the Soviet Union in the early 1960s, the Chinese were able to benefit from international circumstances by playing one superpower off against the other. Skocpol summarises the international context facing the revolutionary Chinese state as follows:

> None of these arguments are meant to imply that anything about the post-World War II international situation positively prompted China to develop as she did after the mid-1950s. But thinking in terms of the comparison to Russia's situation in the European states system after World War I, it does seem valid to say that the Chinese faced circumstances that *allowed* them to develop differently insofar as domestic economic conditions and – especially – their Party-state's accumulated political capacity encouraged them to do so.
>
> (Skocpol 1989: 277, original emphasis)

Again, in Skocpol's account, warfare plays a significant role in the analysis of the old regime's downfall. In the case of China this was primarily a result of the military intrusions by the more developed western powers. However, China was not faced by the counter-revolutionary forces that confronted the new regimes in Russia and France. Skocpol argues that this accounts for the distinctive form of development taken by the post-revolutionary Chinese state.

Japan

Finally, it is worth considering for a moment Japan's position. Skocpol includes it in her discussion as an example of a state not overthrown in a revolutionary upheaval. She accounts for this partly through the success of the reforms instituted following the Meiji Restoration, but also because of the international context. The international context is important in two ways. First, Japan was involved in two wars at the turn of the century, and both of those led to victory, avoiding the dislocations and humiliations of defeat. Second, and for Skocpol a significant point, 'Japan was not fully involved in the European states system and, consequently, was never subjected to the terrible blows of any such prolonged and total modern war as World War I' (1989: 104).

In Skocpol's account of the revolutions in France, Russia and China, war plays a central factor in the downfall of the old regime. By contrast, in the example of Japan it is *success* in war that is part of the reason a successful revolution did not occur. In all these examples, the influence of the international system in Skocpol's analysis is through the state's involvement in fighting wars.

Skocpol, war and revolution

This section argues that although Skocpol's theoretical position provides a strong systemic viewpoint, her application of the historical material that she provides is reductionist. It is reductionist in both senses of the word as described above in Chapter 3. First, it is mono-causal, because she accounts for the influence of the international system on revolution through one factor: involvement in costly overseas war. Second, it is reductionist in the sense that Waltz uses the term. It is reductionist in this sense because an explanation of the whole is provided through an examination of the parts. Skocpol's discussion of the international system becomes an analysis of the impact of war between the units. This is counter to her more systemic theoretical position, which argues that the international system comprises two interrelated structures, plus the effects of world-historical time. The effect of her approach is to reduce the international system to the presence or absence of warfare.

This reductionist position is most noticeable in her discussion of the factors leading up to the French Revolution and the influences on the post-revolutionary regime. This viewpoint is most strongly expressed in the following statement:

> Warfare was far from extrinsic to the development and fate of the French revolution; rather *it was central and constitutive*, just as one would expect from knowing the nature and dilemmas of the Old Regime from which the Revolution sprang.
>
> (Skocpol 1989: 186, my emphasis)

Two conclusions emerge from this statement. The first is that it is not an international system which influences the developments of revolutions, but rather the interactions between states. In addition, the form of this interaction is confined to the occurrence of violence. The second conclusion is that warfare is a determining factor in development rather than an influence. It is worthwhile to compare this position with the discussion of China. With reference to the position of China, it would appear that a much stronger notion of system is implied. China was able to exploit its position in a tripolar system. However, what seems to be significant is the absence of warfare. In this instance the system is only an influence, it *allowed* a certain form of development. By contrast, Skocpol regards warfare as a determining factor. Her analysis of the Japanese example follows a similar pattern. In this instance, success in the limited wars against China and Russia, and the absence of large-scale incursions from western states, had a decisive influence on Japan's avoiding of a revolutionary path.

It was suggested in the discussion of Skocpol's theoretical position that her analysis of the political and economic system provided a valuable approach, but that in her historical account the economic system does not appear. What does appear is a reduction of economic development to war-fighting capacity, as demonstrated in the following statements:

> In the periods before the Revolutions, each of these regimes – Bourbon France, Romanov Russia, and Manchu China – found itself

in a situation of intensifying military competition with nation-states abroad that possessed relatively much greater and more flexible power based upon economic breakthroughs to capitalist industrialization or agriculture and commerce.

(Skocpol 1989: 50)

and with specific regard to Russia:

Industrialization *was* transforming the economies of Western Europe during the early nineteenth century, and its effects soon put Imperial Russia on the defensive in the vital international arenas of war and diplomacy.

(Skocpol 1989: 83, original emphasis)

Despite the impressive record of industrial expansion after 1880, especially in heavy industry, Russian economic development left the country still very far behind other nations with which it had to deal diplomatically and, potentially, militarily.

(*ibid.*: 94)

Statements such as these belie the notion that the political and international systems, though interdependent, are not reducible to each other. Rather, it would appear that Skocpol envisages the economic system as prior to the political. This is contrary to the position that the economic system developed within an international system of states, which was apparently the theoretical position that Skocpol argued in her introductory chapter.

In short, Skocpol's historical discussion does not match up to the power of her theoretical position. The international political system is reduced to the incidence of interstate warfare. The economic system is reduced to the relative levels of industrial development within specific societies rather than the influence exerted by an international economic system. The surviving element of her analysis is that of world-historical time, whose validity is amply demonstrated.

We noted at the beginning of this chapter that, for Skocpol, their failure to take account of the international context was a major problem with previous accounts of revolution. However, I have argued that despite the criticisms she has made of other writers, she has failed to provide a structural account of international relations. What implications does this have for the analysis in *States and Social Revolutions*? In the analysis of the classic revolutions, the ramifications are less than might be expected. Skocpol's formulation that

revolutionary political crises, culminating in administrative and military breakdowns, emerged because the imperial states became caught in cross-pressures between intensified military competition or intrusions from abroad and constraints imposed on monarchical responses by the existing agrarian class structures and political institutions

(1989: 285)

still stands. The point of the criticism is that she fails to analyse what she claims to be analysing. This is a limiting factor for the analysis of developments outside these three classic revolutions. It is not unreasonable to claim a link between military competition and revolution in the French, Russian and Chinese revolutions. However, in situations where such a link does not exist the explanation is harder to sustain. One example would be other revolutions, particularly in the developing world. In her discussions of the Iranian and Third World revolutions the influence of the international system largely disappears from the analysis (Skocpol 1982; Goodwin and Skocpol 1989). It has to, because war is not an influence. The way that Skocpol has operationalised the concept of the international system limits the possibility for including an international perspective in these instances. The same is true for her approach to social policy, where the international perspective almost totally drops from the analysis (Skocpol 1992a). By restricting the international system to the occurrence of war she is unable to include it in this kind of analysis. It would almost seem to imply that, apart from warfare, there is no influence upon societal developments by international events. It is difficult to understand how state welfare policy can be analysed without taking international factors into account. For example, would it be possible to understand European governments' welfare policies in the 1980s and 1990s without considering the world economic system? In effect she is making the same mistake that she criticised Moore for committing – overlooking the importance of international factors.

In terms of the matrix that was introduced in Chapter 1, attempting to place Skocpol is problematic because of this division between her theoretical and empirical positions. It is suggested that in both instances she is on the explaining side of the matrix (see Figure 4.1). This is on account of her claimed scientific approach. It would seem that in her theoretical position she could be placed in the holistic quartile, given her attempts to introduce structural explanations. But in practice, at least with regard to the international system, she has failed to provide a structural analysis. Instead she has used an individualistic explanation, concentrating on the occurrence of war between states. Therefore both positions will be shown.

CONCLUSION

Skocpol has been rightly applauded for her attempt to refine the definition of the state and to bring the notion of the international system into the analysis

	Explaining	Understanding
Holistic	external structures Skocpol theory	collective rules
Individualistic	Skocpol practice rational choices	reasoned choices

Figure 4.1 Skocpol's approach to the international system

of revolution. These theoretical advances have received considerable interest from International Relations scholars. In this chapter the work of Theda Skocpol has been discussed with the intention of analysing her position on the international system. The conclusion drawn is that, although she outlines a strong theoretical position, in practice her analysis reduces the system to warfare. This severely limits her ability to include the analysis of international contexts where warfare does not occur. This means that she is linking the occurrence, or absence, of revolution to the character of a state's involvement in international violence rather than to an international system. There is no international system beyond war in her analysis.

This conclusion has various implications for our investigation. Our central aim is to examine the approach to the international system used by historical sociologists. Skocpol provides a theoretical analysis of her view of the international system, but this is lost in her empirical work. Her *theoretical* position envisages a combination of economic and political structures, combined with the idea of world-historical time. In the *empirical* side of the analysis of revolutions this is reduced to the occurrence of warfare. In her work on social policy, the influence of the international system virtually disappears altogether. She has provided a theory of the international system in her work, but has failed to operationalise it. Skocpol provides a theory of international systems in the first chapter of *States and Social Revolutions*, but in practice this becomes reduced to the use of warfare to explain social change.

With regard to our second purpose, the analysis of the state is central to Skocpol's work. It is this contribution that marks the most important element in her work. Skocpol takes an institutional approach to the state. She sees it as the set of organisations claiming control over a particular territory. These organisations need to compete with other organisations within a territory, and crucially with other states and organisations in the international sphere. Unlike Marxist theorists, Skocpol does not see the state as a product of class relations, but as a semi-autonomous grouping. The state is able to pursue its own agenda and is not restricted to promoting the agenda of any one class interest.

However, it should be noted that this, very coherent, account of the state is bought at the expense of a vaguer notion of international system. Warfare is central to Skocpol's notion of international system. Furthermore it is this warfare that provides much of the explanation for state transformation. Her explanation for the occurrence of revolution is based to a large extent on the old regime's involvement in international war (successful or otherwise). Under the new, revolutionary regime, the state became rationalised, primarily as a result of the need to consolidate in the face of international conflict. Hence Skocpol's notion of state development is dependent on the way that, in practice, she has employed the notion of international system.

Skocpol's work on revolutions was a crucial element in the development of an interest in Historical Sociology by International Relations writers. Her discussion of the state has been the prime focus of interest. This has been seen as providing a way of thinking about the state that does not make a distinction between domestic and international politics. As such it presents an alternative way of thinking about international relations. In contrast to the traditional realist view of a dichotomy between domestic and international relations, Skocpol's work combines an analysis of both realms. Her work demonstrates how developments within one sphere affect the other. Her work also contrasts with the Marxist class-based view of international relations, where the state is seen as representing ruling-class interests. For Skocpol the state is autonomous of class interests, and can use its international activities as a means of strengthening its position domestically.

The next two chapters will demonstrate that Skocpol's institutionally based view of the state is similar to those held by Tilly and Mann. Likewise, we will also find that their coherent view of the state is obtained at the price of a vague notion of international system.

5

CHARLES TILLY

INTRODUCTION

By any standards, Charles Tilly must be rated as one of the most significant writers of contemporary Historical Sociology. He is certainly amongst the most prolific. His contributions to the subject have been extremely wide-ranging. He (1992a: ix) has stated that three of his career-long concerns have been 'the history and dynamics of collective action, the process of urbaniza-tion, and the formation of national states'. This list, however, would ignore his considerable additions to the theoretical basis of Historical Sociology (Tilly 1981, 1984, 1990, 1992c, 1992d).

His work has been described as follows:

> [It is] open-ended and open-minded ... he treats historical soci-ology as a process of never-ending exploration ... his texts are spattered with question marks. His conclusions are rarely dogmatic, usually provisional, and almost always point towards further enquiry.
>
> (Smith, D. 1991: 78)

In this chapter we will discuss Tilly's work in order to examine how he theo-rises state and international system. In Chapter 4 I argued that although Skocpol had produced a strong theoretical position on the international system, she failed to incorporate this successfully into her empirical work. In a superficial way Tilly's approach can be equated to Skocpol's, in that he places great emphasis on the importance of war in state formation. One purpose of this chapter is to determine whether Tilly takes the same reduc-tionist position as Skocpol regarding the international system.

As in the previous chapter, the study of Tilly's work will begin with a survey of his output. Tilly is known primarily for his work on collective action, particularly in France. However, a key feature of all his work is his analysis of social structures and the way in which these constrain the choices of actors. There would appear to be two important trends in Tilly's work.

First, he now gives less attention to the quantitative methods of his earlier investigations. These place great importance on the testing of hypotheses through the use of vast amounts of empirical data. His later work is much more wide-scale and draws on the work of historians rather than the accumulation of data. The second major development in Tilly's work has been an increased use of the international system as an analytical variable in his work. Following the summary of his work we will analyse his position on the international system.

Compared to Skocpol, Tilly provides little in the way of an explicit theoretical discussion of his conception of the international system. Hence it will be necessary here to construct how he conceives it. To do this it will be necessary to consider what forces act both on the construction of the international system and on its influences upon state formation and revolution. I aim to show that, besides placing much causal weight upon the international system, Tilly provides the basis of a more sophisticated account than that provided by Skocpol. However, there appear to be two versions of the international system within Tilly's account, and a major aim of the final section will be to discuss to what extent these two views are compatible.

OVERVIEW OF TILLY'S WORK

We will begin with a broad survey of Tilly's work. First we will discuss his work on collective action. Although this area is not of direct relevance to our overall investigations, its consideration will give us clues to Tilly's methodology, epistemology and ontology. We will then examine Tilly's earlier work on state formation. Finally, we will review Tilly's two most recent works on European state formation and European revolutions. It is in these two works that Tilly makes particular use of the international system as an analytical variable.

Collective action

Tilly (1978: 5) defines collective action as 'the ways that people act together in pursuit of shared interests'. This definition of collective action would seem to imply an individualistic level of analysis. However, as will become apparent, Tilly always analyses collective action in relation to changing social structures.

For example, in his first major published work Tilly examined the rural rebellions in the Vendée during the French Revolution. Here the process of urbanisation acted as the major variable in his analysis. There have been several histories of the Vendée, and the standard practice had been to portray it as a rebellion of peasants opposed to the Revolution. The normal method of explaining the counter-revolution has therefore been to make proposals about what motivated the peasantry to rebel. Tilly suggested that a different approach was possible:

> One may begin with questions about the organization and composi-
> tion of the groups that supported the Revolution and the
> counterrevolution, about the relations among the principle
> segments of the population before and during the Revolution, about
> the connection between the rapid, drastic changes of Revolution
> and counterrevolution and the more general, more gradual changes
> going on in eighteenth-century France.
>
> (Tilly 1964: 9)

Tilly's hypothesis was that opposition to the regime would be at its greatest where the process of urbanisation had been occurring most rapidly. In other words, 'where interests were most deeply divided, factions most sharply defined, change most recent, drastic and disproportionate' (1964: 37). Tilly sought to prove this hypothesis by examining the processes of urbanisation in different regions of France related to the occurrence of counter-revolutionary activity.

This approach led Tilly to suggest several novel factors in the analysis of the Vendée. These factors were primarily counter to the traditional view that the rebellion was simply peasant-inspired. Tilly suggested that previous accounts had overlooked the crucial distinctions between the participants. Hence it was not possible to suggest that a single motivation led to counter-revolutionary activity: different groups had different motivations (1964: 329, 341). By contrast, a study using comparative sociological analysis is capable of providing more results. In this instance Tilly's research pointed to the impact of urbanisation on different social groups. The process resulted in winners and losers between different social groups, with the result that different parties had divergent reactions to the Revolution.

As Tilly's work has progressed, different structural factors have come to prominence in his analysis. In the preface to a reprint of *The Vendée*, he suggests that his concentration on urbanisation in that work obscured other processes such as capitalism and state making (see Hunt 1984: 262). Tilly pursued these structural themes in *From Mobilization to Revolution*, a more theoretical work. Central to his analysis in this work was an examination of the structure–agent debate. Tilly makes a distinction between external forces causing individual actions, a structural explanation, and individual or group decision making, a purposive account. Tilly acknowledges the difficulties involved in synthesising two such different approaches. Even so, this is what he is attempting to do. However, towards the end of the book he concedes that structural models prove more fruitful. He argues this with particular reference to the processes of industrialisation, proletarianisation and state making. Tilly (1978: 229) remarks that he has 'argued repeatedly that the change in question simultaneously affected the interests and organization of various contenders for power, and thereby affected their mobilization and collective action'.

Tilly put these theoretical developments into practice in a further work on collective action in France. This work sought, through an analysis of popular struggle from the seventeenth century through to the 1980s, to show that 'the development of capitalism and the concentration of power in the national state affect the ways that ordinary people contended – or failed to contend for their interests' (Tilly 1986: 5). Tilly argues that the repertoire of collective action has changed as a result of changes in social structures. Existing forms of collective action constrain the possibilities: 'people tend to act within known limits, to innovate at the margins of existing forms, and to miss many opportunities available to them in principle' (ibid.: 390). Hence the rate at which forms of collective action change is imperceptibly slow. Tilly suggests that changes have occurred along two axes. First, in terms of issues, there has been a trend away from local concerns as a source of collective action to national problems. Second, there has been a change in the target of action, from patronised to autonomous. This refers to a change from appealing to local power holders to mediate with national government, to taking up the protest directly. Examples of local patronised collective action would be seizures of grain, attacks on machines, and inter-village battles. Examples of national autonomous forms of collective action would include strikes, demonstrations and public rallies (ibid.: 391–3).

Tilly accounts for this change through two core processes. He (1986: 396) remarks that 'statemaking and capitalism did not merely shape organization and opportunity. They also dominated the fluctuating interests of different groups in collective action'. The process of state making in France resulted in an increasingly centralised state with increased potential to coerce and extract. This affected the population in three direct ways: through making an increased and direct claim on local resources; through competition with and suppression of local power networks; and through the encouragement of competition between different collective organisations. The combined effect of these three elements was to redirect the focus of protest from local to national level. As the state featured more heavily in the daily life of the population, so it became increasingly the focus for protest action.

In the works surveyed so far, Tilly makes no explicit reference to the international system. Even so, some valuable clues as to his theoretical approach have emerged. The common themes in this body of work have been the actions of collective groups and the situations or structures that contain and constrain them. Thus Tilly has been conducting an almost continual version of the agent–structure debate, and his work has proceeded at two levels of analysis. Most of his empirical work has been at the level of recording occurrences of collective action, and he has assembled a vast database of details of unrest, particularly in France. However, it is also apparent that he relates changes in the form of collective action to social processes. We will discover that in his most recent work this includes transformations in the international system. Tilly's work suggests that he views social structures as causal and primary. Individuals and groups act, but the form of the action is heavily influenced by developments in the social structures. We will now assess how he sees these processes operating in the context of state formation.

State formation

Tilly's analysis of the formation of states has developed over time. The starting point came as part of a joint exercise on the study of state formation sponsored by the Committee on Comparative Politics, part of the American Social Science Research Council. This project resulted in a book, *The Formation of Nation States in Western Europe*, to which Tilly contributed the introduction, conclusion and one chapter. The intention of this book was to analyse the process of state building in Western Europe. In this analysis the extractive capabilities of the state in relation to its war-making activities were the centre of attention. Tilly points to various factors that the whole of Europe in 1500 had in common: cultural homogeneity, a peasant base and a decentralised political structure. He sought to explain why the nation state form of political organisation came to dominate the continent rather than any of the possible alternatives: empire, theocratic federation, trading network, or feudal system (Tilly 1975a: 26–7). He pointed to various general conditions in the Europe of the 1500s that enabled the survival of certain states: the availability of extractable resources; a protected position in time and space; a continuous supply of political entrepreneurs; success in war; homogeneity (or the possibility of homogenisation) of the subject population; and the possibility for a strong coalition between the central power and segments of the landed elite (*ibid.*: 40). Success in war would appear to be the most important of these, going by the prominence of the subject in the remainder of Tilly's analysis. At one level this is obvious. States that were not successful for the most part simply disappeared. At another level the process of war making and the increased centralisation of the state were intimately interlinked:

> The building of an effective military machine imposed a heavy burden on the population involved: taxes, conscription, requisitions, and more. The very act of building it – when it worked – produced arrangements which could deliver resources to the government for other purposes . . . it produced the means of enforcing the government's will over stiff resistance: the army. It tended, indeed, to promote territorial consolidation, centralization, differentiation of the instruments of government and monopolization of the means

of coercion, all the fundamental state-making processes. *War made the state and the state made war.*

(Tilly 1975a: 42, my emphasis)

This growth in state power can be regarded as a cycle. An increase in the size of the army in order to meet the pressures of external competition required an increase in taxation. To administer this increase in taxation states required a larger bureaucracy. An increase in the tax burden led to a growth in resistance. This in turn required increased coercion to extract a surplus, requiring an increase in the size of the army. An increase in the size of the army required an increase in taxation . . . and so on (see Figure 5.1).

As the costs increased, so did the size of the bureaucracy. In a subsequent article Tilly equated this process as akin to racketeering. 'The more costly the activity, all other things being equal, the greater was the organisational residue' (Tilly 1985: 181). Tilly (1975a: 74) concludes that 'preparation for war has been the great state-building activity. The process has been going on more or less continuously for five hundred years'.

The process of state formation has gone through a series of phases: first, the emergence of a limited number of national states from amongst a variety of other political structures; second, the transference of this particular model onto the rest of Europe, primarily through the process of war. This was followed by the domination of most of the rest of the world by the states of Western Europe. Following the withdrawal from empire of the Western European states, autonomous states have formed in the rest of the world. In the final stage, the state system has been extended to the rest of the world (Tilly 1975b: 637).

For Tilly, whether the state will retain its current form of political organisation is in doubt. He has argued that a devolution of power has been

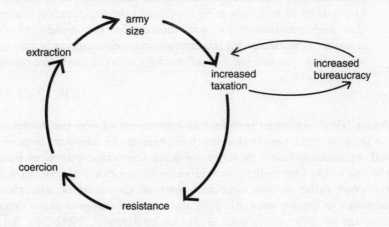

Figure 5.1 War-fighting capacity as a factor in state expansion

occurring. This has pulled the nation state in two directions: upwards, towards a regional grouping, with decisions being taken at a supranational level; and downward, towards the subnational region or ethnic group below the national level (1975b: 638).

The model of state development presented in *The Formation of Nation States in Western Europe* is relatively straightforward. It suggests a unitary theory of state development closely linked to the state's requirement to extract resources from the subject population in order to finance warfare. This model has been developed considerably in Tilly's more recent works. These have concentrated on European history and attempt to bring together his work on collective action and state formation.

European history: state formation and revolution

In his most recent work on the formation of nation states in Europe, Tilly has built on and superseded the outline given above. Tilly is critical of other writers who have worked on state formation and on his own previous work. The criticism of other writers is that the story of the formation of the Western European state is told in a way that assumes that the nineteenth-century state was the intended end-point of the state builders. He criticises his own work for replacing one unilinear story (the intentions of state builders) with another (state building as an accidental by-product of the chain of war, extraction and repression). The reality is considerably more complex. An analysis is required which includes:

> Recognising decisive variations in the paths of change followed by states in different parts of Europe during successive epochs, with the realization that the class coalitions prevailing in a region at a given point in time strongly limited the possibilities of action open to any ruler or would-be ruler . . . placing the organization of coercion and preparation for war squarely in the middle of the analysis . . . insisting that relations among states, especially through war and the preparation for war, strongly affected the entire process of state building.
>
> (Tilly 1992a: 14)

Again, Tilly's intention is to find an explanation of why the nation state as we know it in the twentieth century emerged as the dominant form of political organisation from the variety of other forms that existed in Europe at the end of the first millennium. His central question is: 'what accounts for the great variation over time and space in the kinds of state that have prevailed in Europe since AD 990, and why did European states eventually converge on different variants of the national state?' (1992a: 5). As in his previous work, Tilly finds a central place for the state's extractive and coercive role. However, prominence is also given to class relations, and the role of the international system in conditioning nation-state identities.

Tilly (1992a: 1) defines states as 'coercion-wielding organizations that are distinct from households and kinship groups and exercise clear priority in some respects over all other organizations within substantial territories'. It is possible to trace back the existence of such formations more than five thousand years. He (*ibid.*: 96) suggests that states pursue three minimum activities: state making – the suppression of potential competitors from within the territory claimed by the state; war making – acts of aggression against rivals outside that territory; and protection – the preservation of allies both inside and outside of the territory. Crucial to these three activities is a fourth, the extraction from the subject population of the wherewithal to undertake the previous three. Additionally, over time, a 'civilianization' of the state has occurred. It is has become increasingly involved in activities such as adjudication, distribution and production.

Tilly proposes a simple model for explaining the emergence of the nation state. There are two main variables, capital and coercion. The presence of concentrated capital is generally associated with cities, whilst concentrated coercion coincides with the presence of a state. These two formations exist in a dialectical relationship:

> Cities and their capitalists drew indispensable protection for their commercial and industrial activity from the specialists in coercion who ran states, but rightly feared interference in their money-making and diversion of their resources to war, preparation for war, or payment for past wars. States and military men depended on city-based capitalists for the financial means to recruit and sustain armed force, yet properly worried about the resistance to state power engendered by cities, their commercial interests, and their working classes.
>
> (Tilly 1992a: 58–9)

Different combinations of the concentration of capital and coercion resulted in the emergence of different forms of nation state. Tilly points to a continuum from coercion-intensive states on the one hand to capital-intensive states on the other. Despite the infinite variety of possible combinations of capital and coercion, Tilly suggests that it is useful to reduce the possibilities to three main 'ideal' types.

First, there is the example of a coercive-intensive/capital-sparse state. Under conditions of capital shortage state rulers were forced to extract the wherewithal to pursue their war-making activities from their subject populations, including those which had been conquered. In this process it was necessary to construct large state mechanisms to carry out the extraction. Tilly cites Russia as a prime example.

At the other end of the spectrum lies the situation where capital was more concentrated and coercion less prevalent. In these instances state rulers were forced into compacts with capitalists to provide the funds for war making. As a result there was less necessity for the creation of an extensive state. The Italian city-states provide the example here.

In between these two extremes lay the examples where the concentrations of capital and coercion were more balanced. In these instances rulers pursued a combination of the above activities. Capitalists were typically co-opted into the state structures. Tilly (1992a: 30) remarks that 'holders of capital and coercion interacted on terms of relative equality'. Britain and France represent the clearest examples of this path.

In the competitive system that has typified Europe of the past millennium, of the three ideal types, the capitalised-coercion state proved to be the most effective in overcoming its opponents. Tilly argues that this is because of the central requirement of capital for war making. In order to be able to compete in terms of fighting wars, states need a source of capital. States also need to be able to extract that capital. In coercive-intensive locations, although the potential to extract capital was present, there was little to extract. In capital-intensive locations, the capital was there, but the means to extract it was absent. Only in capitalised-coercion states did a balance exist between the presence of capital and the means to extract it. Such a combination was the most efficient for the pursuit of war-making activities.

The implication of Tilly's position is clear. War making is the force that has driven state making. The capitalised-coercion form of nation state came to represent the model that other states followed because it proved successful in war making. The balance of capital and coercion represented the most efficient means of mobilising the resources needed to vanquish other states and retain sovereignty. Tilly (1992a: 76) makes this explicit when he remarks that 'war wove the European network of national states, and preparation for war created the internal structures of the states within it'.

This central position of war making in his analysis has prompted considerable criticism, and his entire schema has been accused of being over-simplified. Goldstone, for example, argues that other factors apart from war making could be equally important in influencing state formation. He writes that:

Tilly's insistence that war making alone drove states begs too many questions. England's state was arguably shaped more by the reformation (in 1531–4), by conflict over the religion of the dynasty (in 1688–9), and by the conflict over the state between landlords and nonlandlords (in 1828–32) than by military exigencies.

(Goldstone 1991: 177)

Mann makes a similar point. He points out that some states have not only appeared to their subjects in the form of tax collectors and military recruiters, but also as social workers, teachers and other providers of services. Tilly's approach is not able to explain this divergence. 'Had he defined the state otherwise', suggests Mann (1991: 1261), 'perhaps in terms of political regulation, he would be better placed to explain this'.

Kasza argues that Tilly fails to provide a differentiated account of war. Instead, war is presented as a constant, and different aspects or types of war are not analysed. This provides an over-simplified account, with the result that different features of war and their impacts on state formation are not considered:

> His assumption that war is always the prime mover causes him to overlook distinctions that are useful in formulating theory. Tilly does not specify precisely which aspects of war have had which effects on the state's extractive policies or institutional development. Because he assumes that war is behind all efforts to increase extraction and to build state institutions, he does not break down the causal variable of war as sharply as he might.
>
> (Kasza 1996: 366)

McNeill also criticises Tilly for producing an over-simplified model. He suggests that Tilly should have included an account of agricultural differences between states. He (1992: 584) argues that 'until very recently the great majority of Europeans lived on the land; and differences in the techniques of cultivation, property law, and harvest results probably had more to do with European state building than commercial capital and cities did'. He also suggests that Tilly has failed to include an analysis of political legitimacy, religion, demography and changes in technology.

Claessen takes a more positive view of Tilly's work. He agrees that war played a fundamental role in the emergence of European states, but argues that it cannot be treated as an independent variable. 'War is the derivative of underlying causes: demographic, economic or ideological (and every possible combination of the three)' (Claessen 1992: 101). Without an analysis of these factors, the view of war taking the central role in state development is misleading.

Tilly's model is undoubtedly very simple, and perhaps a better way of approaching it is to ask how useful it is as a model, rather than whether it is historically accurate. Reality is obviously more complex, and his critics have found it easy to point out what Tilly has omitted from the analysis, as noted above. This would seem to miss the point. Tilly's later work is a progression from his earlier theorising on state formation, and provides a useful platform either to react against, or to build upon. It would seem to be more constructive to criticise the model in its own terms.[1] One area of weakness might be the lack of an explanation of how a state that lacks the winning combination makes the transition to a state of capitalised coercion. Additionally, Russia, offered as an example of a coercive-intensive/capital-sparse state, is presumably still within that categorisation. Even so, it has been a dominating influence in Europe for over one hundred years, and even in its current chaotic condition remains a major element of the European state system.

In the final chapter of *Coercion, Capital, and European States* Tilly analyses states in the developing world. He claims that a particular type of state, the national state, was exported from Europe by the colonial powers and now constitutes a worldwide model. His intention is to examine whether his model can explain the predominance of military governments or extensive military influence. He suggests that:

> The new entrants, on the average, were following coercion-intensive paths to statehood. The departing colonial powers left little accumulated capital behind them, but bequeathed to their successor states military forces drawn from and modelled on the repressive forces they had previously established to maintain their own local administrations.
>
> (Tilly 1992a: 199–200)

In his more recent work, Tilly has focused more on the role of cities as sites of the concentration of capital. In the introduction to a collected edition on state–city relations in Europe, he notes that the purpose of the book is to explore 'the possibility that the variable distribution of cities and systems of cities by region and era significantly and independently constrained the multiple paths of state transformation' (1994: 6). This is a development of the position outlined in *Coercion, Capital, and European States*, and marks a further development in his thinking regarding the role of capital in state formation.

Concerning the future of European states, Tilly sees two processes at work. On the one hand the break-up of the Soviet empire has resulted in the emergence of a plethora of new political formations claiming statehood. This has reversed the long-term trend in Europe for a decrease in the number of states. On the other hand, the European Union represents a project to undermine the distinctiveness and sovereignty of its member states. Tilly ponders which of these processes will become dominant. He suggests that it is possible to imagine three possible futures: that there might be a proliferation of state forms representing distinctive nationalist aspirations; or that there could be a continuation of the process towards the consolidation of a single homogenous state; alternatively, ideas of cultural distinctiveness could become separated from claims to statehood. He argues that in the short term the first two contradictory forces will predominate, whilst over the long run the third possibility will prevail. In other words, the state is being undermined in two directions, from national demands at sub-state level, and from the pressure to consolidate at supra-state level (Tilly 1992b).

Besides writing on the history of European states, Tilly has also recently produced a Europe-wide analysis of European revolutions covering the last five hundred years. This offers a very general account of revolutions and is concerned with three main clusters of issues:

- How the character of revolutions has changed in line with changes of social structure and relations between states.
- How changes in revolutionary processes connect with non-revolutionary conflict.
- How revolutions work and whether systematic changes in the mechanisms have occurred over the last five hundred years (Tilly 1993: 5).

Tilly takes a broad definition of revolution and makes a clear distinction between revolutionary situations and revolutionary outcomes. A revolutionary situation 'entails multiple sovereignty: two or more blocs make effective, incompatible claims to control the state, or to be the state' (1993: 10). This can happen under a variety of circumstances: an existing polity can split (Tilly gives the example of the English Revolution, where a division occurred between the Roundheads and Cavaliers); a previously subordinate authority can exert its autonomy (for example, as when the Baltic states made the break from Soviet control); or a coalition of forces not in control of the state can threaten the existing rulers or take control of some part of the state (as in the French Revolution).

There is a tendency to associate revolutionary situations with revolutionary outcomes. However, as Tilly is at some pains to point out, the history of Europe is littered with examples of cases where the former did not translate into the latter. To cover this phenomenon, Tilly (1993: 14) argues that a revolutionary outcome occurs 'with transfer of state power from those who held it before the start of multiple sovereignty to a new ruling coalition'.

Tilly relates differences in the character of revolution to differences in the form of state development based on the model discussed above. For example, in high-coercion/low capital states, revolutions normally took the form of peasant rebellions. In high-capital/low-coercion states, revolutions generally originated around the struggles of guilds for power (1993: 38). Combined with these differences are the processes, as discussed in *The Contentious French*, that led to a development from local patronised forms of collective action to national autonomous patterns.

To pursue his ideas about revolution, Tilly discusses a number of case studies, examining France, Britain and Russia. But the most instructive chapter is his comparison between the Netherlands, Iberia and the Balkans. This particular study crystallises the major issues that Tilly is addressing:

First, the character of revolutions altered greatly over the 500 years in question, as a function of the same processes that eventually created consolidated states. Second, the organization and incidence of revolution varied substantially from one region of Europe to another, especially as a function of the relative predominance of capital and coercion in each region. Third, revolutions and other non-revolutionary political conflicts varied in parallel from region to region and period to period.

(Tilly 1993: 53)

The Netherlands represents an example of state formation in the presence of a high concentration of capital and a low concentration of coercion. In this instance the forms that revolution took were heavily influenced by the relations between capitalists and landlords, workers and rulers. As a result, the form that revolutionary struggles took was neither peasant rebellion nor struggle for the royal succession. International factors also played their part in the form of the frequent invasions and occupations of the area, most notably by the French forces under Napoleon.

State development in the Iberian peninsula, by contrast, was more consistent with Tilly's coercion-intensive path. Here revolution primarily took the form of dynastic struggle. Revolutionary processes in the Balkans were largely related to the ebb and flow of the imperial regimes that dominated the region. In this instance revolutionary struggles typically took the form of peasant rebellions. Hence, in his work on revolutions, Tilly has sought to incorporate his work on the paths of state formation and an analysis of international factors.

I wish to highlight three main points from this overview of Tilly's work. First, Tilly attaches great importance to the use of historical methods in the study of social processes. Second, he gives a central position to an approach that stresses the study of structures.[2] Third, he introduces international factors into his social analysis. All of these three elements will be taken into account in the discussion of Tilly's concept of the international system.

CHARLES TILLY AND THE CONCEPT OF INTERNATIONAL SYSTEM

We now turn to a more thorough analysis of Tilly's position *vis-à-vis* the international system. He makes frequent references to the international system in his more recent work, but he fails to provide a clear definition. Hence it will be necessary to construct from his statements what he means by the international system, and how it affects and/or is affected by other social processes. Unfortunately, Tilly's writings on the international system are somewhat contradictory and it is thus possible to draw more than one conclusion. However, this section takes Tilly's enthusiasm for structural explanations as its starting point.

The argument will proceed as follows. First, I intend to show that Tilly takes the international system to be a causal element in his explanation of social processes. We will then examine his theoretical comments on international systems. These explain very little about how he understands the international system or how it affects other social processes. It will therefore be necessary first to examine the causal role that Tilly assigns to the international system. It will then be possible to see how the international system is conceptualised. Finally, I will argue that Tilly does produce a structural view of the international system. However, he appears to have two different positions, and it will be necessary to consider the relation between these.

For Tilly the system is causal . . .

A causal view of international systems has been a consistent element in Tilly's analysis of state formation. In earlier work on state formation he (1975b: 625) talks about the need to incorporate in the analysis 'the influence of the changing international structure of power'. But what he means by 'international structure of power' is not apparent, nor is its influence, nor is the form in which this influence is manifested.

In *Coercion, Capital, and European States* Tilly (1992a: 26) argues that 'other states – and eventually the entire system of states – strongly affected the path of change followed by any particular state'. In addition, he notes that European states exist 'as a set of interacting parties, a system whose operation constrains the actions of its members' (*ibid.*: 37). However, the effect of this influence has not been historically consistent. He notes that 'on the average state formation moved from a relatively "internal" to a strongly "external" process' (*ibid.*: 181). Whilst war has always been an external factor, there has been a trend away from internal struggle as a prominent force in state making to 'the increasing salience of concerts among states for the fate of any particular state' (*ibid.*).

The role of the international system has become apparent in his work on European revolutions. Tilly argues that besides the organisation of any particular state affecting the likelihood of the occurrence of revolution, 'it is also that relations *among* states affect the locus, likelihood, character and outcome of revolution' (1993: 6, original emphasis). However, after this remark he gives the example, following Skocpol, that the Russian revolutions of 1905 and 1917 were directly linked to defeat by Japanese and German forces respectively. The immediate reaction here might be that Tilly's position is very close to that of Skocpol: in other words, the reduction of the international system to the occurrence of war. This discussion will be pursued below.

Tilly has also made reference to current changes in the international system. He has stated that 'right now the international system is undergoing one of those deep mutations that not only alter politics in individual states, but change the character and incidence of war itself' (1992c: 187–8). In other words, he appears to be arguing that changes in the international system lead to changes in domestic politics. Moreover, such changes affect the character of relations between states.

It would seem apparent, then, that Tilly does base some causal explanation in the international system. It influences state development and affects the nature of politics within nations. Additionally, relations between states are, to a certain degree, conditioned by it. Its importance as a causal variable begs the question of what Tilly understands by the international system. Therefore it is necessary to consider Tilly's remarks on how he defines the international system.

. . . but he offers little in the way of definition . . .

The statements quoted above suggest that Tilly bases some of his account of state formation and revolution on the international system. Although he has made frequent reference to the international system as a causal variable, he offers little in the way of explanation of what he understands by the international system or how its effects operate.

In his earlier work on state formation, Tilly pointed to two international contexts to state formation: the changing structure of the European economy, and the emergence of an international system of states. Concerning the former, he points approvingly to the work of Wallerstein. Regarding the latter, he notes that the Treaty of Westphalia 'first made it clear that all of Europe was to be divided into distinct and sovereign states whose boundaries were defined by international agreement' (1975a: 45). This position is, in summary form, very close to that of Skocpol, as outlined in the previous chapter.

By the time of *Coercion, Capital, and European States*, Tilly had simplified this formulation to the following: 'states form *systems* to the extent that they interact, and to the degree that their interaction significantly affects each party's fate' (1992a: 4, original emphasis). This may sound familiar. It is very close to the definition of the international system given by Bull, as discussed in Chapter 3 of this book. It will be recalled that Bull made a distinction between an international system and an international society. He argued that a system exists whereby states interact to the extent that they have to take each other into account in their calculations. This was as distinct from an international society, where state activities were constrained by the existence of norms, common rules and institutions. However, Tilly does not make such a distinction, at least not explicitly.

Tilly's discussion of the international system is, then, somewhat limited. A little further assistance is given, however, in his discussion of existing theories of state formation. He argues that existing theories can be distinguished by their position on two issues: the relation of state formation to economic change; and the extent of exterior influences on state formation. This two-by-two classification yields four pole positions.

1   *Statist positions:* These argue for primarily internal forces affecting state development, autonomous of economic developments. Tilly includes writers such as Samuel Huntington and Paul Kennedy under this heading, as well as International Relations writers in the realist tradition who base their analysis of state actions on notions such as national interest (1992a: 6). Tilly notes that he draws much of his raw material from such writers. But such an analysis fails to explain why state formation followed such divergent paths, yet finally converged on a single model. He argues as follows:

> They dissolve into particularisms and teleologies, explaining why the 'modern' form of a given state emerged on the basis of the special character of a national population and economy. They neglect, furthermore, the hundreds of states that once flourished but then disappeared – Moravia, Bohemia, Burgundy, Aragon, Milan, Savoy, and many more.
>
> (Tilly 1992a: 9)

2   *Mode of production positions:* This approach again concentrates on internal factors, but relates state development to economic change. In essence, the form of the state is derived from the form of the relations of production active within a particular territory at a particular time. Tilly points to writers such as Perry Anderson as typical of this approach. While agreeing that some insights have emerged from this type of analysis, Tilly suggests that it fails to explain why different forms of state have been in control of territories operating under the same mode of production (1992a: 8).

3   *Geopolitical positions:* These give emphasis to external factors in determining state formation, though independent of economic change. Writers such as Waltz provide this kind of analysis. Tilly (1992a: 10) suggests that this approach 'provides a valuable corrective to the internalism of statist analyses, but gives unclear guidance to the search for mechanisms that link particular forms of state to specific positions within the international system'. What Tilly appears to be arguing here is that he finds value in 'geopolitical' positions, but that they have been unable to demonstrate links between the system and the state.

4   *World systems positions:* The final group of analyses link state development with external and economic forces, namely the world economic system. Here Tilly is referring primarily to the work of Wallerstein, whose work will be discussed in Chapter 7. Tilly clearly admires this work, but argues that it fails to reveal the mechanisms that determine a particular

state's form based on its position in the international economic system. One example is the Dutch case. How is it possible to account for the diminutive size of the Dutch state in the seventeenth century? At that time the Netherlands was the dominant country and most of its competitors were creating large bureaucratic states with standing armies (1992a: 11).

This discussion of alternative approaches does not advance our understanding of Tilly's view of the international system. But it does provide clues about what, in his eyes, it is not. He sees value in all four approaches, but argues that none gives a complete set of answers, and rejects the idea of combining them (1992a: 11). He is therefore rejecting the holist positions of Waltz on the one hand and Wallerstein on the other. The system may be important, as has already been argued, but it is not as determinist as others have argued.

Having exhausted Tilly's theoretical positions on the international system, it is now time to take another tack, and to consider the forms that the system takes and how it affects state development.

... hence it is necessary to consider what the system does ...

It is possible to make two readings of Tilly's approach to the international system. In the first the relationship between the system and war will be considered. Does Tilly reduce the international system to war, as Skocpol appears to do, or is it possible to distinguish them? This will be followed with a reading that equates Tilly with a more constructivist position. The next section will consider whether these two positions are incompatible.

It is easy to link war to the international system in Tilly's writings. Consider, for example, the following two statements:

> War wove the European network of national states, and preparation for war created the internal structures of the states within it.
>
> (Tilly 1992a: 76)

> War drove not only the state system and the formation of individual states, but also the distribution of power over the state. Even with the last few centuries' civilization of Western governments, war has remained the defining activity of national states.
>
> (*ibid.*: 187)

In these two statements it is war that is doing all the work. However, also note that war is not the same as the international system. This was the conclusion drawn about Skocpol's work in the previous chapter. Instead, it would appear to be Tilly's view that war leads to the creation of an international system. Not only did the states make war and war made the state, it would appear that war also made the system. Remember, though, that Tilly is attempting to explain why one particular form of state, the capitalised-coercion model, became dominant. The explanation would appear to be a process of socialisation, and at this point Tilly's analysis comes very close to that of Waltz:

> After centuries of divergences among capital-intensive, coercion-intensive, and capitalized-coercion paths of state formation, European states began to converge a few centuries ago; war and mutual influence caused the convergence.
>
> (Tilly 1992a: 195)[3]

In other words, the capitalised-coercion model proved to be the winning formula for state formation – other states had to adapt to this path or face extinction. However, it may be jumping to too quick a conclusion to equate this socialising power to the structure of the international system, as Waltz would do. Tilly considers war to be the reason for the convergence. A particular state formation was more effective at fighting war and provided a model to emulate.

For Tilly, competition would seem to be a feature of the system. In the following statement, which appears to point to the international system being anarchic, he again seems close to Waltz: 'in the nature of the case, national states always appear in competition with each other' (1992a: 23). This is presumably a reference to an anarchical international system.

In this reading, then, war becomes the most important variable, but, as suggested above, it is also possible to derive another interpretation. At other points Tilly talks about the international system being 'made', first in Europe and then through the export of the state form that developed there. He remarks that:

> Five hundred years ago, Europeans were busy *creating* a pair of arrangements that were then unique: first a system of interconnected states linked by treaties, embassies, marriages and extensive communication; second, declared wars fought by large, disciplined military forces and ended by formal peace settlements.
>
> (Tilly 1992a: 163, my emphasis)

These remarks seem to be in direct contrast to what has gone before. The international system has now become defined in terms of negotiation, understanding, norms and rules. It would be tempting to link this with Bull's views of international society. In addition, wars now become less important than the settlements that follow them. Tilly subsequently notes that the Treaty of Westphalia at the end of the Thirty Years War consolidated the international system (1992a: 167).

This interpretation of the international system would seem to be comparable to a constructivist position. In other words, the international system is a social construction, with Tilly giving the emphasis to treaties, marriages and peace settlements. This theme is not entirely new in Tilly's work. He had previously noted (1975b: 601) that 'Europeans and their offspring played the dominant part in creating the international system within which all states of the contemporary world are now operating'. This theme is taken up in *Coercion, Capital, and European States*. Tilly notes that after the end of World War I the victorious powers created their own version of the international system. This was through a process of 'deliberate collective mapping of the entire state system, right down to the boundaries, rulers and constitutions of individual states' (1992a: 169). This process is presumably part, or perhaps all, of the reason why state formation has proceeded from an internal to an external process. Subsequently Tilly develops this point as follows:

> Over the last three centuries, compacts of powerful states have increasingly narrowed the limits within which any national struggle for power occurred. They have done so through imposition of international war settlements, organization of colonies, diffusion of standard models for armies, bureaucracies, and other elements of the state apparatus, creation of international organizations charged with tending the state system, collective guarantee of national borders, and intervention to maintain domestic order.
>
> (Tilly 1992a: 182)

This then would appear to be closer to a constructivist position, and somewhat at odds with the view of the international system presented earlier. Tilly does not appear to be aware of these two versions of the international system that he presents, or if he is aware he does not point out the distinctions and/or relations. Perhaps these two positions are incompatible. The next section considers this question.

. . . in order to understand what Tilly means

So far we have seen that it is possible to make two readings of Tilly's position on international systems. The first position appeared to equate the international system closely to war. However, I argued that this was not the reductionist position occupied by Skocpol as suggested in the previous chapter. Tilly was successful in separating war from the system. The second appeared to be more of a constructivist position, implying that the international system is a social construction.

In order to get a clearer idea of what underlies Tilly's analysis, two further steps are required. The first move is to more distinctly separate war from the system. In *Coercion, Capital and European States*, Tilly's statements are open to either interpretation, but the following quotation from *European Revolutions* suggests that he does make such a distinction:

> Wars generally had a strong influence on the prospects for revolution in Europe. War does not result from the actions of a single state, however aggressive; it results from interactions among states, from alignments in the state system as a whole.
>
> (Tilly 1993: 6)

This statement implies that war is subordinate, a function of an anarchical international system, and strengthens the view being developed in the previous section. Is it possible to link this to the constructivist position that Tilly also seems to suggest? Is it feasible to make a connection between a system purely of interacting states and a system of embassies, peace proposals, norms and rules? The second move would need the introduction of a historical element.

As noted, Tilly makes reference on more than one occasion to the Treaty of Westphalia. This seems to have a special significance for him. Perhaps this treaty represents a turning point, with the development from a simple system of interacting states, to a considerably more complex one based on rules and norms. The primary feature of the earlier system would seem to be warfare, whilst in the latter system, although war is still a major feature it is somewhat moderated by the growth of international norms. An additional factor would also be the 'civilianization' of states previously alluded to. A possible model here could be Bull's work on international society. The problem is that Bull makes a clear distinction between system and society. It is not possible to have a society without a system. Tilly's lack of clarity on this point leads to some confusion about what he means.

If there was a historical development of the international system, is it possible to suggest how this change came about? One way of envisaging this development could be as follows. In the medieval European system, norms of state behaviour took less priority, and war was a result of an anarchical system. The resources needed for warfare led to the steady growth of state formations, and the greater success of a particular model resulted in the emulation of a capitalised-coercion model of the state. War drove state formation, but was itself a function of the system. The development of states eventually resulted in a gradual transformation of the system, to one constructed by the states themselves. Hence the view that Tilly's two positions on the international system are contradictory might be less important. It is possible to argue that the system has taken different forms in different historical epochs.

CONCLUSION

To conclude, it may be useful to locate Tilly's position on the international system within the context of his overall writings. The summary of Tilly's work on collective action pointed to two key elements in his method of analysis. First, he uses two levels of analysis. His procedure has been to analyse the actions of individuals and groups, but within the second level of analysis: the circumstances that constrain them. Second, he examines the change over time of structures and the repertoire of rejoinders that actors are able to make in response to these developments.

These elements can be seen in Tilly's analysis of the international system. The international system acts as a causal mechanism on the development of states and as a constraining factor on their activities.

The role of war as a central factor in state formation is crucial to Tilly's work. As was noted in the discussion of his views on the international system, he makes a clear link between war and the international system. He perceives the international system as a product of warfare. However, he does have a stronger notion of system than Skocpol. It would appear from some of Tilly's statements on war and the international system that he does make a distinction between the two. He does not reduce the system to the occurrence of war. Rather, he sees war as constitutive of international systems. Therefore there is a strong argument for locating Tilly's view of the international system in the top left hand corner of the Hollis and Smith matrix (see Figure 5.2). This would see Tilly taking a holist position on the international system, and seeing it as an external structure.

However, as already argued, it is also possible to situate Tilly as a constructivist, which suggests that he can be located on the right-hand side of the matrix. As well as relating war to the international system, Tilly, at times, also depicts the international system as a web of rules and norms that

	Explaining	Understanding
Holistic	external structures Tilly	collective rules Tilly
Individualistic	rational choices	reasoned choices

Figure 5.2 Tilly's approach to the international system

act to constrain state actions. There would appear to be a set of collective rules that are a factor in understanding state development. The causal and constraining weight that Tilly gives to this aspect of the international system also suggests a holist approach, which would place him in the upper-right quarter of the matrix. This position is also represented in Figure 5.2.

This assessment might seem strange when compared to Skocpol's position, given the great weight that both writers give to warfare. However, Tilly extends his analysis further than Skocpol. He makes a distinction between war and the international system. Additionally, Tilly has started to make an analysis that could be described as constructivist, which would place him on the understanding side of the matrix as well as the explaining side.

Hence Tilly's approach can be seen to be more holistic than that of Skocpol. However, it is divided between two different views, and Tilly does not attempt to analyse how these contrasting approaches are related. He uses different explanations of the international system to explain different aspects of state development. When he wants to explain the increase in scope of state activities, he focuses on involvement in the fighting of wars. When he wants to explain the way in which state activities are constrained, he uses a more constructivist understanding of the international system. As with Skocpol, coherence at state level is bought with a vague, and in Tilly's case, inconsistent notion of international system.

Tilly's work has covered a large range of topics. Here we have focused on his work on state formation in Europe. This work has a considerable number of implications for International Relations theorists. Tilly's definition of the state is less specific than that offered by Skocpol. However, this reflects the broader timespan that he is considering. In her work on revolutions, Skocpol was concerned with states more directly comparable to their modern forms. Tilly is concerned with state-like formations dating back over the past millennium. His aim is to trace the trajectory of a diversity of state forms and to analyse why the modern state form has emerged as it has. His explanation combines a discussion of states as sites of concentrated coercion, cities as sites of concentrated capital, and an international system typified both by war and as a network of constraining norms and rules. The key insights that he has introduced are:

- Making a link between war and state growth.
- Showing that in the creation of the European state system various different kinds of state formation converged on one particular form.
- In the process various other forms of state and even states themselves came to an end.
- The introduction of cities as central actors, both internationally and in terms of state formation.

In this examination of Tilly's work, and the previous chapter's discussion of

Skocpol, a similar argument has been made. This is that a degree of coherence of analysis at the state level has been achieved through the use of vague notions of international system. Much of Skocpol's explanation of state development relied on the reduction of the international system to the occurrence of warfare. Tilly employed two views of international system. One view was used to explain the growth of the state; another was used to explain restrictions on state activities. The next chapter examines the work of Michael Mann. Again, a reliance on war for explaining state development will be observed. However, Mann's account also includes other views of international systems.

6

MICHAEL MANN

INTRODUCTION

In the previous two chapters we have considered the work of historical sociologists who have incorporated a concept of the international system in their analyses. In both cases we found that the approach to analysing international systems was problematic. In Skocpol's analysis of revolution, she claims to be employing a structural approach, including the international system. In her theoretical discussion, Skocpol proposed a model of the international system based on the relations between states and the effects of international capitalism. However, in her empirical work the international system was reduced to the presence or absence of warfare between states. Compared to Skocpol, Tilly provides little in the way of a theoretical discussion of the international system. However, his incorporation of the international system in his analysis did imply a holistic position, though the form of the international system did not appear to be consistent or thoroughly analysed. In contrast to Skocpol, Tilly has maintained the international system as a variable in his analyses.

In this chapter we turn to the work of Michael Mann. Mann is internationally famous for his work on the history of social power (Mann 1986a, 1993a), a ground-breaking study of how different combinations of power relations have structured human societies. Compared to the scope of his recent writing, his earlier work, however, reflected more traditional sociological concerns (Mann 1973a, 1973b; Blackburn and Mann 1979). Additionally he has written on the subject of sociological methodology (Mann 1981, 1994). The present chapter will follow the pattern of the previous two. It will begin with a survey of Mann's work. This will concentrate on the volumes on social power and will include a discussion of the critiques of this undertaking. The discussion will then go on to a more detailed analysis of his views of the international system.

I will argue that inherent in Mann's analysis is a serious challenge to International Relations. This challenge takes four main forms. First, he attempts to integrate an analysis of the domestic and the international. In other words, his aim is to break down the national/international dichotomy prevalent in most International Relations theory. Second, he proposes a distinctive theory of change in the international system. Third, he offers a new theory of the state. Although there are some similarities between his analysis and that of the interdependence theorists, this chapter will argue that Mann's theory is more developed. Finally, he argues that none of his sources of social power is ultimately determining. This is a problem for realists, for whom political or military power is ultimately determining, and for Marxists, who place economic power in that role.

However, Mann has failed, so far, to develop his theoretical position. The main manifestation of this failure is a gap between Mann's theoretical position and the presentation of his empirical material. With particular reference to the international aspects of his work, I will argue that the potential of the theoretical position is not fulfilled for two main reasons. First, his failure to resolve the different epistemological and ontological positions that he takes weakens his conception of the international system. Furthermore, realist conceptions heavily influence his view of international systems. This has the result of limiting the development of a framework that can encompass both internal and external factors.

Mann takes a strong position on the role of an international system in structuring human societies. But he has not been able to produce a definite or consistent account of what an international system comprises. My argument is that it is possible to give four readings of the concept of an international system in his work. These four views display different epistemological and ontological assumptions. Although there may be some overlap between these positions, some are mutually exclusive.

A full discussion of Mann's analysis is not possible without a brief summary of his work. This will be our task in the next section. Here we will concentrate on the theoretical aspects of the volumes on social power. In addition we will examine the thoughts of some of Mann's critics. This will lay the foundation for a more detailed analysis of his views on international systems.

THE SOURCES OF SOCIAL POWER

Mann's volumes on the sources of social power are a challenge to summarise. The work is immensely complex, comprehensive, and still in progress. Originally intended to be a short book, it expanded first to three volumes, and now to a planned four. So far the first two volumes have appeared in print. Volume I provides a history of power from the 'beginning' until AD 1760: a history of power in primarily agrarian societies. Volume II extends the analysis to the 'long' nineteenth century (1760–1914) and covers the rise of classes and nation states. The plan is for Volume III to be a history of the twentieth century, whilst Volume IV will be a theoretical work, based on the empirical evidence included in the previous three.

The Sources of Social Power is not a modest work. It has the intention of embracing the entirety of human history. Mann traces the work's origins to a 1972 paper. This paper 'purported not only to refute Karl Marx and reorganise Max Weber but also to offer the outlines of a better general theory of social stratification and social change' (Mann 1986: vii).

Power lies at the centre of Mann's approach. Starting from a simple definition, Mann develops three characteristics of power, and four main sources of social power. Power is a notoriously difficult concept to define. Mann (1986: 6) takes his definition as 'the ability to pursue and attain goals through mastery of one's environment'. Social power has two additional aspects. First there is a distributive, or zero-sum sense. In this aspect one individual's power over another implies a gain for the former and a loss for the latter. Second, there is a collective aspect. This occurs when two or more individuals by combining their resources are able to increase their power over a third party. However, as Mann notes, the relationship between distributive and collective power is not discrete, and in most social relations elements of both are present. He suggests that a dialectical relationship exists between the two:

> In pursuit of their goals humans enter into cooperative, collective power relations with one another. But in implementing collective goals, social organization and a division of labor are set up. Organization and division of function carry an inherent tendency to distributive power, deriving from supervision and coordination.
>
> (Mann 1986: 6–7)

Mann extends his definition of power by making further distinctions between extensive and intensive power, and authoritative and diffused power. Extensive power applies to the possibility of exerting a minimum level of control over far-flung territories. Intensive power is the ability to exert a high level of control, usually over a more restricted area. The distinction is primarily one of logistics. It is much easier to exercise intensive power over a restricted area than over a large territory. Authoritative power is present when a rigid command-obedience environment exists. When authoritative power is present the expectation is that when specific orders are issued they will be obeyed. By contrast, diffuse power refers more to the existence within society of norms that result spontaneously in specific practices rather than as a result of definite commands.

These different types of power are interrelated in different circumstances. For example, religion could be regarded as a form of power that is both diffuse and extensive. A prison is an example of an organisational form that is both authoritative and intensive.

Mann views societies as being made up of networks of organised power. He argues that societies are not unitary, but rather 'are constituted of multiple overlapping and intersecting sociospatial networks of power' (1986: 1). To demonstrate this contention Mann poses the question 'in which society do you live?'. At one level this is a simple question to answer. The reply might, for example, be 'Britain'. Deeper reflection suggests that social life is more complex. An individual is a member of multiple and over-lapping societies. For example, one might be a member of a university in Wales, one might also consider oneself to be a member of industrial society, western society, Europe, the North, a religious society, a political party, a pressure group, and part of a military alliance. Mann suggests that the implication of this is that societies are confederal rather than unitary.

These cross-cutting societies, or socio-spatial networks operate with greater or lesser reach. In the contemporary world Mann (1997: 475) identi-fies five ranges within which socio-spatial networks operate. These are: local networks, which exist at a sub-national level; national networks, which are contained within the borders claimed by a particular state; international networks, which comprise relations between national networks; transna-tional networks, which are unaffected by national borders (for example, religion); and global networks which have expanded to encompass the entire world, or the vast majority of it. Mann (*ibid.*) notes that 'over the centuries local interaction networks have clearly diminished in relative weight; while longer-distance networks – national, international and transnational – have become denser, structuring more of people's lives'.

At the root of these different cross-cutting societies are changing combi-nations of what Mann calls the four sources of social power. He bases his approach to the study of human societies on the analysis of these power sources:

> A general account of societies, their structure, and their history can best be given in terms of the interrelations of what I will call the four sources of social power: ideological, economic, military and political (IEMP) relationships.
>
> (Mann 1986: 2)

These four sources manifest their power through specific organisational forms. Ideological power emerges as a result of the human need to find some meaning to life. Those who control an ideology that purports to provide such meaning gain social power. Ideological power is a good example of a diffuse form of power, as its influence is exerted through the creation of norms of behaviour. It takes two main organisational forms. First, there is a more autonomous form that is 'sociospatially transcendent'. In this instance ideology rises above existing social boundaries and crosses into multiple societies. Religions such as Christianity and Islam are examples of this organisational form. Furthermore, ideology can appear as 'immanent morale'. In this form ideology does not exist in its own right, but as a strengthening factor in what is already there. Nationalism would appear to be a prime example of this organisational form.

Economic power emerges through the organisation of production and exchange to fulfil human needs. Mann argues that economic power is particularly effective and stable because it merges the intensive, extensive, authoritarian and diffuse aspects of power. Different groups emerge as a result of the organisation of these tasks, and these form classes, a central part of Mann's analysis. Mann initially labelled the organisational form of economic power as 'circuits of praxis'. However, this term has subsequently been dropped in favour of expressions more usual for describing forms of economic conflict and cooperation: 'classes and sectional and segmental economic organizations' (Mann 1993a: 7).

Military power originates from the need for protection and the advantages derived from offensive activities. It can appear in both intensive and extensive forms, and those who control it are able to acquire both collective and distributive power. Its main organisational form is 'concentrated-coercive'. This is most apparent in times of warfare, but can also persist into times of peace. Military power is usually 'sociospatially dual'. In the core, military power can be exerted in an intensive, authoritarian form, whilst surrounding this core is a large area where control is less complete. Although the population in this area may find it in their interests to cooperate with the military centre, they are to a certain extent able to exercise a degree of autonomy in their activities (Mann 1986a: 26).

The fourth of Mann's sources of social power is political power. Political power is derived from the usefulness of the centralised regulation of social relations. This centralisation marks a difference between political power and the other three sources. 'Political power is located in that centre and exercised outward' (1986a: 27). Whilst the other power sources have the possibility of transcending territorial boundaries, political power has the tendency to emphasise and define boundaries. Like military power, political power is socio-spatially dual, though in a different way. On the one hand there is a territorially centralised and bounded domestic scene, and on the other hand there is an 'area of regulated interstate relations' or geopolitical diplomacy.

Mann (1993a: 1) argues that different combinations of the four power sources 'fundamentally determine the structure of societies'. None of the four sources of social power has 'ultimate primacy'. Different sources, or different combinations of sources, may be dominant during any particular period, but none is ultimately determining. The changing interrelationships between the power sources constitute the historical process and provide him with a model to explain historical change. Human beings enter into a variety of social relationships in pursuit of the fulfilment of their goals and needs. These social relationships consolidate into different forms of organisational power. At any one point a particular form of power combination becomes institutionalised as a dominant configuration. Outside the dominant configuration lie other networks of power and other aspects of the four sources of power. These forces eventually come together to form a more powerful emergent network that brings about a reorganisation of social life and a new dominant configuration (Mann 1986a: 30).

Central to this notion of change is the concept of 'interstitial emergence'. These are the processes by which new power configurations emerge at the boundaries of existing ones. Mann explains these processes as follows:

> They are the outcome of the translation of human goals into organizational means. Societies have never been sufficiently institutionalized to prevent interstitial emergence. Human beings do not create unitary societies but a diversity of interacting networks of social interaction. The most important of these networks form relatively stably around the four power sources in any given social space. But underneath, human beings are tunnelling ahead to achieve their goals, forming new networks, extending old ones, and emerging most clearly into our view with rival configurations of one or more of the principal power networks.
>
> (Mann 1986a: 16)

As an example of interstitial emergence, Mann points to the analysis by Marx of the development of capitalist relations within feudalism. This occurred as a result of the creation of new networks, between the bourgeoisie, landowners, tenant farmers and rich peasants, within the existing power relations. Capitalism emerged between the 'pores' of feudal society. Changes in the dominant form of power configuration do not occur suddenly, but as a result of the gradual emergence of new networks that eventually come to challenge the existing institutions. Mann argues that history takes the form of a series of such developments. The configuration of power in one period, and the political arrangements set up to institutionalise it, become inappropriate as the subsidiary forms of social power reorganise.[1] In Volume I of *The Sources of Social Power*, Mann attempts to apply this model to the development of social power in agrarian societies, and in Volume II to the rise of classes and nation states.

The second chapter of Volume I covers the vast majority of human history. During this long period 'from the beginning' no permanent power networks emerged. This does not mean that there were no societies, just that they remained broadly egalitarian or that where stratification did emerge it did not persist. Mann accounts for this by arguing that such societies lacked a 'social cage'. Where stratification did appear people had two choices, either to move on or to overthrow those who had taken control. For the vast majority of human existence these were the options that were pursued (1986a: 68). Where stratification states did eventually emerge, this was a result of the cage being closed, removing the possibility of escape.

Alluvial agriculture, especially when irrigation became involved, acted to close the cage. This was because of the economic benefits to be gained from staying in one place, as opposed to moving on once stratification relations emerged. However, not only the immediate area became caged. Mann argues that whole regions became involved, primarily because of trade. As a result, three sets of different socio-spatial, overlapping, intersecting networks developed:

> Alluvial or irrigated core, immediate periphery, and whole region. The first two settled down into small local states, the third into a broader civilisation. All three fixed and made more permanent finite and bounded social and territorial spaces. It was now relatively difficult for the population caged there to turn their backs on emerging authority and inequality, as they had done on countless occasions in prehistory.
>
> (Mann 1986a: 124)

Mann argues that civilisation emerged in the form of what he describes as multi-power-actor civilisations. In multi-power-actor civilisations there are two levels of power: one political, the other ideological. Small political units, often city-states, exist within a wider civilisation, usually based around religious and/or cultural factors (1986a: 76). Within multi-power-actor civilisations, the separate social groupings share a wide range of experience. The diffusion of artistic styles and ideologies occurs between different groups primarily because they seek answers to the same sort of questions. Additionally, and importantly for the subsequent discussion, there is some normative control over the relations between the social groupings.

The opposite of the multi-power-actor civilisation is the empire of domination. Historically, empires of domination usually appeared in the peripheral areas of multi-power-actor civilisations and resulted from the spur of military organisation. Mann (1986a: 130) observes that 'what had been hitherto semiperipheral areas became, in a sense, the new core of civilization'. In the empires of domination, military power becomes the predominant power source, as 'marcher lords' from the periphery conquer the pre-existing multi-power-actor civilisation. Centralised control of empires of domination permits the potential for deriving the benefits from collective and distributional power. Examples of multi-power-actor civilisations include Sumeria, Phoenicia and Greece. Examples of empires of domination include Akkadia and Rome.

The majority of Volume I describes the rise and fall of these different social formations. It concludes with a long discussion of the emergence of industrial capitalism in Europe. Mann locates his explanation for its dynamism in two features of medieval Europe. First, there was no one power dominant over the region. Medieval Europe was a 'multiple acephalous federation'. It 'had no head, no center, yet it was an entity composed of a number of small, crosscutting interaction networks' (1986a: 376). Yet transcending this federation was the ideological power of Christianity. Christianity took the second organisational form of ideological power, in that it provided the immanent morale for the ruling class of lords. Christianity 'helped ensure a basic level of normative pacification, confirming property and market relations within and between the cells' (ibid.: 377).

From the late twelfth century the character of this federation underwent a period of prolonged change, with the gradual emergence of nation states. From a detailed empirical analysis of English state expenditure, Mann draws the conclusion that the growth of the state can be directly linked to its involvement in warfare. In times of war, state spending increased dramatically, and following periods of war there was no comparable decrease. Hence the increase in the size and scope of the state has been incremental. However, warfare has not been the only preserve of the state. Gradually it also became involved in domestic affairs, and through its infrastructural spending provided a boost to industrial capitalism. Mann therefore sees the early sources of European dynamism in Christian ideological pacification over a region of overlapping power networks, given a boost by the emergence of territorially bounded nation states.

Mann concludes his discussion of power in agrarian society with a discussion of the focal question of the first volume: is there a cyclical or even dialectical pattern to history? Mann suggests that the answer is possibly 'yes'. Empires of domination (e.g Akkadia, Assyria, Rome) and multi-power-actor civilisations (e.g. Greece, Europe) have replaced each other in a cyclical fashion.

> Each of these cases was notably creative in its use and development of the sources of social power. . . . Each, therefore, made notable contributions to the single process of world-historical development. . . . Yet each type [empires of domination and multi-power-actor civilizations] eventually reaches the limits of its power capacities. It lacks the adaptability in the face of new opportunities or threats created by the uncontrolled, interstitial development of a new combination of power networks.
>
> (Mann 1986a: 534, 537)

Decentralised power locations emerged within the power configurations of empires of domination. These took the form of landowners, merchants and artisans. Ideological movements usually linked these decentralised power locations. With the destruction or metamorphosis of the empire of domination, these decentralised power locations have usually coalesced into the poles of a new multi-power-actor civilisation. In turn, these civilisations may also contain the seeds that lead to a centralisation and the emergence of a new empire or hegemonic power. The relationship between multi-power-actor civilisations and empires of domination will be reconsidered later, in the discussion of Mann's view of the international system.

The time period covered in Volume II is considerably less than that attempted in the history of agrarian societies, and the geographical location of the analysis centres more exclusively on Europe. Central to Volume II is the production of a theory of the modern state that connects existing state theory to the four sources of social power. Mann's approach is to develop a theory that is partly institutional and partly functional, with the latter leading to the description of the state as 'polymorphous'. His theory of the modern state is an eclectic mixture, drawn from a selection of existing state theory and given an additional twist through his incorporation of the four sources of social power. From Marxism he takes the view that the modern state is capitalist and that class conflict drives politics. However, he rejects the view that the capitalist class, or any other, is ultimately determining. From pluralism he accepts the position that there are multiple actors in the state. Nonetheless he refuses to accept the view that conflict between actors is resolved through democratic means. Power forms other than voting and democracy are active in determining outcomes. From elite theory he appro-priates the view that state personnel can act autonomously. Finally, from cock-up theorists he adopts the view that states are much 'messier' than any single theory can encompass.

Mann models his institutional analysis of the state very closely on Weber's views. However, he views the issue of the state's monopoly of violence differently. Mann's position is as follows:

1   The state is a differentiated set of institutions and personnel
2   embodying centrality, in the sense that political relations radiate to and from a centre, to cover a
3   territorially demarcated area over which it exercises
4   some degree of authoritative, binding rule making, backed up by some organised physical force (Mann 1993a: 55).

Mann takes the term 'polymorphous' from chemistry, where it is used to describe a substance that crystallises in multiple different forms. The concept of the polymorphous state develops from the differentiated institu-tions and personnel of the state. Different parts of the state pursue different issues and represent different groups and interests from within its territory: *the state need have no final unity or even consistency*' (1993a: 56, original emphasis). The term polymorphous is relevant because it 'conveys the way states crystallize as the center – but in each case as a different center – of a number of power networks. States have multiple institutions, charged with multiple tasks, mobilizing constituencies both through their territories and geopolitically' (*ibid.*: 75). Different constituencies crystallise in different forms. At different times one or more different crystallisations may be ultimately determining. Mann calls these forms 'higher-level crystallizations'. During the long nineteenth century Mann identifies six higher-level crystallisations: capitalist, militarist, representative, national, ideological-moral and patriarchal. The majority of the remainder of Volume II examines the ways in which different combinations of the higher-level crystallisations formed in different European states. Mann concentrates on France, Germany and, especially, Britain.

During the period covered in Volume II a major change occurred in the relationship between state and society. In the period up to 1800 the primary activity of the state had been making war (as suggested by the evidence offered in Volume I). During the nineteenth century the scope of state activities broadened considerably, incorporating an increasing range of domestic responsibilities. Mann (1993a: 504) comments that 'by 1914, they were dual military-civil states'. This had two major consequences. First, there was a marked increase in bureaucratisation and representation as states endeavoured to manage their increased responsibilities. Second, civil society became, to use Mann's term, 'naturalised', in that it was increasingly caged by the activities of the state and the boundedness of the nation state.

World War I marks the conclusion of the historical period considered in Volume II, in more than one sense. Besides marking the end of the expansion of influence of the European states that typified the long nineteenth century, 'its leading philosophies of hope, liberalism and socialism, appeared to be extinguished in one crazed week in August 1914' (1993a: 740). Mann attempts to account for the causes of the cataclysm in terms of his analysis so far developed.

Mann's argument is that the war resulted from contradictions between the higher-level crystallisations. 'It resulted from the unintended consequences of the interaction of overlapping, intersecting power networks. Actors pursued and drifted between strategies whose interactions were unpredictable and eventually devastating' (1993a: 796). Mann argues that polymorphous crystallisation was most extreme in Germany and Austria. In both, crystallisations formed that were centred on the monarchy, the military and classes. In Britain and France, the prime crystallisations were different, concentrating around capitalism and classes. As a result 'it became difficult to predict the reactions of other Powers to one's own diplomacy. The problem was not irrational actors but plural actors with plural identities pursuing diverse strategies whose interactions were unpredictable and eventually devastating' (*ibid.*: 757).

Before proceeding, it is worth highlighting some of the aspects of Mann's analysis that are of particular relevance to International Relations. His theoretical discussion of the cross-cutting character of societies is clearly a

126

challenge to a realist analysis. However, this is an aspect of his analysis that disappears in the historical account. The discussions of societal developments and the analysis of the origins of World War I in Volume II are very tied to specific societies.

His analysis of the state is related to that of the interdependence writers. Mann develops an analysis of the state that stresses the potential for inconsistency and, perhaps more importantly, offers an explanation of how it is possible for different states to completely misunderstand each other's actions.

The discussion of the dialectical relationship between empires of domination and multi-power-actor civilisations is an element of Mann's work that has received less comment than perhaps it deserves. Mann suggests that this might represent a world-historical process. However, it might also offer a theory of change between hierarchical and anarchical international systems. This point will be developed later.

Mann's work also leads us to question the multi-dimensional characteristics of power. Rather than a single source of power, such as economic power, or political power, Mann argues that different sources of power are more significant in different historical epochs. The changing relationship between the sources of social power gives him a theoretical framework for the analysis of change in human societies.

Further light can be cast on Mann's analysis by examining some of the criticisms that it has generated. This is the purpose of the next section.

CRITICAL REACTIONS TO MANN'S WORK

Most reviews of Mann's work have praised its ambition and scope. Vaughan (1987) has described it as a 'neo-Victorian venture', but with an un-Victorian underlying theoretical design. Wickham (1988: 63) suggested that Volume I was a book 'which few historians or sociologists can afford to ignore'. Rengger (1995: 167) describes Volume I as 'a gem of modern social science'. Giddens (1994: 37) has described Volume II as 'a study bursting with interesting ideas as well as covering a rich sweep of empirical materials'. Not surprisingly, the majority of criticism of Mann's project has concentrated on his concept of the four sources of social power and their relative autonomy. But there have been other criticisms.

Critics have suggested that Mann's work is Euro-centric. Giddens (1994: 38) makes this point with specific reference to Volume II, where he claims that 'modern history becomes the history of the west'. He also notes that Mann largely overlooks the colonial history of Europe during the nineteenth century, concentrating instead on the building of states and nations. Anderson (1986) notes the relative absence of the analysis of China in Volume I. This seems a little unjustified, given Mann's discussion of Shang

China as one of his examples of the emergence of a pristine civilisation, his discussion of Confucianism as an example of a world religion, and his examination of the reasons for China's lack of dynamism when compared to medieval Europe (Mann 1986a: 106–8, 342–4, 501–2). Volume II is decidedly Euro-centric however, though perhaps this is justified, given the author's intention to focus on the 'leading edge of power' (Mann 1993a: 1). This is a point made by Moore, who notes that 'if one were to write a history of the violin there would be no reason to say much about those parts of the world that had no violins' (Moore 1998: 171). Whatever position is taken on this debate, it does seem reasonable to agree with Moore's observation that Mann is over-reliant on source texts in the English language (*ibid.*: 174). Moore suggests that this has led him to overlook in particular works in German on medieval history.

Both Gellner and Giddens have accused Mann of evolutionism. This is a very important point, as it strikes right at the heart of Mann's project. He (1986a: 1) rejects the concept of societies as systems and as a result rules out the possibility of an evolutionary process. Yet as Gellner (1988: 206) notes, despite Mann's anti-evolutionist stance, his work proceeds sequentially, 'following the familiar ladder of man's ascent'. In a similar vein, Giddens (1994: 38) notes 'an evolutionist ring' to the work.

Mann's work has also been attacked from a Foucauldian perspective. What narratives have been silenced in Mann's approach? Stillman (1987: 311) remarks that it is very much a product of its time and sees 'its concerns as typical of the late twentieth century: power and organisation, shot through by chance and contingency'. He goes on to comment that 'it so reflects those dominant patterns that I wonder what has been suppressed by his theoretical framework and what "interstitial emergence", what new and unexpected dynamic, may occur to upset the world that he presents'.

One voice that is largely suppressed is that of gender relations. In the history of agrarian societies Mann justifies this by arguing that gender relations remained constant in the form of patriarchy, and that the power relations discussed concern those in the 'public sphere' between male heads of households. But this admission ignores the issue of power relations within the household. The consequences of excluding them should be considered. More telling is the absence of an analysis of gender relations in Volume II. This was promised in Volume I, but is put aside with the comment that 'gender relations have their own history, currently being rewritten by feminist scholarship. Now is not the time for a grand synthesis' (Mann 1986a: 31).[2]

Most criticism, however, has been directed at Mann's concept of social power. The criticism can be divided into two groups. First there are those who criticise Mann's definition and application of his concepts, and second there are those who dispute his arguments about autonomy and primacy.

Tilly criticises Mann for presenting a vague definition of power. Mann's initial definition of power is very simple and in his theoretical discussion he makes no reference to some of the standard material on the two, three, or even four dimensions of power.[3] Mann does extend his initial definition of power considerably, with his introduction of the concepts of collective, distributive, intensive, extensive, authoritarian and diffuse power. However, he does not appear to enter the debate on second or third dimensions of power. These dimensions refer to the ability to set the agenda or to influence or determine the aspirations of other actors. It is possible, though, that Mann might argue that these issues would be incorporated under ideological power.

Other critics have suggested that his concept of four sources of social power is only of limited value or represents no significant theoretical advance (Moore 1988: 170). Munz, though less critical of Mann's 'conceptology', expresses doubts about its application. He suggests that Mann's narrative, based around the four sources of social power, offers little, if any, increase in an understanding of history. He suggests that 'the story it tells is not new and that the explanatory value of the classification scheme it uses is negligible' (1991: 264). In a similar vein, Sanderson (1988: 311) is critical of the 'promulgation of an unnecessarily complicated theory of history', and he calls for a more parsimonious approach that explains more by telling less.

Finally, Mann has been criticised for his failure to allocate ultimate primacy to one of his four sources of social power. Wickham disputes Mann's analysis of the role of Christianity in the dynamism of medieval Europe, and disputes the autonomy of military and political from economic power. He (1988: 77) argues that 'it is not true that political/military power floats free from the economy; it merely extracts from the economic base and intervenes in it at different levels from those operated by the producer'. Haldon also argues that the economic sphere is ultimately determining. He (1993: 267) argues that 'power in the political, military and ideological spheres is ultimately dependent upon access to and control over the distribution of economic resources'. Similarly, Anderson argues that political power cannot be regarded as autonomous. He (1986: 1405) contends that 'any exercise of it manifestly depends on the possession of either ideological or military power, and normally a combination of both force and belief – while the converse does not hold'.

These arguments about primacy do not hold too great a problem for Mann, as he would maintain that different sources of social power are ultimately determining in different historical epochs. In recent periods, economic power has been particularly important, though according to Mann always in combination with one of the other sources. During the eighteenth century, economic and military sources of power were predominant, whilst in the nineteenth century this changed to a combination of economic and political (Mann 1993a: 1). Marxist critics complain that Mann fails to award the economic power source the distinction of being ultimately determining. Mann would reply that it is, but only within specific historical periods. The distinction here is that Mann is not ultimately reductionist to one source of power. In different historical epochs different sources of power may be determining, alone or in combination. However, no one source has been in that position indefinitely.

Having considered some of the critiques of Mann's work, we will proceed to an examination of his view of the international system.

MICHAEL MANN AND THE CONCEPT OF INTERNATIONAL SYSTEM

Mann criticises the discipline of International Relations for its failure to analyse the integration between the national and the international. He argues that the concepts of international space held by what he describes as the two main traditions of International Relations are limited. He argues that Realism is restricted to a view of the international system as structured by the interests of states. In contrast, 'interdependence' writers concentrate on the mutuality of economic interests. Mann (1988: ix) argues that both these positions are limited, because 'the international arena is clearly some kind of combination of both these (as well as other) phenomena, and both impact greatly upon domestic societies, states and economies'.

The implication of this position is that Mann has been able to develop a more comprehensive approach to the international system, one that includes all these phenomena and integrates the national and the international. We will now look in more detail at Mann's conception of the international system. This process is complicated by the proliferation of terms that he uses. Things are made more difficult by the extent to which Mann uses the idea of the international system as a residual concept, piling into it any number of transnational interactions (the 'other phenomena') without evaluating what they are, or how they are related.

As an example, consider this quotation from a review by Mann of a work by Wallerstein. Mann's criticisms of Wallerstein's work are similar to those made by Skocpol: that Wallerstein places too much emphasis on an economic analysis. He maintains that:

> Capitalism, even world system capitalism, is not the only 'society' occupying the world. The nation-state, the civilization, the Church, the ethnic community, gender etc., are also human communities contributing their own logics of development, alongside market capitalism, each helping structure all others.
>
> (Mann 1993c: 363)

Such a position would seem to develop from Mann's analysis, but how is it possible to combine these into a conception of the international system? My argument is that Mann's analysis requires a conception of the international system to take the causal weight that he places in the international arena. In short, he suggests that the international system comprises a multitude of relationships, looks to the international system to explain a wide range of phenomena (such as the development of the state, social classes and capitalism), but fails to provide an analysis that can fulfil what he requires.

My argument will be built as follows. First, the range of descriptions that Mann uses to describe international space will be outlined. Four approaches to the international system that can be found in Mann's work will then be outlined: a geopolitical view, a rule-based/norms view, a rational actor view, and a reasoned choices view. These four positions can be related to each of the quadrants of the matrix that was discussed in Chapter 1 (see Figure 6.1). One purpose of the remainder of this chapter will be to argue that these four accounts are incompatible and rely on different approaches to theorising the social world.

Different terms for the international system

As already noted, Mann uses various terms to describe the international system. Several of these have already been encountered in the overview of his work. Mann makes comparatively little use of the term 'system'. It is used occasionally in his analysis of the European dynamic. Discussing the increasing centralisation of the state, and increasing consolidation of territory, both in response to war-fighting activities, he notes that 'these eliminations ensured that Europe moved toward a *state* system, in other words, that the surviving units would be relatively centred and relatively territorial' (Mann 1986a: 455, original emphasis). It is significant that Mann places the emphasis on 'state'. As the second half of the sentence indicates, it

	Explaining	Understanding
Holistic	geopolitical account	norms and roles account
Individualistic	rational actor account	social actor account

Figure 6.1 Four different accounts of the international system in Michael Mann's *The Sources of Social Power*

is the centralisation of state activities and the increasing boundedness of territorialities that he is stressing, rather than any significance to an international system as such. He (*ibid.*, original emphasis) goes on to remark that 'Europe also became a more orderly *multi*state system in which the actors were more nearly equal, more similar in their interests, and more formally rational in their diplomacy'. At this point, where the stress is on shared interests and diplomacy, he appears to be using the term in the sense of his frequently used phrase multi-power-actor civilisation. Finally, he points to an important characteristic of multistate systems: diffusion. 'Whereas the leading power stumbles across new power techniques, the more successful of its rivals react in a more ordered, planned fashion. The advantage of late entry is not a trait of multistate systems that began with industrialization' (*ibid.*: 456). This characteristic of the international system would seem to have much in common with Skocpol's analysis of world-historical time, where later actors are able to benefit from advances made elsewhere.

The relative infrequency with which Mann uses the term 'system' is not surprising. What is perhaps more surprising is that he uses it at all. He is at great pains to reject the notion of system with relation to society. This is detailed most succinctly as follows:

> It is a basic tenet of my work that societies are not systems. There is no ultimately determining structure to human existence – at least none that social actors or sociological observers, situated in its midst, can discern. What we call societies are only loose aggregates of diverse, overlapping, intersecting power networks.
>
> (Mann 1993a: 506)[4]

The societies referred to here are domestic societies, but clearly Mann attaches an element of determinism to the word 'system'. Given his overall theoretical stance, this would be an understanding that he would probably choose to avoid with reference to the relations between states.

An alternative term that Mann uses is 'arena'. This has already been seen in the quotation above with reference to International Relations. The following reference comes from a discussion of the importance of leadership as a power process, here with specific reference to crisis: 'Diplomatic and military decisions in crises become critical. Then the international arena resembles the normless "anarchy" favored by realism' (1993a: 260). Mann gives no explanation of what he means by 'arena', but it conjures up images of competition and conflict, especially when combined with the concept of normless anarchy.

More useful are the two geopolitical types that Mann employs; namely multi-power-actor civilisations and empires of domination. It will be argued here that these constitute descriptions of Mann's view of, in International Relations terms, international systems. What is important to consider is whether these are examples of two manifestations of an international system, or whether they constitute two separate systems.

The prime characteristic of multi-power-actor civilisations is the degree of shared norms amongst a number of actors. Despite the existence of multiple actors, there is a sense from Mann's descriptions that there are more similarities between the actors than there are differences. There are various examples of these civilisations, and in each one Mann suggests that there are norms that constrain the actors in relations with each other.

By contrast, for empires of domination, a shared environment based on common norms is replaced by what Mann terms 'compulsory cooperation'. 'Empires of domination combined military concentrated coercion with an attempt at state territorial centralization and geopolitical hegemony' (Mann 1986a: 533). A complicated mix of power relations exists in such empires: at the centre, intensive authoritarian power, based on military coercion; toward the periphery, extensive power, though still authoritarian.

Mann clearly does see a relationship between these two forms of organising geopolitical space. He has gone as far as suggesting that there may be a dialectical relationship between the two, based around the concept of interstitial emergence. As an example of this, consider the following description of how multi-power-actor civilisations may emerge from an empire of domination:

> Empires of domination have unintentionally generated more diffuse power relations of two main sorts within their interstices: (1) decentralized, property-owning landlords, merchants, and artisans, that is, upper and middling classes; and (2) ideological movements, located primarily among these classes, but also embodying more diffuse and universal notions of community. If these diffuse power relations continue to grow interstitially, a decentralized multi-power-actor civilization may result, either from the collapse of the empire or from its gradual metamorphosis.
>
> (Mann 1986a: 537)

This process can also proceed in the opposite direction. The multi-power-actor civilisation

> generates its own antithetical, interstitial forces, in this case tendencies toward state centralization and militaristic coercion, coupled perhaps with the emergence of one hegemonic geopolitical state, which may eventually result in the reemergence of an empire of domination.
>
> (Mann 1996a: 537)

Developments in the European state system provide an example of this process. Take, for example, the rise of the European state system, which Mann would describe as a multi-power-actor civilisation. It is one civilisation in the sense that there are more similarities between the states of Europe than differences, and multi-power because (despite various attempts) no single power has been able to exert hegemony over the whole continent. This arose from the debris of the collapsed Roman Empire, an empire of domination. Although there was a relatively long period between the collapse of the Roman Empire and the emergence of the European system as it would be recognised today, the Roman system clearly influenced and laid the foundations for the European system that did appear. The progress of the European community could be seen as a contrary process. The possibilities of further development of a multi-power-actor civilisation being exhausted, the opposite dynamic towards a single political entity could be seen to be coming into effect.

Hence Mann clearly sees a close relationship between these two forms of ordering of geopolitical space. The general term that Mann uses to describe these forms of ordering is 'geopolitical organisation', which constitutes political organisation in its international as opposed to domestic manifestation. Perhaps within International Relations theory the closest parallel might be to Waltz's anarchic and hierarchical systems: the multi-power-actor civilisation being an example of the former; and the empire of domination being an example of the latter (Waltz 1979: 106–16).

Having looked at some of the terms that Mann uses to describe the international system, we will now consider the ways in which the system is typified at different points in the text.

International system as external structure

In his discussion of the four sources of social power and their organisational forms, Mann (1986a: 27) notes that geopolitical organisation, the international aspect of political organisation, is 'an essential part of social life and it is not reducible to the "internal" power configurations of its component states'. In other words, the form of the structure of the relations between states is distinct from the power relations within individual states. It is an entity that has to be analysed in its own right.

Mann places a particularly strong emphasis on the role of geopolitical organisation in his analysis of the development of the European state. He (1986a: 511) notes that 'states and the multistate civilization developed primarily in response to pressures emanating from the geopolitical and military spheres'.[5] The implication of this statement is that the system is prior to the states. States, and the relations between them, developed as a result of pressures from the international system. As already noted above, Mann claims to have produced empirical evidence detailing the relation between the growth of the English state and its involvement in warfare.

But it is not only in the growth of the state that geopolitical organisation had an impact. Its influence was also evident in the development of classes. Mann (1986a: 513) notes that 'the process and outcome of class struggles became significantly determined by the nature and interrelations of states'.[6] Furthermore, the relations between states have decisively shaped capitalism itself. Mann (1993a: 31) states that 'capitalism actually emerged within and between the territories of states. It became sociospatially structured by their domestic and geopolitical relations'.

Mann is making very strong claims regarding the influences of geopolitical organisation. He uses the concept as a causal factor in his account of states, classes and capitalism. However, it is less clear what he means by geopolitical organisation and how this influence comes about. The main way that Mann documents is through 'military-fiscal extraction'. Briefly, the demands of warfare require the state to extract resources from its domestic population. But these extractions are not made without cost. Mann argues that the tax burden imposed to pay for war-fighting activities resulted in domestic class conflict and alterations in domestic political systems (Mann 1993a: 214–15, 224, 225).[7]

This is a reductionist position. Mann relates changes in the state and in classes to the occurrence of war. This implies that the international system is the equivalent of war, and the explanation of domestic developments is related to the circumstances of war. This raises the question of what effect the international system can have when there is no war. Is there no international system without war? This problem arises because of the view of the international system that Mann employs when discussing developments in society. Concentration on a view of the international system as an arena of geopolitical conflict, a realist viewpoint, restricts the possibilities of pursuing an analysis except through the use of war as the central element.

However, this view of geopolitical space is only one position that Mann takes regarding the international system. We now turn to another portrayal which features a vision of the international system as a set of norms that govern state behaviour. I will argue that this represents an insider account with a holistic ontology.

Rules and norms in multi-power-actor civilisations

We now turn to an examination of the role and importance of rules and norms. Mann suggests that the role of rules and norms in interstate relations forms a particular characteristic of all multi-power-actor civilisations, even the earliest examples. We will find that, for Mann, international norms are a constraining factor on state actions.

The first mention of norms is with reference to the degree of normative constraint over the actors in the Mesopotamian civilisation. Mann (1986a: 92) notes that 'as in modern relations between nation-states, some degree of normative regulation between the individual states existed. There was

warfare, but there were rules of war. There were boundary disputes, but proce-
dures for settling them'. Such normative control over states is even more
notable in the case of the Greek civilisation. Mann notes that the conduct of
warfare was determined by particular rules. For example, war was publicly
declared, removing the possibility of surprise attacks, and norms of behaviour
existed which determined the relationship between victor and vanquished.
Greece comprised a 'broader culture, one that provided explicit regulation
and legitimation of a multistate system' (*ibid.*: 202). In other words the
actions of states were confined, to a greater or lesser degree, by the existence of
norms of behaviour in relations between the various Greek states.

However, it is with regard to Europe that Mann is able to extend his analysis the furthest. He notes that

> European diplomats inhabited a 'multi-power-actor civilisation', not
> an anarchic black hole (as envisaged by some realists) but a normative
> community of shared norms and perceptions, some very general,
> others shared by specific transnational classes or religions; some
> peaceful, others violent. . . . Thus diplomacy and geopolitics were
> rule-governed. Some rules defined what reasonable national interests
> were and were shared by statesmen across the civilization. Others
> added normative understandings among kin-related aristocrats,
> among Catholics, among 'Europeans', 'Westerners', even occasionally
> among 'human beings'. Even war was rule-governed, 'limited' in
> relation to some, righteously savage in relation to others.
>
> (Mann 1993a: 69)[8]

The international norms that affected the European multi-power-actor civilisation concerned religion, culture, philosophy, political institutions,
economy, monarchical rulers and, increasingly through the nineteenth
century, racism. All of these acted to increase a normative solidarity amongst
the European states (1993a: 753). The effect of such norms is to constrain
the action of states. In an article on the future of the nation state, Mann
(1993b: 119) observes that 'geopolitical relations restrict the sovereignty of
states which are parties to binding agreements, and they more persistently
undercut the sovereignty of weaker states'.

The usual approach to norms in International Relations is that they are a
source of order. However, Mann maintains that norms can possibly come in
both positive and negative forms. Most interdependence writers stress the
positive nature of international norms. For Mann, however, they are not
necessarily benign. They might represent repressive class interests, or
encourage or even idealise war. He notes that 'normative solidarities might
lead to disorder' (1993a: 50).

Despite the existence of norms with the potential to generate instability,
Mann clearly attaches great importance to the role of norms in the maintenance

of peaceful relations between states. He (1993a: 293) notes that international peace 'needs shared norms and careful multistate diplomacy'. Additionally, 'lack of shared norms worsens the misunderstandings of downward diplomatic spirals' (*ibid*.: 769–70). Therefore, despite the existence of norms that are far from benign, Mann argues that the presence of norms is essential for international order.

Mann attributes a significant and important role to norms. But it is far from clear how norms come into existence, or how they are created, or how their influence is manifested. As with the view of the international system as a form of geopolitical organisation, Mann fails to give a definition, but only argues through the provision of examples.

Individualistic views of the international system

We have now examined two holistic accounts of international systems: a geopolitical outsider account that reduced the international system to the occurrence of warfare; and an insider norms-based account. Both of these views can be regarded as holistic. In the first, causal factors were located in external geopolitical space. In the second, causal factors were derived from the constraining effects of shared understandings.

It is also possible to derive two accounts from Mann's work at an individualistic level. We will find too that at this level of analysis Mann's work is also divided by insider and outsider accounts.

First, it is possible to view some of Mann's analysis in terms of the international system as a creation of social actors. Clearly this would relate very closely to the existence of norms, but at this point the analysis would seem to be centred on the social actors themselves. Mann at several points discusses the realist views held by European diplomats and derived from their social upbringing. This realist viewpoint provided the foundation for their beliefs about the world and the international system. With reference to the nineteenth century, Mann remarks that

> The statesmen of this period were drawn overwhelmingly from the old regime class. Their common social identity reinforced balance of power realism. They constructed an elaborate alliance system to prevent any repetition of the alarming conjunction of devastating war and revolutionary class and national mobilization.
>
> (Mann 1993a: 278–9)[9]

This position emphasises the role of individual actors in the creation of the social world. Their beliefs about how the world is constituted result in the reproduction of that world. The international system becomes the creation of what specific actors believe it to be.

Alongside this view, it is also possible to find statements where Mann is suggesting a rational actor position for political leaders, forever calculating the best available option. For example, at one point he (1993a: 416) notes that 'multistate diplomacy involves autonomous states with only limited normative ties, continuously recalculating geopolitical options'. In this statement Mann appears to downplay the role of norms that have featured so highly elsewhere. Here the emphasis appears to be on diplomats making apparently rational decisions, based on their continuous recalculation of the external situation.

The sense of views of the international system at an individualistic level is heightened by Mann's account of the causes of the First World War in the final chapter of Volume II of *The Sources of Social Power*. In this account there is an almost total concentration on specific groups of actors, particularly the form of the crystallisations in different polymorphous states, with no mention of the international system in a holistic sense.

Hence it is possible to derive two individualistic readings of Mann's approach to the international system, as well as the two holistic approaches discussed in the previous sections.

Insider and outsider accounts

Although it is possible to make four readings of international systems in Mann's work, he has not indicated a preference for one view over another, nor discussed the relationship between these positions. It is possible that a concluding statement on his view of the international system will be included in Volume IV of *The Sources of Social Power*, which will deal with theoretical material in more detail.

In the meantime it is necessary to make some sense of these different positions. This raises a number of issues:

- Does Mann really have four different views of the international system?
- Are these views related in any way?
- Are any of these views mutually exclusive?

From Mann's writings it is difficult to outline how he views the international system. This is problematic, given the causal role he gives to it. This is especially the case given his claim to be attempting an analysis of the impact of geopolitics on social developments on a scale never before attempted. It is suggested here that the four views can be reduced to two different accounts from two perspectives: an insider account and an outsider account. The outsider account represents a version of international politics derived, initially, from a realist position.[10] The geopolitical view of the international system and the rational actor account can be looked upon as outsider views from different levels – a holistic and an individualistic level.

On the other hand, the norms and rules based account and the social constructivist view amount to different levels of analysis in an insider account. Such a position would derive more directly from a sociological analysis. It is easier to see how these two levels of analysis might be interrelated. Common understandings between diplomats (having similar backgrounds and views) result in the creation of a system of norms and rules that act to constrain the actions of individual diplomats. Although the norms derive from individuals, the result is a system that constrains all.

These insider and outsider accounts sit uneasily together, and do not work together. This is because they are derived from different approaches to the social sciences. The first stresses a scientific approach based on measurement, whilst the second concerns the understandings of the actors. Both of these approaches coexist within Mann's work, resulting in multiple accounts of the international system. The presence of these two versions of the international system amounts to a serious weakness in Mann's analysis. This is because the two different accounts contain elements that are not equivalent. They are talking about different things. It is difficult to aggregate an insider account with an outsider account. In the outsider account it is structures and rational actors which are the object of study. In the insider account it is mutual expectations and actors as social agents that are the basis of analysis.

CONCLUSION

The introduction to this chapter argued that Mann's work had the potential to mount a challenge to International Relations. The purpose of this conclusion is to summarise the nature of that challenge and to assess the extent to which its potential has, so far, been fulfilled.

From an International Relations perspective, the most provocative element of Mann's work is his view of the way in which societies are structured by overlapping power networks. This position is expressed most strongly in the introductory chapter of Volume I of *The Sources of Social Power*. Mann almost goes as far as saying that 'there is no such thing as society'. However, what he means is that a view of society as bounded entities is misleading. They are not billiard balls. Nor is the international system considered to be an autonomous realm. The implication of this position is that International Relations cannot be considered as an independent discipline. In other words, it is not possible to study international relations without considering the power networks that are structuring those societies. It is not possible to study the external without studying the internal. Relations are not between nations, but between individuals involved in many different 'societies' with different loyalties and influenced by the various sources of social power. The character of these societies is structured, according to Mann, by differing combinations of the sources of social power. None of these sources of social power is ultimately determining.

It is a central argument of this chapter that the full implications of this most radical element of Mann's position are not fully developed. There seems to be a distance between the theoretical framework and the empirical material. One source of this divide is the attempt to include an international aspect in the work without clearly defining its characteristics.

A further innovation in Mann's work concerns his approach to the state. The key element of Mann's work regarding the state is to locate its development within particular combinations of the four main sources of social power. The current position of the state is not a historical constant: 'for most of history centralised states had little salience for most social actors' (Mann 1996: 221). However, as with Skocpol and Tilly, much of Mann's analysis focuses on the view of the state as a product of international conflict. In Volume II of *The Sources of Social Power* the analysis is extended to discuss the increasing role of the state as a social agency. However, this is primarily linked to bargains struck between state and society during periods of war. Mann's approach to the state as polymorphous is a new development. His work does build on an existing body of work. Writers within the interdependence paradigm have long pointed to divisions within the state. An example of this would be those who have written on bureaucratic politics. Mann pursues this notion further with his concept of higher-level crystallisations. This is particularly significant in the relations between states. This is because of the potential for misunderstandings between states with different higher-level crystallisations. An apocalyptic example of this is Mann's discussion of the causes of World War I.

A further element of Mann's work that appears to have received little comment is his theory of change from one international system to another.[11] In Volume I of *The Sources of Social Power* he describes at some length the processes through which an empire of domination transforms into a multi-power-actor civilisation. The similarities between these two forms of international system and Waltz's hierarchic and anarchic systems have already been noted.

There is a tension in Mann's work between the elements that undermine a realist approach (his view of societies as conditioned by overlapping networks of power, his account of change, and his analysis of the state) and those that appear to be derived from or to support a realist position. This tension is reflected in his approach to the international system. The discussion of Mann's approach to the international system in the previous section suggests that there is a major weakness in his analysis: the use of two different epistemologies in his account of the international system.

There is firstly an outsider account. This occurs at two levels of analysis. First there is a systemic version. In this form Mann refers to geopolitical forces that shape state and society development. Mann makes several strong statements about the causal impact of these geopolitical forces without elucidating what these forces are or how they come about. There is also an individualistic level in this account. At this level political leaders make rational judgements of the international situation, and make decisions to act based on these calculations. In this account the international system becomes the equivalent of a games-theory matrix.

But Mann also has another epistemological approach, an insider account. As with the outsider account, this can be detected at a holistic and an individualistic level. At the holistic level there is a network of norms, rules and practises that constrain the actions of states. At an individualistic level can be detected a constructivist position, where the beliefs of actors about the system create the system itself.

Hence Mann's approach to theorising the international system can be seen as ill defined and inconsistent. As was noted earlier, he attributes a range of forces to the international system, but fails to provide a coherent framework within which these can be theorised. Instead, his approach to the international system tends to see it as a catch-all area for a variety of factors that cannot be included at a domestic level. This chapter has suggested that he has produced four different accounts of the international system. He employs each of these depending on what he is trying to analyse. As with Tilly, he uses warfare to explain the growth of the state in Europe, and a more constructivist approach to explain the restrictions on state activities.

However, despite the weaknesses in his approach to analysing the international system, Mann's work does have implications for International Relations theorists. He provides alternative ways of thinking about the state and the international system, and suggests ways of theorising the relationship between them. Crucially, he provides a theory of change between one form of international system and another. The strength of his position lies in his analysis of what he regards as the four main sources of social power, and his view of societies as overlapping and cross-cutting. However, his approach is weakened by a failure to provide a coherent account of the international system. The influence of international forces is central to Mann's analysis, but he fails to provide a means of analysing these.

There have been problems found with the approach to the international system taken by all the historical sociologists that we have considered so far. The next chapter considers the work of Wallerstein. Wallerstein has produced a much more coherent account of international relations, but, as will be seen, this clarity has been achieved through a failure to produce an analysis of the state.

7

IMMANUEL WALLERSTEIN

INTRODUCTION

In the previous three chapters we have considered the writings of historical sociologists who have made use of a concept of the international system in their analyses. I have been critical of all three writers because of the vague and contradictory ways in which they have defined and made use of the term. In all three cases, the lack of a clear definition has necessitated an interpretation of their understanding of 'international system' from the role it plays in their writings.

We will now consider the work of a writer whose approach to systems is considerably different: Immanuel Wallerstein. Wallerstein places a systemic approach at the centre of his analysis, and as a result ends up with a considerably different result from the other writers that we have considered.

The extent of Wallerstein's writing is phenomenal. Mokyr (1991: 895) has noted that 'for sheer scope, energy, ambition, and chutzpah, he has no peers'. The impact of his work has been considerable across a range of disciplines, especially in the fields of Geography and International Relations. Little (1995: 76) argues that he 'is one of the few theorists to have developed a distinctively different framework for studying international relations'. His work on the capitalist system has been met with critical acclaim in some quarters, while receiving a barrage of criticism in others. The significance of his work is indicated by the strength of opinion it has generated.

My intention in this chapter is to outline this work and to present the argument that, of all the writers considered, Wallerstein has come the closest to producing a systemic theory. The approach will be as follows. First we will consider the antecedents of Wallerstein's method. This will involve a discussion of how Wallerstein became dissatisfied with non-systemic approaches in his studies of African countries; of the influences of Dependency Theory on his approach; and of the impact of the French *Annales* school, specifically Braudel, on his work. Our attention will then turn to Wallerstein's theory of the world-economy. We will first consider this in the abstract, and then on a more historical basis, though there will be some overlap between the discussions.

We will then consider some of the criticisms of Wallerstein. Finally we will assess his work in relation to the other writers that we have discussed.

EARLY INFLUENCES: THE NEED FOR A SYSTEMIC APPROACH

Wallerstein's first works were studies of African states in the pre- and post-colonial era (Wallerstein 1961, 1964, 1966, 1967). These analyses were of one country at a time, in contrast to his later works. This reflected the dominance of the modernisation paradigm, which viewed the development processes as endogenous, with the same path of modernisation being open to all countries. As he progressed, Wallerstein became increasingly dissatisfied with this kind of approach. There was much that he could not explain about the continued poverty of many African countries through their individual study. It was therefore necessary to pursue an analysis at a different level from the sovereign state or national society: 'I decided that neither one was a social system and that one could only speak of social change in social systems. The only social system in this scheme was the world-system' (Wallerstein 1974: 7).

In other words, to understand development as a whole it was not possible to carry out an analysis at the level of one country. In order to produce such an analysis it would be necessary to study specific countries within one social whole. This one social whole became known as the world-system.

Having reached this conclusion, Wallerstein was confronted with the issue of which methodology to pursue to undertake this form of analysis. Clearly, he has been greatly influenced by the analysis of the Latin American Dependency school, particularly as developed in the work of Andre Gunder Frank. In a series of articles and books in the 1960s and 1970s, Frank's polemical style and analysis provided a major critique of the Modernisation school of development. His work formed the basis for the growth of interest in the Dependency school amongst English-speaking scholars.

Frank in his turn drew from three main influences: Lenin's pamphlet 'Imperialism', which marked the first major break from Marx's view that 'the industrially more developed country shows the less developed one merely an image of its own future' (Marx, quoted in Blomstrom and Hettne 1984: 10); the development of Lenin's views on monopoly capitalism by Baran (1957); and the work of the United Nations Economic Commission for Latin America (UNECLA), especially under its first director, Raúl Prebisch. UNECLA was the source of two key terms, 'centre' and 'periphery'. This analysis drew a marked distinction between the countries of the industrialised centre and those of the primary producing periphery. This was based on the difference between the two regions' access to technology. The Commission also developed the notion of declining terms of trade. They argued that the terms of trade were moving steadily in favour of producers of industrialised goods and against producers of primary goods. In other words, year by year each unit of primary product was able to purchase less in the way of industrialised product from the centre.

Frank developed these two propositions to argue that a chain of relationships exists between the periphery and the centre. Each link of the chain constitutes a 'metropolis–satellite' relationship whereby surplus capital is drained from the periphery to the centre. Hence the relationship between developing and developed countries is injurious to the former and of benefit to the latter. Frank (1969: 3) argues that the relationship between the core and the periphery 'generated underdevelopment in the peripheral satellites whose economic surplus was expropriated, while generating economic development in the metropolitan centres which appropriate that surplus'.

Wallerstein's work shares this view that development within capitalism is uneven and exploitative. However, as McCormick (1990: 126–7) has pointed out, there are major differences between the world-system approach and Dependency Theory. First, the world-systems approach rejects Dependency Theory's strategy of autarchy for escaping from the world capitalist system. For Wallerstein there is no escape from capitalism: domestic markets in developing countries are not large enough. Even though exploited, those that do participate in world markets are more successful than those that do not. Second, and as will be discussed in the review of Wallerstein's work, his view of the system is less static. Mobility between economic regions is a possibility, even if the options are limited.

If Dependency Theory provided Wallerstein with the basis of a theoretical approach to world-systems, then it was to the French *Annales* school that he turned to provide a methodology. In Chapter 2 we briefly reviewed some of the output of this school. Wallerstein was particularly attracted to the work of Braudel,[1] and drew from his work the many-layered approach to historical time. According to Ragin and Chirot (1984), Wallerstein benefited in three ways from his association with the *Annales* school. First, he was able to gain access to the vast historical material that was at their disposal. Second, the association with the French school gave him a degree of credibility. Finally, because the work of the *annalistes* was less well known in the US, it also gave his approach an apparent degree of novelty.

This is not to deny, however, that there are considerable differences between Wallerstein's work and that of the *Annales* school. Writers such as Braudel, Ladurie and Bloch make extensive use of primary sources in their research. Wallerstein relies mostly on secondary sources. As with any approach of this kind, his selection of materials has been open to criticism. This use of secondary sources reflects the second major difference that distinguishes Wallerstein's work from that of the *annalistes*, that is, its strong underpinnings in theory. The writings of the *Annales* school are more distinctly grounded in history, with explicit theorisation taking a subsidiary position. For Wallerstein this position is reversed. He begins with a theoretical position and uses historical material as a means of supporting that theory.

We now turn to an examination of how that theory has developed, and how it has been applied.

OVERVIEW OF WALLERSTEIN'S WORK

The modern world-system: theoretical overview

Central to Wallerstein's theoretical position is his view of a system. There are two defining characteristics of a system for Wallerstein. First, life within the system is more or less self-contained. This means that if the system were cut off from all external influences the internal outcomes would be identical. Second, and by implication from the first, all changes within the system are dependent on internal forces. A further characteristic of world-systems is that they are historical, meaning that they have a beginning, a lifespan and an end. Wallerstein defines a world-system as follows:

> A world-system is a social system, one that has boundaries, structures, member groups, rules of legitimation, and coherence. Its life is made up of the conflicting forces which hold it together by tension, and tear it apart as each group seeks eternally to remould it to its advantage. It has the characteristics of an organism, in that it has a life span over which its characteristics change in some respects and remain stable in others. One can define its structures as being at different times strong or weak in terms of the internal logic of its functioning.
>
> (Wallerstein 1974: 347)[2]

Wallerstein argues that there have been two types of world-system: world-empires and world-economies. An important point to notice initially is that the prefix 'world' does not imply that any particular system has encompassed the entire geographical world (1974: 15). For example, Wallerstein would consider that the Roman Empire was a world-empire even though its boundaries did not extend to the whole world. Having said this, it is a key feature of the current capitalist world-system that it has extended to incorporate the entire globe.

The main distinction between a world-economy and a world-empire concerns political control. In a world-empire there is only one political system, and this extends throughout the empire. In a world-economy there is no single political system, but instead multiple competing centres of control. For this reason world-economies have tended, historically speaking, to be very unstable. They have tended to revert to world-empires when one of the competing centres of political control has overwhelmed all the others. However, the modern world-system, an example of a world-economy, has tended to be comparatively stable. Wallerstein accounts for this stability through the existence of capitalism.[3]

A second distinction that Wallerstein draws between world-empires and world-economies is that the latter are much more efficient. He (1974: 15) regards empires as 'a primitive means of economic domination'. This is because of the inefficiencies involved in extracting resources by coercion for use at the political centre. By contrast, capitalism offers 'an alternative and more lucrative source of surplus appropriation' (*ibid.*: 16).

We are now living within the constraints of what Wallerstein calls the modern world-system. This is an example of a world-economy. It started to emerge in the sixteenth century and has proceeded to incorporate the entire globe. There are two main features of the modern world-system. First, it is a capitalist system. Wallerstein, following Frank and Baran, takes a neo-Marxist[4] definition of capitalism. He describes it as 'a system of production for sale in a market for profit and appropriation of this profit on the basis of individual or collective ownership' (Wallerstein 1979: 66).

The second feature of the modern world-system is the existence of a world-wide division of labour. For Wallerstein (1974: 162) this refers to the situation where different zones of the world-economy 'were assigned specific economic roles, developed different class structures, used consequently different modes of labour control, and profited unequally from the workings of the system'.

The modern world-system, as described by Wallerstein, has both spatial and temporal dimensions (Pieterse 1988: 251). The spatial dimension refers to the allotment of different economic roles to specific areas. Dependency theorists argued that a twofold division could be made between core and periphery. Wallerstein adds two further categories: an intermediate zone between core and periphery, which he calls the semiperiphery; and an external area, which existed outside the world-system before capitalism extended to encompass the whole world.

Within this scheme, Wallerstein's view of the periphery is very close to that posited by Dependency Theory. In other words, the periphery acts as a source of raw materials, and a site of extensive surplus extraction. He describes it as follows:

> The periphery of a world-economy is that geographical sector of it wherein production is primarily of lower-ranking goods (that is, goods whose labor is less well rewarded) but which is an integral part of the overall system of the division of labor, because the commodities involved are essential for daily use.
>
> (Wallerstein 1974: 301–2)

The important feature of the periphery is that it is an integral part of the system. It is peripheral in the sense that labour in these countries is comparatively less well rewarded than in the core or semiperiphery.

Wallerstein's major development over the centre–periphery division of Dependency Theory is the inclusion of a semiperiphery, which for Wallerstein fulfils important political and economic roles. Wallerstein considers the areas of the semiperiphery to be:

> A necessary structural element in a world-economy. . . . They are collection points of vital skills that are often politically unpopular. These middle areas . . . partially deflect the political pressures which groups primarily located in peripheral areas might otherwise direct against core-states.
>
> (Wallerstein 1974: 349–50)

Hence the semiperiphery plays a stabilising role. It provides a source of labour that counteracts any squeeze on wages in the core. It is also used by established industries as a site of production for goods that have reached their limit of profitability in the core (for example, in the present day, car assembly and textiles). It also acts as an area that absorbs political unrest from the periphery that might undermine the position of the core.

The final area within a world-economy is the core area. In countries of the core, production processes requiring the highest levels of skills and the greatest concentrations of capital are found (1974: 350). A process of 'unequal exchange' closely links the three zones of the world-economy. Wallerstein takes this analysis directly from Emmanuel's theory of unequal exchange (Emmanuel 1972).[5] Emmanuel's theory is notoriously complicated. It revolves around three main features: the higher levels of technology available to producers in the core, the relative mobility of capital compared to that of labour, and the institutional ability of workers in the core to achieve pay rises above the level of subsistence. Exchange is unequal because of the different pay levels between core and periphery. As a result, goods from the periphery embodying equal amounts of labour time are available at a lower cost in the centre. Hence workers in the periphery are superexploited compared to those in the centre. The outcome for the world-economy is the drain of surplus from the periphery to the centre, with the consequence that inequalities within the world-economy become more deeply entrenched: the peripheral areas become poorer whilst the core becomes richer.

The core, semiperiphery and periphery make up the spatial dimension of the world-economy. However, described in isolation they would present a static picture of the world-system. On their own they are unable to explain how change occurs within the system. Specifically, these spatial elements would fail to explain how the system could ever end. To do that it is necessary to account for the temporal dimensions of the world-economy.

In terms of the temporal dimensions of the world-economy, Wallerstein draws distinctions between cyclical rhythms, secular trends, contradictions and crisis. These are all closely interrelated and each one influences all the others. These temporal features determine the character of the historical development of the world-economy. The distinction between cyclical rhythms, secular trends, contradictions and crisis can be looked at as different ways of viewing historical time in a manner similar to Braudel. Cyclical rhythms manifest themselves over the very long period, secular trends over the middle period, and contradictions and crisis occupy the level of more immediate events.

Wallerstein finds the explanation of cyclical rhythms in long-wave theory. He points in particular to the effects of so-called Kondratieff waves. These are purported to have a cycle of between fifty and sixty years (Wallerstein 1991a: 163). Such waves, Wallerstein suggests, explain the regular upturns and downturns in the world-economy. These cycles bear a close relationship to the secular trends of the world-economy, which Wallerstein describes as follows:

> It is the dynamics of the system itself that explain its historically changing characteristics. Hence insofar as it is a system, it has structures and these structures manifest themselves in cyclical rhythms, that is, mechanisms which reflect and ensure repetitious patterns. But insofar as this system is historical, no rhythmic movement ever returns the system to an equilibrium point but instead moves the system along various continua which may be called the secular trends of this system.
>
> (Wallerstein 1984: 37)

Hence deep-lying structures within the system are responsible for cyclical developments, but each cycle does not return the system to the point from which it started. Instead, the end-point of each cycle delineates a point, and the mapping of these points allows definition of the trends within the system.

All world-systems face contradictions. These arise because of 'constraints imposed by systemic structures that make one set of behavior optimal for actors in the short run and a different, even opposite set of behavior optimal for the same actors in the middle run' (Wallerstein 1991b: 261). These constraints can best be understood by examining the two main contradictions confronting the capitalist system. First, Wallerstein points to what Marxists would describe as a crisis of underconsumption:

> Whereas in the short run the maximisation of profit requires maximising the withdrawal of surplus from immediate consumption of the majority, in the long run the continued production of

surplus requires a mass demand which can only be created by redistributing the surplus withdrawn.

(Wallerstein 1979: 35)[6]

Wallerstein suggests that in the short term it is in the interests of capitalists to maximise profits by driving down the wages of producers. Although in the short term this might be beneficial for individual or all capitalists, in the long term Wallerstein argues that this would lead to a fall in profits, because wage earners would be able to afford fewer goods.[7]

The second contradiction refers to the manner in which oppositional movements are handled within the system. The characteristics of oppositional or anti-systemic movements will be discussed below. They act as a contradiction because

> Whenever the tenants of privilege seek to coopt an oppositional movement by including them in a minor share of the privilege, they may no doubt eliminate opponents in the short run; but they also up the ante for the next oppositional movement created in the next crisis of the world-economy.
>
> (Wallerstein: 1979: 35)

Wallerstein is suggesting that when oppositional movements are co-opted into the dominant arrangements, although the immediate pressures may be relieved, subsequent opposition movements will have to be more extreme to have any impact.

Wallerstein reserves the term 'crisis' not to refer to periodic downswings of the world-economy, but to dislocations in the rhythm from which the system cannot recover. He outlines his position as follows:

> I shall use 'crisis' to refer to a rare circumstance, the circumstance in which an historical system has evolved to the point where the cumulative effect of its internal contradictions make it impossible for the system to 'resolve' its dilemmas by 'adjustments' in its ongoing institutional patterns. A crisis is a situation in which the demise of the existing historical system is certain.
>
> (Wallerstein 1991a: 104)[8]

Hence crisis refers to a set of circumstances that occur only once during the lifetime of a world-system, and presage its end and replacement by another system. The combination of mounting contradictions provides a destabilising factor that the system is no longer able to contain. The result of these mounting contradictions is the dissolution of the system. As will be seen in the subsequent discussion of the historical material, Wallerstein believes that the world-economy is now in a state of crisis that will end with its eventual replacement by a new system. Such a time is a period of great uncertainty, but also of opportunity.

Outside the period of crisis the possibilities for action are much more restricted. At other times the structures of the world-economy are deeply deterministic. For example, Wallerstein (1991b: 235) claims that 'within a functioning historical system there is no genuine free will. The structures constrain choice and even create choice'. For Wallerstein the world-system is the primary element in his analysis: all other features are products of the system itself. Their appearance and characteristics are dependent on the system. Hence 'it is the world-economy which develops over time and not the subunits within it' (Wallerstein 1989: 33). More specifically, Wallerstein argues that:

> The development of the capitalist world-economy has involved the creation of all the major institutions of the modern world: classes, ethnic/national groups, households – and the 'states'. All of these structures postdate, not antedate capitalism; all are consequence, not cause.
>
> (Wallerstein 1984: 29)[9]

Turning more specifically to the states and the state system, Wallerstein has written about the relationship between the world-economy, the states, and the interstate system. As already noted, Wallerstein sees states as the product of the world-economy, but they are also defined in relationship to each other:

> They defined themselves in function of other states, together with whom they formed an interstate system. The nation-state had boundaries that were fixed not merely by internal decree but just as much by the recognition of other states, a process often formalized in treaties.
>
> (Wallerstein 1991a: 189)[10]

The relationship between states acts as a constraining force between them, 'which limits the abilities of individual state machineries, even the strongest among them, to make decisions' (Wallerstein 1984: 33). There is, however, an inconsistency about the form of these constraints. At one point Wallerstein (ibid.: 38) points to the balance of power, 'a mechanism designed to ensure that no single state ever has the capacity to transform this interstate system into a single world-empire'. Elsewhere he points to the rule-bound nature of the interstate system (ibid.: 33).

A further feature of the interstate system is the periodic appearance of a hegemonic power. Compared to other writers on hegemony, Wallerstein views it as a rare and ephemeral condition. The time period over which hegemonic power is exercised, for Wallerstein, is comparatively short. His definition of hegemony is almost exclusively concerned with production and exchange. 'It may be defined as a situation wherein the products of a given core state are produced so efficiently that they are by and large competitive even in other core states' (Wallerstein 1980a: 38; 1996: 98–102).

In a more detailed analysis of hegemony, Wallerstein (1984: 40) suggests that hegemonic power exists for the period when a particular state has dominance in all three fields of agro-industry, commercial activity and world finance. In such a situation it is in the interest of the hegemonic state to pursue policies of free trade, as in open competition its goods and services will normally beat those of any other contender. For this reason the hegemon is likely pursue a policy of trade liberalism. Such political structures aim 'to lock economic advantages into place and make it function smoothly' (1991a: 26).

Besides the features of the world-economy already mentioned, the structures of the system are also responsible for the production of antisystemic movements (Arrighi *et al.* 1989: 1). These movements are generated by mounting economic constraints resulting from cyclical trends in the world-economy. They have generally appeared in one of two forms: social movements or national movements. Examples of social movements include unions, socialist parties and other worker organisations. These emerged primarily as a result of the growth of the division between bourgeoisie and proletariat, and sought a transformation of the system of inequality. National movements emerged as a result of the growing polarity between centre and periphery. These nationalist movements acted to concentrate activities within particular countries for the purpose of improving their structural position within the world-system (Wallerstein 1980b: 173–4).[11] As already noted, these oppositional movements tend to become co-opted into the system. Even so, the antisystemic movements have had the effect of inspiring other movements and of creating political space in which they are able to develop. As a result there has been 'a secular upward trend of the overall strength of antisystemic movements in the capitalist world-economy over the last 150 years' (*ibid.*: 177). This upward trend is a contributory factor in the crisis of the world-economy.

In his more recent writings Wallerstein has become increasingly interested in the notion of 'geoculture'. He describes it as follows:

> It represents the cultural framework within which the world system operates. . . . I prefer to think of it as its underside, the part that is more hidden from view and therefore more difficult to assess, but the part without which the rest would not be nourished.
>
> (Wallerstein 1991a: 11)

The geoculture provides the underlying legitimation for the world-system, and conflicts over its constitution provide the central ideological battleground. Two main, and contradictory, elements have characterised the geoculture of the modern world-system. The first has been an ideology of universalism. 'By the middle of the nineteenth century, universalism had become the ostensible central organising value of the capitalist world-economy' (Wallerstein 1996: 96). The ideology of universalism provided the notion of equal rights for all. This was manifested primarily through democracy and the creed that the free market guaranteed that this reward would be given to those who played by its rules. The problem was that the ideology of universalism failed to account for the patent inequalities in the world, and this required the institution of the other two elements of the geoculture: racism and sexism. The former legitimised the unequal division of rewards between one group and another. (The definition of the in- and out-groups could be defined as required within any situation.) The latter accounted for the unequal access to resources between men and women. The geoculture provides the justification for the existing inequality within the world-system. Therefore challenges to its central tenets constitute a means of disputing its persistence.

Before turning to a brief discussion of the way in which Wallerstein applies his theoretical approach to the historical material, a brief summary of his theoretical position will be useful. Wallerstein argues that there has been a succession of world-systems, both world-empires and world-economies. Until the advent of the modern world-system, world-empires had been more stable than world-economies. However, the characteristics of capitalism have resulted in the present world-system being particularly stable. The world-economy is ultimately determining. It is responsible for the generation of most of the features of the social world: states, the state-system, classes, households and opposition movements. It is also the source of the generation of a threefold division of the world into core, periphery and semiperiphery. However, the stability of the modern world-system does not mean it will last forever. The sources of change and decay in the system result in a series of cycles, trends and contradictions, all of which contribute to the ultimate breakdown of the system.

We will now turn to a consideration of the way in which Wallerstein approaches the historical record in the light of his theoretical position.

The modern world-system: historical overview

The great majority of Wallerstein's historical writings are concentrated in the three volumes of *The Modern World-System* published to date, which cover, approximately, the period between the beginning of the sixteenth century and the 1840s. In his essays he has dealt with more recent events in the world-economy, especially the collapse of Communist party rule in the Soviet bloc. But there is a lacuna with regard to the latter part of the nineteenth century and the early twentieth century that will only be redressed with the completion of his extensive work.

The first volume of *The Modern World-System* covers the 'long' sixteenth century (1450–1650) and analyses the emergence of a world-economy in Europe. Interestingly, Wallerstein considers the period immediately before the appearance of the modern world-system as neither a world-economy nor a world-empire. Instead, a Christian civilisation existed throughout most of Europe.[12] During the period of the late Middle Ages, feudalism dominated Europe. Wallerstein (1974: 36) describes feudalism as a complex of 'relatively small, relatively self-sufficient economic nodules based on a form of exploitation which involved the relatively direct appropriation of the small agricultural surplus produced within a manorial economy by a small class of nobility'. Here the form of surplus appropriation by the ruling classes was direct, as compared to through exchange, which, for Wallerstein, typifies capitalism.[13]

As with the capitalist world-economy, feudalism experienced cycles of expansion and contraction. Between 1150 and 1300 Europe enjoyed a period of concerted economic growth; however, this was replaced by a marked downturn between 1300 and 1450. This contraction was one of the causes of the crisis of feudalism that permitted the emergence of the capitalist system. Wallerstein argues that, combined with this cyclical economic trend, a secular decline in feudalism occurred. This was because the maximum level of production was reached within the existing technology. Additionally, a climatological change resulted in a decrease in crop yields. Together these elements resulted in a conjuncture. Wallerstein (1964: 37) notes that 'it was precisely the immense pressures of this conjuncture that made possible the enormity of the social change'. The form of the social change that was to occur was the appearance of a new form of surplus appropriation based on capitalism. Three things were needed for this social change to occur:

> An expansion of the geographical size of the world in question, the development of variegated methods of labor control for different products and different zones of the world-economy and the creation of relatively strong state machineries in what would become the core-states of this capitalist world-economy.
>
> (Wallerstein 1974: 38)

All of these three elements developed during the long sixteenth century. Expansion occurred as a result of exploration. There was a growth of a variety of means for controlling labour. Furthermore, 'strong' states gradually began to emerge in the core. These acted to protect the property rights of the capitalist class and to set the rules for the market within the area under their jurisdiction (1974: 355).

The first beneficiary of these developments was the Netherlands, centred on Amsterdam. The second volume of *The Modern World-System* covers 1600–1750. Wallerstein describes a part of this time as a period of Dutch hegemony. A further feature of this period was that, compared to the 'long' sixteenth century, it represented a time of contraction rather than expansion. However, this was not severe enough to represent a period of crisis for the world-economy. Instead, it was a period when the world-economy became more entrenched and state structures were strengthened (Wallerstein 1980a: 26). Wallerstein suggests that the role of the state becomes more important during periods of downturn:

> Alterations of status occur particularly in moments of overall down-turn or stagnation; and for those in the middle of the hierarchical continuum, the semiperiphery, movement is primarily effected and affected by state action. . . . This sounds voluntaristic, and to some degree it is. . . . But two caveats must immediately be added. First, state policies are not prime movers but intervening processes. Secondly, not every state machinery can utilize any given set of policies with the same expectation of a happy result.
>
> (Wallerstein 1980a: 179)

Wallerstein cites policies of the Swedish state as an example of how a country's position in the world division of labour can be affected. During this period Sweden was able to make the transition from the semiperiphery to the core through the pursuance of particular state policies (1980a: 217–25).

Meanwhile, in the core, the prime feature of the period covered by Volume II of *The Modern World-System* was the intensity of rivalry between the dominant states. Britain and France sought to overthrow Dutch hegemony and to succeed to its position. In this process pressure was increased on the peripheral regions as a source of increased surplus. The semiperiphery became increasingly incorporated in their intermediary role of 'conveyor belts of surplus value' (1980a: 241).

The third volume of *The Modern World-System* charts the period following the end of Dutch hegemony. The main feature of this period is the inter-core rivalry between England and France in pursuit of the number one position. Furthermore, there was a period of upturn in the world-economy between 1730 and the 1840s. Wallerstein's intention is to locate the three important revolutions of the period – the French, the Industrial, and that of the North American settlers – within the context of the developing world-economy. The central argument of the volume is that these revolutions, rather than comprising a threat to the world-economy, 'represented its further consolidation and entrenchment' (Wallerstein 1989: 256).

In his essays Wallerstein has written repeatedly about the world-economy in the post-World War II era and its prospects for the next century. He represents the period 1945–67 as the period of US hegemony, and the time of the greatest expansion of the capitalist world-economy. Wallerstein equates this period to a typical Kondratieff wave A-phase (upswing), which has been replaced by a downturn, or Kondratieff wave B-phase. He has suggested (1984: 58–68) that an upturn will occur starting in the 1990s, though with possible realignments in interstate alliances. Wallerstein has stated, however, that the system is in a state of crisis, caused by the inherent contradictions that will eventually lead to its demise. In earlier works Wallerstein was more confident that the capitalist world-system would be replaced by a socialist system. In more recent writings he has been more circumspect. An interesting feature of his discussion about the transition period from one system to another is that the structural constraints on actors become relaxed. During these periods it is possible to influence the outcome of the transition. For example, regarding the period of crisis he has written that

> Although we are indeed in a systemic crisis, this crisis is a long one that is unfolding at a visible but less hasty pace than we might wish. We can guess about its direction but we cannot be certain. We can nevertheless influence its direction.
>
> (Wallerstein 1991b: 34)

Additionally, he has noted that 'when the system enters that band of time marking its period of demise or rupture (which by definition only happens once and only at its end), everything (or almost everything) is up for grabs' (1991b: 235).

Wallerstein's analysis of the socialist states and the collapse of Communist party rule has also attracted considerable attention. The prime feature of his analysis is that he regards the socialist states as having always been part of the capitalist world-economy. In 1979 he claimed that 'there are today no socialist systems in the world-economy any more than there are feudal systems because there is only *one* world-system' (1979: 35, original emphasis). Revolution was an option for a country located in the semiperiphery and heavily penetrated by foreign capital, as a means to move towards core status:

> The Russian revolution was essentially that of a semiperipheral country whose internal balance of forces had been such that as of the late nineteenth century it began on a decline towards a peripheral status. This was the result of the marked penetration of foreign capital into the industrial sector which was on its way to eliminating all indigenous capitalist forces, the resistance to the mechanization of the agricultural sector, the decline of relative military power (as evidenced by the defeat by the Japanese in 1905). The revolution brought to power a group of state managers who reversed each one of these trends by using the classic technique of

mercantilist semiwithdrawal from the world-economy. In the process of doing this, the now USSR mobilized considerable support, especially in the urban sector. At the end of the Second World War, Russia was reinstated as a very strong member of the semiperiphery and could begin to seek core status.

(Wallerstein 1979: 30–1)

Wallerstein sees the collapse of Communist party regimes as a feature of the crisis in the capitalist world-economy. Instead of representing the triumph of the liberal capitalist ideal, it represents 'the final collapse of liberalism as a hegemonic idealism' (Wallerstein 1992: 104). This collapse of the Soviet bloc leads to a more unstable world-system because it deprives the US of the ideological weapon with which to dominate Europe and Japan culturally. Wallerstein (1993: 4) remarks that 'it lifts the Leninist justification of the status quo without replacing it with any viable substitute'. For Wallerstein, the close of the twentieth century is a time marked by what he considers to be the terminal crisis of the capitalist world-system. Despite occasional upturns, the ability of the system to adjust to dislocations has now become increasingly undermined.

Having examined Wallerstein's theory of the world-system, and briefly reviewed his analysis of the capitalist world-economy, we will now consider some of the criticisms made of his work.

CRITICS OF WORLD-SYSTEMS THEORY

This section will mirror the previous one by first examining the criticisms of Wallerstein's theory, and then looking at some the problems that have arisen which challenge his historical interpretation. Again there will be, of necessity, a certain degree of overlap between the two areas.

Theoretical criticisms of world-systems theory

The theoretical criticisms of world-systems theory have concentrated on several of Wallerstein's propositions. Marxists in particular have been especially critical of his definition of capitalism. Others have been critical of his use of systems theory, while several writers have raised the issue of agency. Finally, the question of whether his approach is teleological has been posed. We will now consider these issues in turn.

As has already been noted, Wallerstein locates his definition of capitalism in the sphere of exchange. For Wallerstein, the prime characteristic of capitalism is the existence of the appropriation of profit from exchange. In other words, the main feature of capitalism is the practice of making a profit from selling goods at a higher price than they were purchased. Hence Wallerstein would distinguish feudalism from capitalism by pointing to the direct appropriation of an agricultural surplus as the prime characteristic of the former, and the exchange of goods as the prime characteristic of the latter.

However, for Marxists it is the production process, and the appropriation of a portion of labour value that is the prime feature of capitalism. The labourer does not receive the full value of the goods that she or he produces; the capitalist expropriates a proportion of that value. Worsley (1980: 304) argues that Wallerstein 'mistakenly locates the defining properties of capitalism in exchange and not in the relations that govern the way commodities are produced: in trade rather than in production'.

Are differences in the definition of capitalism important? Writers such as Brenner suggest that they are. Brenner (1977: 32) argues that production for exchange has been a feature of many societies that are generally regarded as pre-capitalist. By implication, to describe these societies as capitalist makes nonsense of the term. Brenner argues that the approach taken by neo-Marxists represents a reversion to a model of economics derived from Adam Smith. This model neglects the insights of Marx (Brenner 1977: 27). Harvey makes a similar point. He (1987: 44) argues that the traditional view of capitalism as a mode of production gives 'a very firm basis for understanding the internal contradictions of that mode of production that force its dynamisms (in technology, organization of class relations, relations between factions of capital) and spawn its contradictions (particularly periodic)'. Although these factors might be open to different interpretations, all 'see internal contradictions as a product of class relations in production with manifestations in the realm of exchange rather than as products of the contradictions of market exchange'. All of this analysis, Marxist critics suggest, is lost in Wallerstein's work.

This argument can be see in terms of different epistemologies and ontologies. For Wallerstein world development has to be studied at the international level. By contrast, an analysis of class relations has tended to be at national level (though this need not necessarily be the case). Wallerstein's epistemological position is that there is more to be gained from a top-down, systemic account. In terms of his ontology he is examining the world-system. Wallerstein argues that it is the structures that emerge from exchange relations that are central to his analysis. For traditional Marxists it is the analysis of class relations that permit the examination of historical developments. Hence there is not only much at stake in the definition of capitalism, but also in what lies behind that definition. It is Wallerstein's definition of capitalism in terms of exchange relations that permits him to pursue a systemic approach. This is because he sees all other social formations as a product of the modern world-system, rather than seeing systemic effects as a consequence of social relations.

Wallerstein's work has also been criticised in terms of the agent–structure debate. As we have seen, Wallerstein comes down very heavily on the structure side of this debate. It is the structures of the world-economy that do the work in his analysis. However, this position has come under attack, especially concerning the autonomy of the state.

Various writers have complained that Wallerstein's approach is overly deterministic, and leaves no room for state agency. Klink, for example, argues that:

> If the properties of the world system are ontologically prior to the states embedded within that system and if state behavior is a function of systemic reproductive imperatives, then it must be the case that states, or state decision makers are not goal-directed entities.
>
> (Klink 1990: 184)

As Driver (1991: 275) notes, in Wallerstein's formulation 'states appear to become mere tools of the system as a whole'.[14]

Wallerstein sees the capitalist world-system as prior to states, classes and other structures at the national level, but he does allow for agency under certain circumstances. For example, state initiatives have permitted certain states to move from one zone of the world-economy to another. This is within very specific constraints, however. As Wallerstein pointed out, the same policies followed by another state may not lead to the same results. Additionally, during the transition between one system and another the structures weaken, allowing much more room for agency. Therefore to say that Wallerstein leaves no room for agency is incorrect. However, particularly when a world-system is functioning smoothly, agency is severely restricted.

Related to the accusation that Wallerstein allows no room for agency in his work is the view that his conception of the world-system is teleological: that there is only one point at which the world-system could end. Wallerstein's critics claim that he had a view of the contemporary world-system in mind and projected it back into history so that it would have to end up with the system as currently constituted. As Kimmel observes:

> Systems theory . . . lends itself to a certain historical teleology in which events occur because there is a systemic need for them to happen, and the dynamic internal engine of social change is replaced by a static, reactive capacity for adaptation and system maintenance. In part, this is a problem with any theoretical account of historical development that knows the outcome and seeks to generate its causes from what seems decisive at the end-point.
>
> (Kimmel 1990: 110)

Friedmann argues that Wallerstein's teleology is inevitable, given his use of an analogy with astronomical methods. In such approaches, the status of a system at one point allows the possibility of deriving the condition of the system at a given point in the past. From this line of reasoning it is not surprising, she claims, that having posited a three-level hierarchy in the twentieth century Wallerstein is able to find the same chains of exploitation in the sixteenth century (Friedmann 1983: 500–1). In a similar vein it has been claimed that 'Wallerstein's decisions about history were made before he began the book, on the basis of his theory' (Chirot 1982: 562). Zolberg suggests that Wallerstein falls into the trap of transforming the past into a metaphor of the present:

> Past and present are made to mirror each other, and what is said about each appears to substantiate what is said about the other. His depiction of the world of the sixteenth century appears credible because it bears an uncanny resemblance to the familiar representation of the world of the late twentieth century in the literature on dependency; and the realism of the latter portrait is in turn vouchsafed by its resemblance to the ancestor.
>
> (Zolberg 1981: 255)

The criticisms of Wallerstein's theoretical position have therefore centred on three main issues, and all of these relate to the systemic approach that he adopts. The most sustained attack has related to his definition of capitalism, and the implications of choosing a definition in the realm of exchange rather than of production. Wallerstein's position allows a systemic approach to be followed, but reduces the potential for the analysis of class conflict as a source of social development. His systemic approach also largely rejects the possibility of the analysis of agency. Wallerstein has been criticised for overlooking the possibility of autonomous state action. Finally, it has been suggested that his systemic approach results in a degree of teleology, with the current world-system being the only possible end-point of the analysis, and other potential outcomes not being considered.

Having explored some of the theoretical critiques of Wallerstein's work, some of the discussions of the historical aspects will now be examined.

Historical criticisms of world-systems theory

The final theoretical criticism discussed above suggested that Wallerstein derived his view of the sixteenth-century world-economy from his analysis of the contemporary world. Historians who have examined his work have also taken up this point. They argue that Wallerstein has exaggerated the historical evidence that suggests a close link between the world-system of the sixteenth century and the contemporary world-system. These arguments have primarily related to trade, which lies at the heart of Wallerstein's analysis.

O'Brien (1984: 53), for example, has argued that the levels of trade in the sixteenth century were much lower than implied by Wallerstein. He estimates that less than one per cent of Europe's output was sold to Africa, Asia, Latin America, the Caribbean and the slave states of America. Furthermore, only a very low proportion of consumption by Europeans comprised imports from these areas. DuPlessis develops this point as follows:

> Between 1450 and 1750, historians now generally agree, core-periphery trade was neither extensive nor unusually profitable, and as few industries relied upon imported raw materials foreign trade exerted little pressure toward specialization in the domestic economies.
>
> (DuPlessis 1987: 20)[15]

This kind of critique raises the question of whether it is possible to talk about a world-economy in the sixteenth century. Without significant levels of trade there can be no division of labour and no unequal exchange – two central parts of Wallerstein's theory. Without these there can be no structuring of the world-economy into different zones. Stinchcombe suggests that the evidence implies that it is only possible to talk about a world-system in very vague terms:

> If the world was a system at all in the 17th century, and I suppose it was, it was a ramshackle affair with a lot of random motion and ill-fitting parts going in their own orbits, banging into each other occasionally to produce sporadic systemic behavior.
>
> (Stinchcombe 1982: 1395)

Washbrook raises an argument with similar implications. He suggests that Wallerstein has overlooked the role of indigenous roots in the implementation of colonialism. Washbrook uses India as an example. He argues that there were institutions – for example, an emerging marketplace-type economy – which predated inclusion in the British economy. He (1990: 490) suggests that 'it was an empire that, in critical ways was as much Indian as British and contributed a strong Indian component to the world capitalist system it helped to develop'.

Such views undermine Wallerstein's system considerably. This is because it would appear that the impact of trade was much less than that necessary to cause the structuring of societies in a way that his theory requires. Furthermore, there is an implication of much greater agency at the sub-unit level. Finally, there is the argument that capitalist-type economies were not exported to India as a result of its incorporation into the world-economy. Instead, institutions of a capitalist economy already existed there.

Wallerstein's views on the semiperiphery, and particularly the role of the socialist bloc in the capitalist system, have led to considerable criticism (Worsley 1980; Gorin 1985; Sen 1985). But this debate would now seem to be somewhat academic. Even societies in which Communist parties remain in power (e.g. China, Vietnam, Cuba) are now increasing their trading links with the capitalist world. This does not mean that they have always been incorporated into the world-economy, but they clearly are now. This appears to vindicate Wallerstein's position (Little 1995: 85–6).

As for the issue of the semiperiphery, Washbrook has questioned the value of the concept. He argues that there is little evidence of the semiperiphery providing a site for capital to avoid a wage-productivity squeeze in the core. Additionally, contrary to the view that the semiperiphery provides a zone of political stability between the core the periphery 'it would appear to be the most politically unstable of the three sectors of the world system and the source of the few dangers that threaten it' (Washbrook 1990: 484). This, however, is not necessarily inconsistent with the view that pressures are deflected into the semiperiphery.

Finally, it has been suggested that Wallerstein has failed to take account of developments in the world-economy that would have implications for its future development. Tooze (1986: 176) points to the impact of the internationalisation of banking, which has the impact of divorcing the creation of credit from the extraction of surplus value. Strange (1985: 497) makes a similar point. She also points to the structural power of the United States, which she claims allows it to maintain its hegemonic power even though it may have lost its supremacy in manufacturing competitiveness.

Most of the criticisms that we have discussed here hinge on the use of systems theory in general. For example, criticisms of Wallerstein's definition of capitalism. His definition is predicated by the choice of a systemic approach. To adopt a more traditional view would imply an analysis at a different level. Hence there are costs and benefits to the use of a systemic approach, a point that will be developed in the next section.

WALLERSTEIN AS A SYSTEMS THEORIST

Wallerstein's view of international relations is markedly different from any other that we have discussed; though in certain senses it is the clearest. However, he makes comparatively little use of the term 'international system' itself. He (1991a: 163) describes 'international' as 'a bad term, but one in common use'. The term he prefers is 'interstate' system. The interstate system for Wallerstein is the closest equivalent in his work to the realist International Relations idea of an international system. Where he has used it, he refers to relations between states. In these instances he hovers between a view of these as being driven by a balance-of-power mechanism, or as governed by common rules. The point that needs to be emphasised here is that, for Wallerstein, this 'international system', in a narrower sense, is a product of what he labels the 'world-system'. It is the world-system that is primary. The interstate system is a product of the modern world-system. For this reason the intention throughout this chapter has been to discuss this world-system in the same terms that the international system has been discussed in other chapters. For Wallerstein it is the modern world-system that is the causal factor in social relations. Hence this becomes the appropriate variable to discuss in his work.

Wallerstein's work is in many ways notably different from that of the other historical sociologists that we have studied. In many respects it could be considered to be closer to International Relations theory. This suspicion is confirmed by the version of world-system theory that is described as Globalism or Structuralism in discussions of the three-paradigm debate that marked the way that the discipline was characterised in the 1980s. Despite this incorporation into the discipline of International Relations, Wallerstein's work is still primarily regarded as sociological in origin (Ragin and Chirot 1984).

Wallerstein himself would probably regard with some disdain attempts to pigeonhole his work, given his espousal of a multidisciplinary approach. He has remarked that he was trained as a social scientist, has a Sociology PhD and is a Professor in that discipline, is politically active, but that his major work is regarded as History or Economic History. He does not regard this as a contradiction:

> I myself feel that I am being thoroughly consistent and that my concern with history, with social science, and with politics is not a matter of engaging in three separate, even if related, activities, but is a *single* concern, informed by the belief that the strands cannot be separated, nor should they if they could.
>
> (Wallerstein 1979: vii)

We have considered Wallerstein to be amongst the ranks of historical sociologists, and I argue that he has more in common with them than with International Relations theorists. Having said that, he has produced a theory that is more systemic than the most systemic theory in International Relations.

Wallerstein is closest to the other historical sociologists that we have considered in terms of his use of a multidisciplinary approach. All the writers discussed so far combine insights from more than one discipline, as is obvious from the term itself. All would probably agree that the division between disciplines is arbitrary and misleading. This is a significant point of similarity between Wallerstein, and Skocpol, Tilly and Mann.

A further major point of similarity relates to methodology. They all make use of written history to test and verify their theories. All the writers considered as historical sociologists so far have had a theory that has been outlined and which they have sought to verify by, in the main, secondary historical sources. Theory, for all these scholars, has preceded evidence: they are deductive rather than inductive.

Where Wallerstein differs primarily is in terms of epistemology and ontology. Again, reference to the Hollis and Smith matrix makes this point much clearer (see Figure 7.1). Wallerstein's work belongs in the very top left corner. His work is much less ambiguous than that of any other writer that we have considered. His work is avowedly top-down, a position that has hardly altered since his earliest writings on the world-system. It is the system, as he frequently remarks, that is primary and is responsible for the production of other social phenomena. His work, at least on the economic system, refers to external structures. This is an outsider account rather than an insider account, a work of explaining rather than of understanding.

Clearly, the analyst to whom Wallerstein comes closest is Waltz, whose work was examined in Chapter 3. Both have made the production of a systemic theory central to their approach. In a comparison of these two systems theorists, Wendt has been critical of both for failing to adopt a structuration approach that not only proceeds from top-down, but also from bottom-up. Wendt's argument is that Waltz follows an epistemology of systems theory, though his ontology is individualist. By contrast, Wallerstein's epistemology and ontology are both systemic. Wendt (1989) argues that as a result Wallerstein has produced a more systemic theory than Waltz, though the result of this is that Wallerstein's approach leads to a reification of the system.

However, there are other differences between Waltz and Wallerstein. Waltz is proud to claim his as a theory of politics, and rejects the value of a multidisciplinary approach. Additionally, in classical realist spirit he argues that a theory of international politics should treat the national and the international as distinct realms. Wallerstein, as has been discussed above, attempts to include everything in his analysis. Like most other analysts,

	Explaining	Understanding
Holistic	external structures Wallerstein	collective rules
Individualistic	rational choices	reasoned choices

Figure 7.1 Wallerstein's approach to the world-system

Wallerstein uses the term international system to describe the relationship between states. However, he sees states and the state system as generated by the world-economy. A schematic version of this approach is depicted in Figure 7.2.

A further distinction between Neorealism and World-Systems Theory is the issue of change. As was noted in Chapter 3, Neorealism is frequently accused of lacking a theory of change. World-systems theory does contain an analysis of change. World-systems are regarded as historical. Change from one system to another results from internal developments. These take the form of trends and contradictions.

The political positions underlying these two theories would also appear to be different. Neorealism is generally regarded as a conservative doctrine. It celebrates the bipolarity of the 1970s, and regards inequalities between nations as a positive factor in international relations (Waltz 1979: 170–6, 132). World-systems theory could be regarded as conservative in the sense that structures are extremely determinist. However, it deplores the current inequalities in the world-economy, and anticipates its eventual demise. Wallerstein (1996: 106) argues that it is down to individual action and conscience to ensure that the next system is more equitable than the current one.

Wallerstein's systemic approach involves a conscious decision to pursue a holistic approach, and this involves costs and benefits. The prime benefit is the parsimony of his approach. Although it involves several elements, Wallerstein's world-system is a relatively clear and simple theory, from which he is able to derive a considerable amount of explanatory and predictive mileage.

On the deficit side is a lack of clarity at the sub-unit level. As many writers have indicated, Wallerstein does not have much of a theory of the state. States are either strong or weak, depending on their position in the world economic hierarchy. However, his approach to the state is more developed than that of Waltz. In particular, Wallerstein's work does cross the

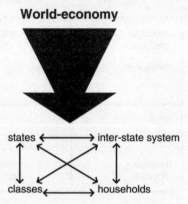

Figure 7.2 Interrelation of the elements of the world-economy

internal/external divide when he discusses the impacts of the modern world-system. However, the details of the formation of states, classes and households are rather vague.

To summarise, Wallerstein's approach to the characteristics of international relations is distinct from any other that we have considered. His starting point is the character of a worldwide capitalist system, which is responsible for the other social formations of the contemporary world. This is a very ambitious project, a grand theory on a grand scale. Given this scale of undertaking, it is perhaps not surprising that some elements of the analysis are less successful than others.

CONCLUSION

Wallerstein's work has generated and continues to generate great interest within the International Relations community. Despite the many criticisms of his work, this interest is not without foundation. In his 1980 *Foreign Policy* essay, 'Friends as foes', Wallerstein predicted a major realignment of world powers. This is not an accurate prediction of the nature of the end of the Cold War. However, at least in the sense of anticipating a major upheaval, it came closer than many within the International Relations community.[16] Perhaps this was just coincidental, but there does seem to be some logic in the view, given his position that the socialist states were part of the world-economy. In a 1981 special edition of *International Studies Quarterly*, the editors pointed to a renewed interest in world-systems theory, 'in the surfacing of political economy issues high on the global agenda and a corresponding decline in the relative predominance of military-security issues' (Hollist and Rosenau 1981: 6). With the end of the Cold War it seems appropriate that within International Relations there should be an interest in economic issues within the global system. Wallerstein's work might well be on the receiving end of such attention.

In epistemological terms Wallerstein's work is closest to that of Waltz. Both have pursued a systemic approach, and have followed it determinedly. But in ontological terms their work is markedly different. Waltz studies political structures, while Wallerstein studies economic structures. Wallerstein has a theory of change, caused by the rhythms of the world-economy, whereas Waltz's vision is much more static. Having a theory of change suggests that Wallerstein has produced a more sophisticated account of international relations than Waltz has been able to provide. Perhaps he has also been more successful than others writing in the field in anticipating the major changes of the post-Cold War world.

A central difference between Wallerstein and Skocpol, Tilly and Mann is the former's concentration on economic structures. The other writers have adopted a multi-logic approach. Wallerstein's approach has been to consider a single logic. He also has much less of an analysis of the state. The state is much less of an autonomous actor within the world-system. It exists primarily to protect the interests of capitalists. The main differentiating factor is between strong states and weak states: strong states inhabit the core, weak states the periphery.

The key weakness of Wallerstein's approach is its determinism. This is a result of his focusing attention on systemic factors rather than on actors. Actors appear only capable of autonomous action during the times between world-systems, when they are capable of influencing the form that a new system will take. He gets a lot of explanatory mileage from this approach. However, for many this determinism is unattractive. The key factor of his work is the extent to which he highlights economic forces as a significant factor in the analysis of international relations.

The argument of the previous three chapters has been that the writers considered employed a vague and inconsistent view of the international system. Clarity at the state level has only been achieved by reducing the system to warfare (in Skocpol's case) or through using different accounts of international systems depending on the particular factor in the analysis of the state that was being examined. Wallerstein's approach is completely different. Clarity at system level has been acquired through an under-theorised account of the state. In this respect Wallerstein's work has much in common with that of Waltz. As was noted in Chapter 3, Waltz has a definite notion of the international system, but lacks a theory of the state.

Consequently, the theorists on whom we have concentrated have made one of two analytical moves. Waltz and Wallerstein have produced systemic theories, but this has been achieved by retaining a primitive view of the state. Skocpol, Tilly and Mann have produced sophisticated theories of the state, but have under-theorised the international system. Does this imply that there are problems with producing a theory of international relations that can provide sophisticated accounts of both system and units? This is one issue that we consider in the final chapter.

8

HISTORICAL SOCIOLOGY AND INTERNATIONAL RELATIONS

INTRODUCTION

In the previous four chapters we have considered the work of a selection of contemporary historical sociologists. Although involved in different areas of research, a central link between these four writers is that they have all attempted to incorporate the idea of an international system in their writings. All four have argued that an international system has had an impact on domestic events and developments. However, each has put forward a different account. Our discussion in each of the four chapters suggested that, with the exception of Wallerstein, the notion of international system being used by each of these writers is under-theorised. A key component linking the first three writers considered has been the analysis of the state. Skocpol, Tilly and Mann all have a similar idea of the state. Wallerstein, the fourth writer discussed, had a much weaker notion of state, but a much more definite notion of a (world-)system.

State and international system are both central concepts in International Relations theory. In Chapter 3 we examined the analysis of the international system produced by Kenneth Waltz. Waltz's approach is generally known as Neorealism. Since the publication of his *Theory of International Politics* in 1979, Neorealism has become the dominant approach to theorising the international system within the discipline. However, despite its dominant position, Waltz's structural theory suffers from a serious deficiency: it does not have the capacity to explain change. In Chapter 3 I argued that a central source of this problem is Neorealism's lack of a theory of the state.

Our purpose in this chapter is to draw these strands together and to answer the three core questions posed in the introduction:

- How is the international system theorised in recent Historical Sociology writing?
- Can Historical Sociology provide Neorealism with a theory of the state?
- What is the character of the relationship between Historical Sociology and International Relations?

The approach taken in this chapter will be as follows. First we will address the issue of the analysis of the international system by historical sociologists. Our assessments of the works of Skocpol, Tilly, Mann and Wallerstein will be summarised. This will provide us with a basis on which to build the analysis in the rest of this chapter. I will then outline three main problems with the approaches to international systems adopted by these writers: inconsistency, incompatibility and a heavy reliance on realist approaches to international politics. This last problem returns us to an issue raised in the introduction: the influence of realist thinking on Historical Sociology. The chapter will therefore consider the issue of whether Historical Sociology should be rejected for assimilating too many realist assumptions about international relations. I will argue that, counter to this view, the work of the historical sociologists that we have considered undermines realist and neorealist theorising. The core issue is regarding the historicisation of social forms that Historical Sociology provides. The approach of Historical Sociology to the state and international system undermines Realism's claim to provide a 'timeless wisdom'.

We will then address the second major question: the possibility of combining a view of the state derived from Historical Sociology with a neorealist account of the international system. The intention of such a synthesis would be to provide Neorealism with a theory of the state, while providing Historical Sociology with a more robust account of the international system. If such a synthesis were possible, it would appear to provide a means of overcoming the weaknesses in both approaches to the study of international relations. However, I will argue that such a combination is problematic because the effect of adding a theory of the state to Neorealism results in a fundamental undermining of the entire approach. A radical rethinking of the concept of the international system is required in order to gain most from the approach to the state that Historical Sociology provides.

This is an issue that we will take up in the final section of the chapter, where we will discuss the character of the relationship between Historical Sociology and International Relations. We will examine the implications of the work of writers such as Skocpol, Tilly, Mann and Wallerstein for International Relations theorists. Finally I propose an agenda for future research into 'global structures' which aims to overcome the weaknesses in international systems theorising that we have highlighted.

HOW ARE INTERNATIONAL SYSTEMS
THEORISED IN HISTORICAL SOCIOLOGY?

Theda Skocpol

In Chapter 4 we considered the work of Theda Skocpol, and concentrated on her study of three classical social revolutions in France, China and Russia. Her approach developed several novel themes in the examination of social revolutions. Of prime interest was her inclusion of the state and the international system as variables in her analysis. Skocpol suggests that the international system is not only a central causal factor in the revolutions that she studies, but also plays a central role in the form that state development takes in the post-revolutionary phase.

Skocpol defines the state as the set of institutions at the political centre of a particular territory. The state looks both outwards and inwards, and is in competition with actors both in the international and domestic sphere. Skocpol claims that domestic and international factors were involved in the revolutions that she examines. On the international front, states confronted political and economic pressures. Domestically, they had to deal with unrest amongst the agrarian population. In the instances that she examines, the accumulation of these problems was sufficient to overwhelm state structures, permitting a successful revolution to occur. During the post-revolutionary phase, state structures were strengthened and centralised as a result of similar pressures.

Her theoretical analysis of the international system comprises two elements. First, she argues that there are two structures: a world capitalist economy, and a system of competing states. Skocpol argues that these two structures are interdependent, but neither is ultimately reducible to the other. Parallel to these two structures lies the context of world-historical time. This refers to the diffusion of ideas and breakthroughs from previous generations to subsequent ones. For example, the ideas and events of the French Revolution were an important influence on the actors in the Russian and Chinese revolutions. Hence her theoretical position contains elements of an economic analysis, a political analysis and a concept of historical diffusion.

Chapter 4 argued, however, that in the empirical work on the three revolutions Skocpol overlooked certain elements of her theoretical position in favour of others. The economic analysis and the element of diffusion became less significant, and the system of competing states became central. This in turn became reduced to the occurrence of warfare. Hence warfare is the main feature of the international system that Skocpol employs in her work. In her analysis of international factors this becomes the central causal factor to explain revolutions and their aftermaths. For example, in her analysis of the French Revolution, Skocpol's analysis concentrated on the effects of France's involvement in the American War of Independence, and the impact that this had on the country's finances. Following the revolution, involvement in counter-revolutionary wars resulted in the centralisation of the state.

The chapter concluded by arguing that there was a conflict in Skocpol's work between her theoretical analysis, which takes a holistic approach, and her empirical work, which places the international system at an individualistic level and reduces it to the occurrence of warfare. The result of this is to place a block on her use of the international system in her analysis. It also explains why this factor drops out as an element in her account of the Iranian Revolution, and in her more recent work on social policy. This is a crucial point, because in her analysis of revolutions the international system provides a necessary causal factor. It also provides a necessary causal factor in analysing the rationalisation of the state that occurs following a revolutionary take-over. Therefore her analysis of the state is directly linked to her reductionist approach to the international system. The coherent account of the state that Skocpol provides is dependent on the approach that she takes to the international system.

Charles Tilly

Tilly has written extensively on the processes of state formation in Europe, and on collective action, with particular reference to France. His most recent work has been a study of European revolutions during the last five hundred years. As with Skocpol's work, Tilly regards the international system as a causal element.

Tilly's definition of the state is comparable to that of Skocpol: namely a set of organisations claiming a degree of priority over all other institutions within a given territory. Central to Tilly's work has been the analysis of the relationship between war and state building. In its simplest version this amounts to seeing a direct relationship between the growth of the state and its involvement in fighting wars. A more sophisticated account has emerged from his recent writings. Two variables have now become central to his analysis of state formation: the fluctuating concentrations in different locations of coercive power and of capital. Different combinations of these variables, he argues, resulted in different types of state formation.

This type of analysis has drawn especially on the notion of an international system. In his earlier work, Tilly's view of the international system appeared to be very similar to that adopted by Skocpol. He employed a dualistic approach, part economic and part political – a formation of competing states. In his later work he changed this position to the view that it is state interactions that are important. The interactions between states lead to the generation of a system.

These different views coexist uneasily in his work. Tilly is famous for the phrase that 'war made the state and the state made war'. The implication of this is that his position is very close to that of Skocpol. However, Chapter 5 argued that Tilly had developed a less reductionist position than that of Skocpol. Tilly achieves a separation of war from the system. Furthermore, alongside this position is another which appears to take a constructivist view. Here the international system appears to be the construction of a web of interrelationships between states. This web has a constraining effect on state actions.

In Chapter 5 we attempted to unravel the puzzle that these two positions present. For Tilly the international system is a causal element in his analysis, though he does not offer much by way of a definition. There are two accounts of international system present in his work, and he fails to examine how these are related. A possible solution is that Tilly is attempting to provide a historical analysis of the system. His analysis of the international system implies a development from being a product of war to being a product of norms and rules. Tilly appears to be providing a view of the international system as a developing entity. In other words it is not a constant, but is historically contingent on the character of interrelationships between states.

Tilly has employed different accounts of international systems depending on what he is trying to explain. His account of state growth relies on a view of international systems heavily related to war. There is also a more constructivist view that sees constraints on state action derived from a web of norms and rules operating internationally. As with Skocpol, much of the analysis of the state is dependent on the approach to the international system. Tilly obtains his clarity at the state level through an inconsistency in his approach to the international system.

Michael Mann

In Chapter 6 we turned to the work of Michael Mann. We concentrated on the two volumes of his history of social power published to date. This work attempts to describe how various combinations of four main sources of social power have structured all human societies: ideological, economic, military and political. The chapter discussed his theoretical position and examined the way that he attempts to apply this to the historical material that he introduces.

I argued that there were several elements in his work that challenge traditional views of international relations. His analysis of the cross-cutting and overlapping character of the different forms of social power comprises an attempt to integrate an analysis of the domestic and the international. His analysis of the relationship between empires of domination and multi-power-actor civilisations is a distinctive theory of change in the international system. Additionally, he offers a new theory of the 'polymorphous' state. Although there are some similarities between his analysis and that of the interdependence theorists, the chapter concluded that Mann's theory is more developed. Finally, he argues that none of his sources of social power is ultimately determining.

However, I argued that there are serious problems with his approach, and that these are manifested in the failure to incorporate his theoretical position with his historical material. Part of the problem lies in the analysis of the international system. Mann uses the international system as a residual category. He loads this category with all the phenomena that he cannot incorporate at the state level, but does not attempt to analyse the relationships between different factors. Mann allocates a causal role to the international system in influencing the development of states, classes and capitalism. However, he fails to provide a consistent analysis of what the international system comprises. As with Tilly, he uses different accounts of the international system depending on what he is trying to explain for state development. I suggested that it is possible to outline four readings of the international system in his work. These four positions involve different epistemological and ontological positions. Of these four views, a realist position appears to be doing most of the work, and this primarily reduces to the occurrence of warfare. This lessens the potential of the use of the international system as a variable in his work.

Immanuel Wallerstein

The final writer considered was Wallerstein. Chapter 7 was devoted to a discussion of his account of what he describes as the modern world-system. As with Mann's work on social power, this is a work in progress, with the most recently published volume taking the exposition up to the 1840s. However, this is where any similarity between the two writers' forms of analysis ends. Wallerstein's work is markedly different from that of the other historical sociologists we have considered. Of all of these scholars, Wallerstein has produced the most coherent approach to theorising the international system. His work demonstrates the benefits and weaknesses that result from such an approach.

For Wallerstein, it is the modern world-system that provides the deep structure for his analysis. There have been two types of world-system: world-empires and world-economies. The modern world-system is an example of the latter. There are three main features of the modern world-system that distinguish it from previous examples: it has extended to encompass the entire globe, it is a capitalist system, and it is characterised by a worldwide division of labour. This is manifested by the spatial division of the system into three zones: core, semiperiphery and periphery. Each of these zones plays an essential role in the reproduction and stability of the system.

A key element of Wallerstein's work is that he views the world-system as historical. It has a beginning, middle and end. He argues that all world-systems go through a period of crisis, following which they collapse and are replaced by another system. The modern world-system is in this sense no different from any other.

The world-economy is responsible for the generation of the other phenomena that Wallerstein discusses in his analysis: states, the interstate system, classes and households. The element of an interstate system that appears in his work is closest to that usually analysed in International Relations, but for Wallerstein it is subordinate to the economic system.

In Chapter 7 I argued that of all of the writers that we have examined, Wallerstein had the clearest vision of an international system. However, the trade-off is a weakening in the analysis of domestic features: all actors are primarily influenced by the world-system, and features such as the state are subsidiary. Wallerstein has adopted a completely different approach in his theorising of state-system relations. Skocpol, Tilly and Mann have produced accounts of the international system that provide the causal explanation of what they require for the analysis of the state. When they wish to explain different things they have generated different accounts of the international system. By contrast, it is the state which plays the comparable role in Wallerstein's analysis. The state fulfils the function that Wallerstein requires to allow him to maintain his account of the world-system. These issues will become more apparent through a more generalised critique of these writers' approach to the international system.

General criticisms of Historical Sociology views of the international system

There are three main problems with the way that the historical sociologists whom we have considered have theorised the international system. These are inconsistency, incompatibility and being heavily influenced by realist views. The impact of these problems results in a view of the international system that is not able to provide the form of analysis that these writers are seeking. But it is worth noting that although these criticisms can be addressed generally at the work of Skocpol, Tilly and Mann, they are less appropriate for Wallerstein's work. His view of the international system cannot be regarded as inconsistent, incompatible or heavily influenced Realism.[1] The three general criticisms will now be considered in turn. The approaches employed by Skocpol, Tilly and Mann and the problems that they have encountered will be discussed in relation to Wallerstein.

Inconsistency

I consider the analysis of the international system presented by Skocpol, Tilly and Mann to be inconsistent, because each of them fails to provide a uniform version of what the international system comprises. I have attempted to demonstrate that each of these writers has put forward more than one account of the international system. This raises two questions. First, how have they employed their different accounts? Furthermore, has there been any attempt to differentiate between them?

In Chapter 6 I suggested that it is possible to give four different readings of the international system in Michael Mann's work: a view of the international system as an external structure; a rational actor game-playing version; a view of the system as a set of rules; and a version implying that the international system was a construct of social actors. Mann provides no account of how the relation between these four versions is to be understood, which makes it difficult to understand how he perceives the international system. This makes it harder to see the links between his view of the international system and the phenomena that he claims are heavily influenced by it. For example, he argues that state growth occurred as a response to pressures from the international realm. When it is so unclear what he means by the international realm, it becomes harder to accept this assertion.

This becomes clearer when comparing Mann's account of the international system to Wallerstein's discussion of the world-system. Wallerstein's account, as Chapter 7 demonstrated, is more consistent. For Wallerstein the primary feature of international relations is the capitalist world-system, and this is responsible for the generation of most other features of the social world.

In contrast to Wallerstein, the analyses of the international system provided by Skocpol, Tilly and Mann are less consistent. They suggest that the international system is the source of some of the phenomena that they are attempting to analyse. However, because they give different accounts of what the international system comprises, it becomes hard to see how these influences are exerted. Moreover, there is an additional problem: that of incompatibility between accounts.

Incompatibility

The problem of the inconsistency in accounts of the international system provided by Skocpol, Tilly and Mann is further compounded by the incompatibility between different accounts. Figure 8.1 summarises the different views of the international system that the previous four chapters have discussed.

	Explaining	Understanding
Holistic	external structures Wallerstein Skocpol (theory) Tilly Mann	collective rules Tilly Mann
Individualistic	Skocpol (practice) Mann rational choices	Mann reasoned choices

Figure 8.1 Summary of different approaches to the international system by Skocpol, Tilly, Mann and Wallerstein

In the review of Tilly's work I argued that he provided two different accounts of the international system. These two accounts reflect different epistemological approaches and are difficult to consider as complementing each other. The first account stresses the international system as an external given – an anarchic competitive realm. In this version it is competitive warfare that accounts for the phenomena that Tilly is attempting to explain. The second account is closer to a constructivist one, based on rules and common understandings. Here, it is the norms and rules of state interactions that act as a constricting force on state activities. In this example different features are being examined – on the one hand an outside environment of competitive anarchy, and on the other a collection of shared understandings.

The difference between these two forms of analysis means that it is hard to combine them in a meaningful way. There are problems with combining them to form one account of the international system. The implication is therefore that Tilly presents the reader with incompatible accounts of the international system. This problem was also highlighted in Mann's approach to the international system, though it was less apparent in Skocpol's work.

When Wallerstein's work is considered, because his description of the world-system is more consistent, there is not a problem with the reconciliation of incompatible accounts. Chapter 7 described the world-system as depicted by Wallerstein as an outsider, explanatory account at a holistic level.

Realism

The third general criticism is the over-reliance on realist interpretations of the international system. A realist view of the international system is one that is state-centric, sees the state as a unitary, rational actor, and considers the competition for power and security to be the prime concern of state actors. I will argue below that none of the historical sociologists that we have analysed can be considered wholeheartedly realist. However, their approaches to international systems are heavily influenced by realist work. This heavy influence of Realism is most evident in the choice of references to International Relations writers. Tilly (1992a: 9) cites for his main sources of geopolitical analyses Waltz (1979) and an early work by Rosenau (1970). Mann (1993a: 258) states that for his analysis of geopolitical power he 'draws freely upon' Knorr (1956) and Morgenthau (1978).

The effects of this realist influence are seen most clearly in Skocpol's work. Chapter 4 argued that Skocpol presented a clear and inventive theoretical position on the international system, which attempted to combine an economic approach with a political one. But in her empirical analysis this was forsaken for a discussion of the occurrence of war between states. In this instance Skocpol reduces the international system to traditional realist concerns with war as the central feature of the international system. In a similar way, both Tilly and Mann consider the occurrence of war in the international system to be the most significant variable in the process of state formation.

I consider this to be a weakness, because there are other factors at work in the international system. Significantly, these other factors are highlighted by these three writers' own analyses – particularly the importance of economic factors. The problem with this kind of approach is that it limits the possibility of developing an analysis that takes into account the international system. There is only a certain amount that can be derived from the use of an analysis centred on a realist view of the international system. By relying on a realist-based analysis Mann, Skocpol and Tilly are restricted in where their use of the international system can take them.

Wallerstein's account of the world-system, with its primarily economic base, cannot be considered as excessively reliant on realist formulations. Military force is not an important factor in Wallerstein's work, nor is the state a central actor. By starting with different assumptions, Wallerstein ends up with a different answer, and considers different issues. However, as will be discussed below, his view of the international system is mono-causal, and this generates a different set of problems.

To summarise these general criticisms, although Skocpol, Tilly and Mann claim that they are incorporating the international system as a variable in their analyses, they have all failed to provide a uniform definition of the international system or an explanation of how their different conceptions of the international system can be equated. Furthermore, their different positions rely on incompatible epistemological foundations, making them difficult to combine in one account. Finally, the centrality of the significance of war suggests a heavy reliance on realist explanations in their accounts.

Does Historical Sociology support a realist view of international relations?

The heavy reliance on realist concepts in their account of the international system poses the question of whether the Historical Sociology of Skocpol, Tilly and Mann is realist. If this is the case, this would open their work to the many criticisms of Realism and undermine the claim that their work provides a 'challenge' to International Relations or is the basis of a 'second agenda'.

As noted in the introduction, writers such as Navari, Scholte and Buzan have indicated that that they have come to this conclusion. Their views support very clearly the criticism made in the previous section: that the views of the international system held by Mann, Skocpol and Tilly are heavily influenced by Realism. But does this amount to a claim that these historical sociologists are realists, and share the main assumptions of Realism, as has been suggested by Buzan? If this is the case, then it is understandable why writers such as Navari and Scholte are critical of their work. But this section will make a contrary argument. It will be contended that Historical Sociology, far from affirming Realism, can be used as a tool to undermine Realism and Neorealism.

First, the extent of the influence of Realism has varied. The positions of all the writers that we have considered are not equivalent. The separate chapters on each writer have demonstrated that they have different positions on the character of the international system. They would all appear to be influenced by realist notions of the international system (with the possible exception of Wallerstein), but the level of influence is not the same. Perhaps it is possible to say that Skocpol is more influenced by Realism than, for example, Tilly. However, to rank Historical Sociology in terms of the level of influence from Realism is not a particularly useful activity. The important point is that the impact varies.

A second point is that those who point to the Realism of the work of Skocpol, Tilly, Mann and Wallerstein, miss a central point about the discipline of Historical Sociology: the centrality of the notion of time and change. A central tenet of Realism is its claim to be timeless. It is easy to find examples – from Thucydides to Buzan. This is contrary to the position of historical sociologists. The central aim of Historical Sociology is to provide an analysis of context and development of social forms. For Historical Sociology there are no givens – the development of all social phenomena is open to analysis. By contrast, realists are much less concerned with the issue of change – continuity characterises their work. Hence central to the work of historical sociologists is the analysis of change.

A third point refers to the degree of state-centricity of these writers. Here again it is possible to indicate varying levels of their concentration on the state. For Wallerstein the state is clearly not a central actor. By contrast, the state is a much more significant actor for Skocpol. However, none of the writers considered here exclude the significance of alternate actors. For example, all consider the importance of classes acting on an international level. Additionally, the state is not taken as a given. Their work seeks to analyse state development. These writers see the state as a social formation whose existence is restricted to a particular historical period.

Linked to the last point is the crucial distinction between the writers we have considered and realist approaches to International Relations. That is to say, for the former there is no dichotomy between the domestic and the international, whereas for most realists a crucial distinction exists between social relations inside the state and outside. Anarchy and the absence of morality mark the external realm. The structure of the internal realm is less important, and the relations of one on the other are not considered. For historical sociologists, the social world is considered as a whole, and such a division between behaviour within a society and outside is not made. This is probably the major point that distinguishes historical sociologists from realists.

Therefore, despite the criticism that Historical Sociology views of the international system are highly influenced by realist descriptions, there are certain key points that mark Historical Sociology apart from Realism, namely the historical element in their account, the inclusion of other actors in their analyses, and, crucially, the absence of a dichotomy between the domestic and the international. Finally, their views of the international system are different. Although heavily influenced by a realist, competitive view, the previous four chapters have brought out other elements, in particular economic relations, and the impact of norms and rules.

One of our central aims has been to examine how recent writings by historical sociologists have incorporated the notion of an international system into their works. The main contrast comes between Wallerstein's view of the international system and that of Skocpol, Tilly, and Mann. Wallerstein has provided a much more systemic account. However, this is at the cost of a less developed notion of the state. For Wallerstein, the state is a product of the modern world-system. A state is either weak or strong dependent on its location in the world-economy. Wallerstein achieves a clear notion of a world-system by producing an under-theorised account of the state. He has held the state as a primitive factor, which fulfils the requirements that he needs to produce his account of the system. Skocpol, Tilly and Mann have less defined accounts; compared to Wallerstein their approach to the international system appears more ambiguous. However, in Wallerstein's work analysis of the (world)-system overwhelms the other elements of the social world.

The approach to the international system is the other way round for Skocpol, Tilly and Mann. They have held the system as a primitive concept, and have introduced it into their analysis of the state when, and in the form that they have required. Their coherence at the state level is dependent on an inconsistent approach to theorising the international system.

Hence there are problems with the way in which the international system has been used in Historical Sociology. The accounts provided by Skocpol, Tilly and Mann are inconsistent because they have used them to bolster their analysis of the state. The international system has fulfilled the role that they have required to keep their account of the state consistent. The account provided by Wallerstein is dependent on an under-theorised account of the state. To have developed his theory of the state further would have undermined his account of the world-system.

In contrast to their analysis of the international system, Skocpol, Tilly and Mann have provided a much more detailed exposition of the development of the state. These three writers have comparable notions of the state as a set of institutions. Hence, compared to Wallerstein these writers have a developed notion of the state and a rather under-theorised notion of the international system. This opens the question of whether their work complements that of Neorealism, which has a developed notion of an international system and a less defined view of the state.

CAN HISTORICAL SOCIOLOGY PROVIDE
NEOREALISM WITH A THEORY OF THE STATE?

In Chapter 3 I argued that a central problem for Neorealism was its inability to analyse processes of change. It was argued that the source of this problem lay in the lack of an analysis of the state. As Waltz has conceded, in order to understand a change in the system, an analysis at unit level is required. Hence to provide Neorealism with a theory of change it is necessary to look to the units: for Waltz, the states. The previous four chapters have argued that some historical sociologists provide a theory of the state, but that their attempts to locate this state within an international environment have been less successful. This begs the question of whether it might be possible to combine a notion of the state derived from Historical Sociology with the analysis of the international system from Neorealism. The aim of such a match would be to provide a theory of the state for Neorealism and a theory of the international system for Historical Sociology. Both of these outcomes would have the goal of overcoming the perceived weaknesses in each approach.

Before attempting such a merger it is necessary to summarise what both sides are offering. Historical Sociology could provide a theory of the state. Writers such as Tilly, Skocpol and Mann depict the state as a set of institutions. These institutions exist within a territorial area and, with a greater or lesser degree of success, claim to maintain control over that area. There is no necessary coincidence between state and nation. For example, the British state asserts a right to rule over Wales, Scotland, England and Northern Ireland, a claim that is disputed by Welsh, Irish, Scottish, and perhaps even Cornish, nationalists. A central claim of states is a monopoly on the legitimate use of violence within the territory under its control. The right to exercise violence in its dealings with the citizens under its control is a prime indication of statehood. The institutions which comprise a state are not in any way constant, but are a product of both domestic social relations and international relations. These international relations comprise both interactions with other state formations and the impact of systemic forces such as the world-economy, or norms and conventions. Hence states affect, and are affected by, both domestic and international actors. On occasion, states can also make appeals to the subject populations of other states. These different sets of interrelations influence the ways in which states develop. The characteristics of any particular state change over time and, as Tilly (1992a: 38–45) points out, at the extremes states can even expire. Hence the character of the institutions that comprise the state is affected by both domestic and international forces. In turn, developments within states, for example revolution, influence the character of international and domestic forces.

On the other side of the equation there is Waltz's conception of international system. Waltz describes his system as comprising a structure plus a set of interacting units. The key point for Waltz is that the structure should be defined without reference to the units, in other words, the states. If this is not done it will not be possible to tell whether international forces originate from the units or the system, and the explanation will be reductionist. Waltz argues that there are three levels of structure: ordering principle, character of units, and distribution of capabilities. For the international system the ordering principle is anarchy. The character of the units is that they are undifferentiated. All states have to fulfil the same functions internationally and hence this level can be ignored. The distribution of capabilities refers to the comparative spread of power across the system, with particular reference to the great powers. As argued in Chapter 3, Waltz's main contribution to theorising International Relations was the provision of a means by which forces operating internationally could be isolated. State actions could be understood in the context of the character of the international system at any one time. His argument is that states act differently in a bipolar system than in a multipolar one. However, this theoretical advance is also the source of his greatest weakness: the difficulty of explaining change within his framework.

One possible way of overcoming this problem would be to replace Waltz's undifferentiated second level with a more developed notion of the state, as provided by Historical Sociology. What would be the implications of such a move? As noted in Chapter 3, Waltz does have a theory of the state, albeit a minimal one. Introducing a notion of the state from Historical Sociology into Waltz's structure would involve the replacement of his black box view of the state with something much more intricate, adding a considerably greater level of complexity to the structure.

The structure would now comprise

- The ordering principle – anarchy.
- The character of the units – differentiated states made up of sets of institutions.
- The distribution of capabilities across states.

What advantages might be derived from this merger? First, instead of treating the state as a black box, this move would open up the 'state' and allow the possibility of investigating issues of state development and change. By considering the state as a set of institutions it becomes possible to address questions such as:

- How have the institutions of the state developed as a result of interactions with the international system?
- How has the size of the state varied?
- How have relations between the different institutions of the state changed over time?

For example, it would become possible to discuss issues such as why the state has developed from being primarily concerned with the mobilisation of resources to engage in warfare, to being principally directed towards social welfare and infrastructural services.

A second benefit would be that the inclusion of a more developed notion of the state would permit an analysis of how state forms affect the international system. This would go some way to answering Ruggie's criticism of Neorealism: that the form of the international system in the medieval era was heteronomous as opposed to the modern heterogeneous international system. The core of his point is that in the medieval system there were constantly shifting and overlapping claims to sovereignty that the modern state system largely superseded. By considering the state more carefully in place of the neorealist black box formulation, it becomes possible to consider that states may take different forms, and may make competing claims on the loyalty of subordinate populations.

Third, and crucially, such a merger would enable the possibility of explaining change. Through considering the state form, the balance of its activities, and the two-way relation between system and units, the possibility of explaining change becomes much more feasible than in Neorealism, where the issue of the form of the state is not even addressed. A more developed theory of the state permits the possibility of examining the processes of change. Change can be analysed through the variations in state form and its impact on the international system. So, for example, the internal crisis of a state and the resultant impact on the international system is within the scope of such a formulation. It becomes possible to analyse one issue in particular when a more developed notion of state is introduced into Waltz's structure: the question of whether states came before systems or vice-versa. For Waltz, states seem to appear fully formed. It is the interactions of states that create a system. By considering the state as a changing social form rather than as a given, it is possible to consider state and system as co-constituting, with neither assuming priority. For example, has the development of the state in Europe, as discussed by Tilly and Mann, had an impact on the characteristics of the European international system?

Hence the incorporation of a more developed notion of the state would seem to open up a range of advantages in the theory of international relations. The impact of the international system on the form that the state takes at any historical period can be considered, whilst the impact of changes in state formations on the international system can also be analysed. Finally, the issue of change can be addressed, either by examining the impact of the international system on state forms, or the influence of changes in state form on the international system.

However, despite opening up these possibilities, the proposed merger confronts a number of problems. The first problem is that, from Waltz's perspective, the inclusion of a more developed notion of state into the second level of structure would act to undermine the parsimony of Neorealism.

Perhaps more importantly from Waltz's point of view, the introduction of a discussion of the state into the outline of structure would constitute reductionism. By Waltz's definition of reductionism, as discussed in Chapter 3, the inclusion of unit features into the account of the structure means that the theory can no longer be regarded as systemic. However, as Chapter 3 also argued, Waltz's definition of reductionism is rather specific, and might not be accepted by all.

Waltz claims that in order for his definition of structure to be systemic it must not include any element derived from the units. He argues that the inclusion of any description of state characteristics in the definition of structure results in reductionism. The purpose of avoiding this reductionism is to be able to isolate those forces that are active at an international level. Incorporation of state-level characteristics would mean that it would not be possible to determine whether forces could be explained by systemic or state-level factors. However, as discussed in Chapter 3, the term reductionism can be used in more than one way. Reductionism in Waltz's sense refers to a practice of explaining the whole through an analysis of the parts. But in a second sense, reductionism can also refer to monocausal explanations: those explanations that rely on giving privilege to one factor. For example, Marxism is often accused of reductionism because of its alleged reliance on economic factors as the ultimate means of explanation. As will be discussed below, Neorealism can be considered as reductionist because the explanation of international action is derived solely from a political structure. However, the move that Waltz is making to avoid reductionism can be likened to making an abstraction. The process of abstraction is one where isolation of certain factors allows conclusions about their influence to be drawn. Waltz is abstracting the international system from all other social phenomena in order to be able to separate and analyse international factors. Whether the incorporation of a more detailed analysis of the state at the second level results in reductionism is largely a matter of how the term is defined. A more important criterion might be the extent to which modifications to the theory on the one hand increase its explanatory potential but on the other reduce its elegance. The potential gains to be achieved by neorealists from taking the state more seriously might outweigh the reduction in parsimony.[2]

The incorporation of a notion of the state from Historical Sociology into Neorealism would, in Waltz's terms, constitute reductionism. However, this is not in itself a problem for the merger. More serious problems arise when considering the ontological and epistemological aspects of combining the two approaches. Additionally, there are difficulties with abstracting a notion of the state from Historical Sociology.

On the epistemological front, Waltz and the historical sociologists that we have considered have different conceptions about the character of structures and the way to analyse them. For Waltz, the structures of the international system are timeless. Their impact is always the same. This is regardless of whether they are being studied in the days of Thucydides or in the post-Cold War world. It is this conception of timelessness that allows Waltz to make the abstraction move discussed above. For historical sociologists structures are not timeless, and their impact and character vary through historical time. For example, in Mann's work the four main sources of social power are not constant. At different times one source or a combination of sources are dominant. Hence the way to attain knowledge is markedly different between Waltz and historical sociologists. For Waltz a move of abstraction can be made and the characteristics of the international system studied and isolated both from history and from other factors. This contrasts with Historical Sociology, where knowledge is gained through historical study. The aim is to situate structures within a historical context. For Neorealism, structures are timeless and constant; for Historical Sociology structures are contingent and need to be analysed within a historical framework.

Besides this problem of epistemology, there is also a related ontological issue. This concerns the direction of influence between system and actors. An implication of Waltz's move to abstraction is that it is only possible to analyse influence in one direction: from system to units. Waltz does acknowledge that influences are reciprocal, but his definition of structure only permits analysis in one direction. For Skocpol, Tilly and Mann, the influence between structures and agents is most definitely in both directions. Furthermore, agents and structures are co-constitutive: state and international system cannot be considered as separate entities, they are both products of each other. Hence between Historical Sociology and Neorealism there are ontological conflicts about the character of system and units.

Finally, there are problems with attempting to abstract Historical Sociology's notion of the state from the rest of the approach. For historical sociologists, the form that the state takes is a product of both domestic and international social relations. One of the central insights of more recent writing in Historical Sociology is to locate the state both within civil society, *and* within an international system. Attempting to abstract their notion of the state undermines much of this advance. It is not possible to see states as isolated from the rest of domestic society. States constantly need to negotiate with other actors on the domestic scene to gain the resources required to act internationally. Consider, for example, Tilly's discussion of the negotiations required between state and civil society to mobilise the resources required to fund international activities. Alternatively, Mann argues that increases in social provision to domestic populations were part of a 'deal' and the price that states paid to ensure popular mobilisation during periods of wartime. Additionally, the upheaval of domestic social relations, as in the case of revolutions, also has impacts beyond the state into the international system, as demonstrated by Skocpol. Therefore the state cannot be seen in isolation from domestic forces. The form of the state in any historical period is a product of domestic social forces as well as international ones.

With relation to the analysis of an international system, a key factor of Historical Sociology approaches is the attempt to produce a multi-logic methodology that does not give primacy to any particular social force. Waltz gives primacy to political structures in his explanation of his international system. This is a reductionist position, in the same sense that Marxists are often accused of rooting their explanations of the social world too exclusively in economic forces. As has been seen in the discussion of the historical sociologists (with the exception of Wallerstein), they do attempt to consider multiple forms of social forces in their work. To abstract their view of the state from this would result in an undermining of the richness of their views.

Thus there are considerable problems with attempting to combine Historical Sociology's approach to the state with Neorealism. It is not a simple case of combining the two to overcome the weaknesses in each. There are epistemological issues that indicate that the two approaches have different views regarding how to gain knowledge. One regards the abstraction of core causal elements as the best way to explain the social world; the other views the investigation of how causal variables are situated within a historical context as the way to analyse structures. There is also a conflict regarding the character of the relationship between structure and agents. Neorealism sees the direction of influence as unidirectional. Historical Sociology sees the relationship as being in more than one direction, with agents and structures being co-constitutive. The attempt to combine the view of the state from Historical Sociology with the view of international system from Neorealism would result in a loss of some of the stronger elements from Historical Sociology. This would undermine the potential gains that International Relations scholars can potentially achieve from the study of Historical Sociology.

The second question posed in the introductory chapter was, could Historical Sociology supply Neorealism with a theory of the state? The argument of this section has been that this project, although seeming to offer a variety of positive advances, is beset with a number of epistemological and ontological problems. Comparing Historical Sociology and Neorealism together highlights some of the weaknesses of the latter: its ahistorical view of structures, its reductionism and its unidirectional view of system-state relations.

Historical Sociology cannot provide a theory of the state that complements Neorealism. There are serious epistemological conflicts, and different understandings of the characteristics and influences of structures and units that make a combination problematic. Moreover, it is not a straightforward task to abstract Historical Sociology's notion of the state from the rest of the approach. The understanding of the state is based upon its location within a realm of both domestic and international social relations. Does this conclusion mean that there are no grounds for a dialogue between Historical

Sociology and International Relations? On the contrary, the following section implies that there are considerable grounds for seeing the possibility of a very fertile relationship between International Relations and Historical Sociology.

THE RELATIONSHIP BETWEEN HISTORICAL SOCIOLOGY AND INTERNATIONAL RELATIONS

This section addresses the third question raised in the introductory chapter and assesses the characteristics of the relationship between Historical Sociology and International Relations. Our analysis has suggested that the writings of Skocpol, Tilly and Mann lack a developed theory of international relations. All of these writers argue that there is a need to include the notion of an international system to carry out the kind of analysis that they are attempting. However, so far, they have been less successful at defining the form that the concept should take. They all argue that there are phenomena that can only be explained through the inclusion of an international system as a variable. But they have been less successful in identifying what constitutes an international system, or how its influence is exerted. Of the historical sociologists that we have considered, only Wallerstein provides a full-blown systemic account. His account is detailed where the others are sketchy, it is consistent where the others are inconsistent, it does not contain incompatible elements, and it is not heavily influenced by realist approaches. However, this, in its own way, has led to problems. By weighting his analysis so heavily at the systemic level, his theory has become excessively deterministic.

This raises the issue of to what extent the view of the international system adopted by Skocpol, Tilly and Mann directs their analysis in a particular direction. All these three writers incorporate a notion of the international system as a competitive arena, and all suggest that the prime factor in explaining state development has been its involvement in interstate conflict. A particular view of the international system, a rather realist viewpoint, has directed their investigations. Starting from a different initial analysis of international relations would have led to a different view. In Wallerstein's work, with its economics-based approach to the system, the fighting of wars plays a much smaller role in the analysis of state development. By starting from a different set of underlying assumptions, the analysis leads to a different set of conclusions. Accepting a realist notion of international system has implications for the entire analysis. The implication for International Relations scholars is the need to be aware of this underlying supposition at work in the writings of historical sociologists. A realist notion of the international system affects their view of state development. Where their work is used in International Relations, allowance needs to be made for that influence. The realist influence on certain writers within Historical Sociology means that their work should be treated with caution rather than rejected.

Irrespective of the shortcomings of the attempt by historical sociologists to incorporate the international system as a variable in their analysis, their work does raise a number of points concerning the study of international relations.

Prime amongst these is the issue of the inclusion of history as a variable. The key point about Historical Sociology, as discussed in Chapter 2, is that all social institutions and structures require the element of time in their analysis. To return to Braudel's point, there is no escape from history. Historical Sociology does provide a historical analysis of the development of the state, and to a lesser degree of the international system. This historical analysis has various implications for the study of International Relations.

It is with regard to the historicisation of the units of the international system that the works of historical sociologists are most recognised. It is this analysis of state development that has provided the impetus for International Relations to take an interest in Historical Sociology, as discussed in the introductory chapter. Historical Sociology does not take the state as a given. It examines its development, and suggests that the present world of states is a unique feature of human social relations. It is also a feature that is constantly developing and being transformed. Historical sociologists have studied the emergence of state forms, and have discussed how the world of states, which is now so familiar, has come about. A part of this analysis has involved discussing how states interact with each other, and how these inter-actions have influenced state developments. The way that states have transformed cannot be understood outside of this context. Furthermore, state development has affected and is affected by relations with other actors domestically.

Historical sociologists' analysis of the state also raises issues concerning territoriality. The realist notion of the state, as discussed in Chapter 1, relies heavily on the notion of fixed borders. This reflects its concentration on political aspects of international affairs. Historical Sociology questions the form and permanence of these borders. They are not 'natural' and they are not impermeable. Social arrangements are overlapping and cross-cutting. The apparent boundedness of societies is a recent and possibly short-lived phenomenon. It is a function of the dominant role played by the territorial state within a particular historical epoch.

A historicisation of the international system is most clearly seen in Wallerstein's work. Of the writers examined, his is the most explicit attempt to provide a historical account of the international system. He argues that all world-systems must be seen in a historical context in the sense that they have a beginning, middle and end. Wallerstein has also provided an account of the internal forces that ultimately bring about the demise of the system.

Less explicitly, Mann provides a historical account of how the transition occurs between empires of domination and multi-power-actor civilisations using his concept of interstitial emergence. It is possible to equate the two forms of ordering geopolitical space that he describes to hierarchical and non-hierarchical forms of international system.

Hence Historical Sociology signals the requirement to treat all social formations historically. It is necessary to see the state as a social formation embedded in a particular set of historical social relations, rather than as something outside time. Likewise, the borders that mark territories are temporary boundaries rather than the hard outer shells of states.

Not only does Historical Sociology open up the question of the development of the state, it places on the agenda a wide range of other social phenomena, and the international system. All the historical sociologists that we have discussed consider the links between class and the international system. The link between revolutions and the international system is a central issue for Skocpol, Tilly and Wallerstein. A central concern for Mann and Wallerstein is the connection between capitalist development and the international system. An element of particular importance in Tilly's work is the emphasis that he directs towards an inclusion of cities in his analysis of the development of the international system. Hence Historical Sociology provides examples of how the scope of International Relations can and should be widened to include a variety of other social phenomena.

Finally, Historical Sociology provides different methodologies that could be harnessed to the study of international relations. Skocpol uses a comparative approach to isolate key factors in her analysis of revolution. The revolutions in France, Russia and China are compared both with each other, and with other societies where revolution did not occur successfully (e.g. Britain). This allows Skocpol to isolate the elements that are common to her three examples. Mann, Wallerstein and Tilly employ more of a historical narrative approach. The aim here is to develop a historical narrative that illustrates the theoretical position that they are advocating.

So there are various implications from the work of historical sociologists for International Relations scholars. Historical sociologists have recently become concerned with two social forms that have been core to the study of International Relations: the state and the international system. Historical sociologists have demonstrated that it is possible to historicise both these formations. Their work shows that neither of these forms can be taken as a given. Both have a history, and it cannot be assumed that the future of either will be a reflection of its present or past form. To use Mann's phrase, all social theorists must be aware of the possibility of interstitial surprise. The work of historical sociologists also provides an example of how other actors, such as cities and classes, can be incorporated into the study of International Relations. Finally, the writers that we have examined employ methodological approaches that could be used by International Relations scholars interested in adopting a more historical approach. But there are also lessons to learn about the way that the international system is theorised. I have argued that there have been problems in the way that recent works of Historical Sociology have approached theorising the international system. These are factors of which those attempting to develop more historical approaches in International Relations should be wary.

How, then, might the relationship between the two disciplines be typified? Does Historical Sociology represent a challenge to International Relations? Does it provide a second agenda? Or does it act to reinforce Realism? Are they involved in different projects?

None of these positions provides an entirely accurate description of the form of the current relationship between Historical Sociology and International Relations. A central argument of this chapter has been that, although historical sociologists have been influenced by realist approaches to the study of international relations, there is much in their work that undermines a realist viewpoint. Hence it is not possible to argue that their work reinforces Realism. The state has always been a central element of International Relations theorising. Hence the attention drawn to the state by historical sociologists does not in itself provide a second agenda for International Relations. The work of historical sociologists on international relations is at an initial stage and is their least developed area of analysis. Hence Historical Sociology does not provide a challenge to International Relations in the sense of swallowing it whole. It does, however, provide a challenge in the senses of being more curious about the characteristics of the state, and the need to think about the historical development of social formations.

The historical sociologists and International Relations theorists who are interested in this kind of approach are part of an overlapping agenda. This project highlights the extent to which disciplinary boundaries are not helpful. Historical Sociology in itself represents the erosion of a rigid boundary between History and Sociology. Historical sociologists tend additionally to draw on the work of, amongst others, political scientists and economists. Hence subsets of Historical Sociology and International Relations are studying the same subjects, using the same methodologies, but starting with different sets of assumptions. The best way to depict the relationship between the two disciplines is as a catalyst for each other. International Relations theorists have much to gain from the study of works by writers such as those that we have considered. This kind of work can give insights into state development, historical structures and methodology. In turn, historical sociologists can gain much from International Relations about the theorising of global interactions. However, these 'borrowings' need to be selective. A problem in the past is that both disciplines have used work from the other indiscriminately. Mann has likened the interaction between the two disciplines to two raiding parties:

Each raiding party was tempted by the other's richest goods, their dominating orthodoxies. Sociologists immediately grabbed for the Realist
state. IR raiders went straight for sociology's 'hardest' structures, at that
time classes, modes of production, and world systems. Though the two
raiding parties had much in common, they passed each other in the
night, carrying off the loot that the other did not actually want.

(Mann 1995: 555)

The potential exists for a much more fruitful dialogue between these two
approaches to theorising the social world. They share an interest in the theorising of the state, and the international system, and potentially have much
to contribute to the other.

What then are the implications of this analysis for International Relations
theory? There are many examples of writers within the discipline who are
looking at similar issues, using similar methodologies and taking on the
agenda set by historical sociologists.

As we saw in the introduction, Halliday has been at the forefront of calls
for a greater consideration of the work of historical sociologists. He has developed his (1987) call for a wider engagement with the Historical Sociology
literature in articles on the homogenisation of international society and the
analysis of revolution. At the core of his argument is the need to include an
analysis of an 'interactive chain' between international and domestic societies.
This allows the tracing of events through the international system to
domestic systems and then back to the international system. 'Following interstate competition and its impact within society, changes occur that then lead
to further inter-state conflict. . . . This is *the* formative interaction that has
shaped so much of international history' (Halliday 1994: 140). To date
Halliday has proposed a potential research agenda but has not pursued this
with an in-depth research project.[3] Several other writers have engaged with
the Historical Sociology agenda more directly.

Rosenberg (1990, 1994a, 1994b) for example, has sought to provide a
critique of realist International Relations, and to put Sociology, and particularly a Marxist Sociology, at the centre of International Political Theory. His
intention is to develop an alternative history of the international system
based on a Marxist methodology. Rosenberg argues that the existing realist
notion of the international system is flawed because it fails to take account
the impact of different sociological structures. Rosenberg seeks to demonstrate this by comparing the modern capitalist state-system to that of the
Greek and Italian city states. His intention is to show that each of these
societies have had particular types of state. 'This is an interrelation which
also has important consequences for both the character of inter-state power
and the developmental trajectory of the geopolitical system as a whole'
(Rosenberg 1994a: 6). Rosenberg argues that Realism does not provide the
tools to pursue this type of analysis. Instead he argues that Historical

Materialism can provide an alternative framework for an analysis of the international system, in particular by providing a redefinition of the terms sovereignty and anarchy.

Spruyt (1994a, 1994b), working in a similar area to Rosenberg, has criticised Neorealism for its inability to explain system change. This is because of its failure to provide an analysis at unit level. For Spruyt, unit type will provide part of the answer to the form that the international system will take at any particular time. He centres his analysis at the unit level and aims to answer a question similar to that posed by Tilly: why, from the variety of institutional forms existing in the early modern period, did the sovereign state become dominant?

The notion of the state and its changing form in the international system is central to Thomson's work (1994, 1995). Her concern is to analyse the variety of ways that the notion of sovereignty has manifested itself and how this relates to non-state forms of violence on the international scene. Definitions of the state derived from Weber (e.g those employed by Skocpol, Tilly and Mann) lay great stress on states' claim to a monopoly on the legitimate use of violence. Thomson argues that this is a very recent development, and a feature of the change in the form of sovereignty that has occurred during the last two hundred years. Before the emergence of the modern system of sovereign states, an array of non-state actors – such as pirates, mercenaries, filibusters and mercantile companies – was responsible for a large proportion of international violence, as opposed to state-controlled armed forces. During the last two hundred years these non-state forms of violence have been almost completely eradicated from the international system. Coercion on the international scene is now almost entirely state-directed.

There are several points of contact between the work of Rasler and Thompson and the agenda of Historical Sociology. Their work has largely revolved around the study of 'global wars'. These are wars that occur infrequently, though on a fairly regular basis (approximately every eighty years) and signal a major struggle for systemic leadership (Thompson, W. R. 1988: 5). Rasler and Thompson have sought to understand the international structures that they believe to underlie the regular occurrence of global war. They suggest that the periods of global war have been: 1494–1516; 1580–1608; 1688–1713; 1792–1815; and 1914–45. Their work has been concerned with understanding the circumstances that lead to these periods of systemic warfare, and the wider impacts of these global wars. It is this latter topic that comes closest to the work of the historical sociologists discussed in this book. Rasler and Thompson argue that the link between war and state growth is most significant for 'global powers'. In other words, those states that are most involved in the power struggles that result in 'global wars'. The development of these states has been most closely affected by their involvement in warfare. Rasler and Thompson's view is that this link does not necessarily hold for all state making activities, but that 'global wars and global power state making . . . are inextricably bound together' (Rasler and Thompson 1989: 205).

Ferguson and Mansbach have gone a long way to address the issues raised by historical sociologists. Their starting point is a rejection of the focus of International Relations on the state (Ferguson and Mansbach 1989). They suggest that the state as an analytical concept has done more to hinder the development of International Relations theory than to promote it. The central problem is that there is no agreement on what constitutes the state. ' "The state" has little substance as an empirical concept and virtually no utility as an analytical concept; it obscures far more than it clarifies' (*ibid.*: 81). Instead they argue that the focus of study should be the polity. 'A polity (or political authority)', they argue, 'has a distinct identity; a capacity to mobilize persons and their resources for political purposes, that is, for value satisfaction; and a degree of institutionalization and hierarchy (leaders and constituents)' (Ferguson and Mansbach 1996: 34). Their work draws considerable inspiration from that of Michael Mann, particularly on his focus on cross-cutting social systems; but they are critical of his focus on the state (*ibid.*: 32). An examination of a range of pre-Westphalian polities leads them to conclude that the 'Westphalian moment', the division of the world into legally sovereign, territorially bounded entities, is the exception, rather than a transhistorical reality. An important theoretical concept that they develop as a result of their empirical research is the notion of nested or layered polities. Not only do social systems overlap, Mansbach and Ferguson suggest, they also overlay each other. The analysis of the interactions between polities may provide a way of providing an analysis of change, as well as providing an alternative focus to the system of states. International relations at the end of the Cold War are characterised by threats to states from within their own territorial borders. An analysis of the polity will lead us to better understanding of these phenomena.

Perhaps the International Relations theorist who has come closest to engaging with the agenda from Historical Sociology is Hobson.[4] In his most recent work (Hobson 1997) he attempts to develop one of the key insights of writers such as Mann and Tilly: the significance of a state's extractive system. A state's ability to raise revenue from its own subject population will dictate its policy regarding international trade, and greatly affect its capabilities to wage war internationally. In this sense, extractive capabilities act as a connecting rod between domestic and international realms. States need to generate revenue to be able to compete internationally. Involvement in international war requires states to raise finance, which inevitably requires interaction of some form with the domestic population.

A study of the fiscal sociology of a variety of states at the end of the last and the beginning of the current century allows Hobson to draw a number of conclusions regarding state capacity in international relations. The capability of a state to raise revenue is linked to its degree of 'embedded autonomy' and institutional factors, such as the degree of centralisation and the ability of the state to logistically reach into society. 'Embedded autonomy' refers to the extent of cooperation between a state and other actors operating within its territory. For Hobson, 'strong' states are those which enjoy a high degree of cooperation with other actors. They are able to enjoy the benefits of collective power. 'Weak' states, on the other hand, employ despotic power in order to extract the resources that they require. From his empirical analysis, Hobson argues that at the two extremes, Britain at the turn of the twentieth century was an example of a strong state, whilst Tsarist Russia provided an example of a weak state. The degree of its embeddedness will give an indication of the likely trade policy of a state. The British state, enjoying an essentially cooperative relationship with class power, was able to rely on direct forms of taxation to raise its required revenue. As a result trade policy favoured lower tariff levels – there was less requirement to raise revenue through an imposition on the trading of goods. Direct taxation augments state capacity more than indirect taxation, because it is less vulnerable to external shocks. The state's ability to raise direct taxation, Hobson argues, was a key factor in British victory in the First World War. By contrast, in Russia, where a more antagonistic relationship existed between the state and other class actors, direct taxation was much harder to collect and so there was a greater need to impose tariffs on traded goods. In between the two extremes lie the other states that Hobson examines. The German state, for example, was only partially embedded within its society – able to profit from collective power relations with the Junkers class, but having to rely on despotic power relations with the German working class. Hence a central conclusion of Hobson's study is that 'state capacity is positively related to the degree of a state's interactive embeddedness within society; the broader and deeper the social embeddedness, the stronger the state's capacity' (ibid.: 237).

His conclusions also lead to wider implications for the study of international relations. Because states straddle both domestic and international realms, an analysis of their characteristics and policies requires an examination of 'state capacity/state–society relations on the one hand, and international political and economic systems on the other' (ibid.: 275).

All of these writers are working in similar subject areas to the historical sociologists that we have been considering, and there is a considerable degree of overlap in subject and methodology. A comparison between these works and those of Skocpol, Tilly, Mann and Wallerstein suggests that that the disciplinary boundaries between Historical Sociology and International Relations are rather false. In terms of agenda and approach there is a great deal that unites the two approaches, and I would argue that this is to be welcomed and encouraged.

However, so far there have been few methodical attempts to produce a historicised account of the international system. Watson's work on the evolution of international society, discussed in Chapter 3, is one example. The work of Buzan and Little also attempts to consider international systems in historical context. The works briefly summarised above take on the notion of the historical development of the state, but their views of the international system remain ahistorical. Spruyt is attempting to combine a historical notion of the state with a neorealist notion of international systems. There are weaknesses in this approach for the reasons discussed in the previous section. Rosenberg develops a notion of the system as a product of the relations of production, but he does not treat it as a causal variable in its own right. Thomson views the international system as a causal variable, but has not so far provided a historical account of its development. The requirement is for an approach that treats both the international system and actors as coherent, co-constitutive, and historical social forms. Ferguson and Mansbach provide a valuable exercise in the utilisation of Michael Mann's ideas within an International Relations framework. Their work does not extend to an analysis of systemic effects on the development of polities, but the analysis of nested polities may provide a way of extending the analysis.

Towards the study of global structures?

Historical sociologists have included the international system as a causal variable, and have suggested ways in which it could be theorised historically. The challenge for International Relations theorists is to further consider those two issues, causality and change, and develop a more coherent analysis of what constitutes an international system. What might such an analysis comprise?

Following on from one of the arguments we have pursued, and the work of Hollis and Smith, such an analysis would require a sensitivity to different accounts, and to the problems of combining insider and outsider versions. I have argued that part of the reason why some historical sociologists have failed to provide a coherent reading of the international system is because they attempted to combine different types of accounts without considering the implications. This does not mean that different accounts cannot be addressed within one analysis. Rather, there needs to be an awareness that different structures can comprise elements that it is difficult to combine directly. Problems start to emerge when a view of structures as external forces is combined with a view of structures as rules and norms. An account of global structures might want to include both of these factors, but it is not simply a case of adding accounts together.

A further element in such an approach would be to build on the multi-logic approach used by Mann. This would envision multiple forces at work internationally, none of which were ultimately determining. It would replace both the political reductionism of Waltz and the economic reductionism of Wallerstein. The suggestion made by Buzan, Jones and Little to develop a sectoral approach would provide a positive step towards such an aim. As discussed in Chapter 3, they suggest developing an approach based on economic, societal, strategic and political sectors. Each of these sectors would require its own structural analysis. It would also need an analysis of:

- *The form of the units within each sector.* This needs to consider who the actors are within each sector, and how they interrelate. Some actors may be active in more than one sector, or even in all.
- *The constitution of units and structures in each sector.* There is also a requirement to consider the units and the structures as historical entities, and to trace the form in which they have developed. The research by historical sociologists on the development of the state would provide a model for this endeavour.
- *How the structures and units change historically.* There is also a requirement for explaining change within sectors. To begin with, this requires an analysis of what constitutes change. This needs to be followed by a discussion of what factors generate change.
- *How the sectors interact.* Finally there is a need to understand the relationships between different sectors. This is a particularly difficult exercise, given the constraints discussed above. However, there are links between the different sectors, for example, political and economic, and including them in the analysis would add depth. A multi-logic approach suggests that at any particular time one or a combination of factors might be dominant, but that this would change historically.

Evidently, this is not a minor undertaking. However, any analysis of an international system requires the awareness of historical contingency and the existence of a variety of structures and units. Hence the unravelling of these structures and the analysis of their interrelations would be a huge task. Nevertheless, doing this might not only provide a richer account of international events, but could also furnish historical sociologists with a systemic theory that could overcome their current impasse. What is being proposed here is more than an analysis of the international system. In practice the term 'international system' might not be that useful, as it suggests both an analysis exclusively between nations, and a certain degree of determinism. A better phrase could be 'global structures'. This term would aim to encompass the different actors (states, nations, classes, TNCs) involved in the analysis. It would also suggest the existence of a number of frameworks within which actors have to function. Furthermore, it would imply that actors and structures are co-constitutive, and that a degree of autonomy is possible.

CONCLUSION

Waltz's *Theory of International Politics* was published in 1979, at a time when tension between the two Cold War superpowers was again on the increase. It spoke to a world dominated by the stasis of bipolarity. Its stress on continuity and stability seemed appropriate to an international system that showed no sign of changing. When *Theory of International Politics* appeared there seemed to be no indication of the size of the international upheaval that was about to occur. However, this was a world that did change. The Cold War ended. Almost overnight the Soviet Union disappeared peacefully (at least from a western perspective). This was a clear example of an 'interstitial surprise' which caught International Relations theorists looking the wrong way. Concerned with institutionalised political and military power, neorealists were caught unawares by a new emergent power network based on economic and ideological power. Neorealist analysis concentrated on the military power and political centralisation of the Soviet Union, and overlooked changes in the economic and ideological spheres. Waltz's Neorealism neither predicted nor could provide an explanation for these changes. Even if a theory cannot predict changes, there is surely some requirement that it be able to offer some comprehension of change. In a time of change, a theory is needed that is capable of explaining transformations. Some International Relations theorists have looked to Historical Sociology as a possible fruitful avenue for developing an analysis of change.

We have assessed to what extent there is a potential for a dialogue between Historical Sociology and International Relations. This concluding chapter has provided answers to the questions posed in Chapter 1. Our central finding is that there is no single approach to the study of the international system by historical sociologists. Three general criticisms were made concerning the way in which historical sociologists have attempted to incorporate a notion of the international system in their work. These were summarised as inconsistency, incompatibility, and being heavily influenced by Realism. As a result of these problems, historical sociologists have been able to provide neither a coherent account of international systems, nor one that can provide the causal explanations that they seek. However, these problems seem less appropriate with regard to Wallerstein's work. His modern world-system approach seems to provide an indication of the result of a more systemic approach within Historical Sociology. Although his account has much to recommend it, ultimately it is reductionist, to economic factors, and deterministic, leaving little room for agency. A related claim is that for Skocpol, Tilly and Mann, the consistent account of the state that they provide relies on under-theorised and inconsistent accounts of the international system. For Skocpol, much of her explanation of revolutions requires her account of the international system as the occurrence of war. Tilly and Mann provide different versions of the international system, depending on what factor of state development they are trying to explain. Mann's account of the international system is of a residual category where he places a number of elements that he cannot include elsewhere. For

Wallerstein the problem is the other way round. Clarity at system level is achieved only through treatment of the state as a primitive variable.

Despite these problems, Historical Sociology can be seen to be undermining of a realist approach to International Relations. The central contribution of Historical Sociology is to argue that the state cannot be taken as a given. State development has to be located within a range of social developments located within a historical context. The work of Mann, Tilly and Wallerstein also points to an historicisation of the international system. Mann, for example, has analysed the transition from empires of domination to multi-power-actor civilisations. Furthermore, their work breaks down two boundaries: the dichotomy, posited by realist writers, between domestic and international; and the notion that societies are encased in the hard shells of their borders. Societies overlap and interact. The social world is much messier than suggested by Realism. For historical sociologists the social world is a totality and cannot be understood in any other way.

Given the coherent reading of the state in Historical Sociology, and the account of international systems in Neorealism, we considered the possibility of combining the two approaches. Although such a partnership, at least on the surface, appeared to offer valuable advances to both bodies of literature, the analysis uncovered considerable epistemological and ontological problems. This suggested that such a merger would be very problematic. The outcome of this experiment suggests that there are serious limitations in Neorealism, and that of the two approaches Historical Sociology provides a more fruitful way of theorising international relations. The prime reason for this is that it includes a historical account of social formations which, by implication, allows for an analysis of change.

As such, Historical Sociology provides various lessons to International Relations. Primarily it demonstrates the necessity for the inclusion of time as a variable in the understanding of social formations. It also suggests ways in which the state and the international system can be historicised, and how the dichotomy between international and domestic, prevalent in International Relations theorising, can be overcome. Some of the insights from this approach have been developed in the work of writers such as Halliday, Spruyt, Rosenberg, Thomson, Rasler and Thompson, Ferguson and Mansbach, and Hobson. The boundaries between those writers in International Relations who are interested in taking a historical approach and the macro-sociologists in Historical Sociology are also breaking down. There are similarities in the areas of study and the ways of going about it. The most important contribution to this project that International Relations scholars can provide is the provision of an approach to global structures that allows for an understanding of change and of causality. There is much potential for a dialogue between these disciplines. However, to achieve the potential of both, an account of global structures is required which provides a consistent account of both systemic and unit-level features.

NOTES

1 INTRODUCTION

1 I will adopt the convention of capitalising International Relations to refer to the discipline, whilst uncapitalised international relations will be used to apply to that which is studied.
2 The phrase 'bringing the state back in' comes from the title of a collection of essays reflecting this renewal of interest in the state (Evans *et al.* 1985).
3 As an example of the differences between the insider and outsider approaches with reference to International Relations, consider the so-called second great debate between scientists and traditionalists (Bull 1966; Kaplan 1966).

2 HISTORY, SOCIOLOGY AND HISTORICAL SOCIOLOGY

1 For examples of the range of subjects examined, consider the following: Jackson (1992) examines the changing relationship between women and housework in differing historical contexts; MacKenzie (1991) explores how social processes shape and are shaped by the development of nuclear technologies; Erikson (1966) discusses patterns of deviance within a seventeenth-century Puritan community in Massachusetts Bay.
2 See Collingwood (1961: 165–83, 205–31) and Elton (1969: 20–4). For a similar view, though put by a sociologist, see Bierstedt 1959. However, Bierstedt argues that the two subjects are complementary.
3 Goldthorpe's attack on what he described as Grand Historical Sociology generated a lively debate in the pages of the *British Journal of Sociology*. See the responses to his article by Bryant, Hart, Mouzelis and Mann, and Goldthorpe's spirited reply to his critics (Bryant *et al.* 1994). A similar criticism has been made of Tilly's work. Taylor argues that Tilly selects facts from the historical literature to fit his framework. He asks, 'where are the fundamental debates about the meaning of the events described?' (Taylor 1994: 89).
4 International Relations scholars might dispute this statement!
5 It should be noted though that Helmes-Hayes (1992) suggests that Ginsberg's position on empirical research is more ambiguous than is suggested by this quotation. This does not, however, undermine the main point of the text with regard to the relationship between History and Sociology.

6 Interestingly a similar analogy to building is employed by Cox (1986: 212) with reference to the uses of History by neorealists: 'History becomes for neorealists a quarry providing materials with which to illustrate variations on always recurrent themes'.

7 As examples of the role of theory in History, consider the following statements from historians: 'past events exist, qua events, only in terms of some historically situated conception of them' (Roth, P. A. 1991: 185); 'any selection and arrangement of facts pertaining to any large area of history, either local or world, race or class, is controlled inexorably by the frame of reference in the mind of the selector and arranger' (Beard 1934: 227); 'those historians who today pretend to dispense with a philosophy of history are merely trying, vainly and self-consciously, like members of a nudist colony, to recreate the garden of Eden in their garden suburb' (Carr 1964: 20).

8 For a similar view see Griffin 1995.

9 The discussion of the romantic historians that follows is based on Collingwood's summaries.

10 This is in contrast to the current usage of the term which relates to the study of historical methodology. Atkinson makes a clear distinction between different uses of the term philosophy of history. He refers to an analytical philosophy of history concerned with 'the significance and truth of historical statements, the possibility of objectivity, with explanation, causation and values' (Atkinson 1978: 4) and a substantive philosophy of history concerned with 'the historical process itself' (*ibid.*: 8–9).

11 For an outline of Weber's view of the state see Weber 1968: 54–6.

12 However, note that Parsons attempted to counter the claim that functionalists could not explain social change (Parsons 1966, 1971). The issue of the possibility of explaining social change will become a central feature in the next chapter when the same problem in Waltz's work will be discussed.

3 KENNETH WALTZ AND THE CONCEPT OF SYSTEM IN INTERNATIONAL RELATIONS

1 The tension between these approaches can be compared to that between History and Sociology. See Chapter 2.

2 James argues that in fact society is a more appropriate term to describe the nature of relations between states, and that the division between system and society made by Bull was a false distinction (James, A. 1993).

3 A conclusion shared by Mann, see Chapter 7.

4 In the sense that states are seen as the principle actors, there is a sharp division between domestic and international politics, and the international scene is viewed primarily as being the site of a struggle for power and peace. However, Shimko (1993) argues that Neorealism is influenced more by American Liberalism than Classical Realism, and is more of an alternative to the latter. For a discussion of structuralist approaches in International Relations more generally, and the role of Neorealism in reviving the fortunes of Realism see Little 1985.

5 The term Structural Realism has been adopted by Buzan *et al.* (1993) to describe their modifications to Waltz's work, and so Neorealism will be used here to describe Waltz's work and those closely aligned with him.

6 In a later article Waltz returned to the question of theory and its importance. He stressed the importance of creating an independent zone before the possibility of

creating theory existed. 'Theory becomes possible only if various objects and processes, movements and events, acts and interactions, are viewed as forming a domain that can be studied in its own right' (Waltz 1991: 23). An important result of producing this domain is that assumptions, simplifications and distortions are introduced, and Waltz is very straightforward about accepting this:

> In making assumptions about men's (or states') motivations, the world must be drastically simplified; subtleties must be rudely pushed aside, and reality must be grossly distorted. Descriptions strive for accuracy; assumptions are brazenly force. The assumptions on which theories are built are radical simplifications of the world and are useful only because they are such. Any false simplification conveys a false impression of the world.
>
> *(ibid.*: 27)

One result of this high level of abstraction is that the 'application of theory in any realm is a perplexing and uncertain matter' (*ibid.*: 29). He claims that Neorealism has made a big step forward in the theorising of international politics by isolating a realm in which such theorising could take place, this being one of several advances that Neorealism has made over Classical Realism.

7   Kaplan has disputed Waltz's definition of reductionism. In a polemic reply to the accusation of reductionism in his work he argues that there is more than one type of reductionism. Waltz has confused and conflated these. Additionally he rejects the idea that the system can be analysed without reference to the characteristics of the units. He argues that 'Waltz shows no understanding that, in the absence of theoretically relevant actor characteristics, no theoretical statements could be made or any conditions specified for the application of a theory' (Kaplan 1979: 12).

8   Note that this point marks an important distinction between Classical Realism and Neorealism. In classical Realism the prime aim of states is to gain more and more power, here the prime aim is to survive.

9   Waltz's interpretation of Durkheim has been challenged. See Barkdull 1995.

10 For an indication of the direction that this research is taking, see Buzan and Little 1994.

11 Note that it has been suggested that Neorealism does not provide a very accurate guide to the way that states act at all. See Schroeder 1994.

12 Note also that Waltz seems to imply that a unipolar system is impossible. See Waltz 1979: 136. More recently Waltz (1993: 52) has described the post-Cold War world as one in which 'bipolarity endures'. This is because 'militarily Russia can take care of itself and because no other great powers have yet emerged'.

13 For a similar opinion, though more forcefully expressed, see George 1994: 119.

14 See Figure 3.1 on page 40 and Figure 5.2 on page 100 of Waltz 1979.

4   THEDA SKOCPOL

1   It is interesting to compare Skocpol's call for a structuralist approach with Waltz's (1979: esp. Chapters 2–4) arguments (especially as both books were

published in 1979!). Skocpol, like Waltz, argues that structures provide the possibility of explaining the difference between intentions and outcomes.
2 However for a suggestion that Marx was at least aware of the significance of international factors in studying social change see Scholte 1993b: 12.
3 See also Skocpol 1979: 47.

5 CHARLES TILLY

1 A request that is made by Tilly (1992a: 36) of his critics.
2 The value of historical and structural approaches is discussed in Tilly 1992d.
3 See also Tilly 1992a: 31, 58.

6 MICHAEL MANN

1 In a later essay Mann (1988: 210–37) applied this approach to an analysis of the failure of outmoded political institutions to halt British decline.
2 See also Mann 1993a: 16. Mann has written elsewhere on gender relations. See Mann 1986b; and more briefly, Mann 1998a: 188–209.
3 For a taste of this debate see Bachrach and Baratz 1963; Lukes 1974; Clegg 1989.
4 See also Mann 1993a: 736; 1986a: 1.
5 See also Mann 1986a: 376, 490.
6 See also Mann 1993a: 33, 215.
7 Mann outlines this pattern with regard to Britain (Mann 1993a: 115–16, 131), the US (*ibid.*: 143, 162–63) and France (*ibid.*: 179–87). This argument is very close to that of Skocpol's that the costs of military competition was a factor in the French, Russian and Chinese revolutions. Mann extends the argument to include reforms occurring in non-revolutionary situations. See also Mann 1988: 146–65.
8 It is worth noting, however, that elsewhere Mann has taken a weaker position on the role of norms in the regulation of state activity. In a discussion of war he remarks that 'diplomacy involves a number of autonomous states among whom there are few normative ties, yet continuous re-calculation of the main chance. The actions of one set up ripple reactions among the others, amounting to an unpredictable whole' (Mann 1988: 151–2).
9 See also Mann 1993a: 51, 72.
10 Although it would be incorrect to give the impression that Mann is not critical of realist positions. See for example his critique of realist explanations for World War One (Mann 1993a: 751–7).
11 See however, the discussion of a pendulum swinging between empire and independent states in Watson 1992: 13–18. Watson's position would seem to be close to Mann's, though he lacks the theoretical analysis that Mann provides in his concept of interstitial emergence. Watson's work was discussed briefly in Chapter 3.

NOTES

7 IMMANUEL WALLERSTEIN

1 See the lengthy discussion of Braudel's influence (Wallerstein 1991b: Section V).
2 Wallerstein also provides further discussions of the notion of social systems (Wallerstein 1984: 37; 1991b: 235).
3 The distinction between world-economy and world-empire is comparable to Mann's use of the terms multi-power-actor civilisations and empires of domination. Mann's analysis of the transition from one form of social organisation to the other is much more detailed, however. See Chapter 6 for further details.
4 The neo-Marxist position is taken as defining capitalism in the sphere of exchange, rather than in the sphere of production, as would traditional Marxists. This has, of course, opened Wallerstein's position to considerable Marxist critiques, as will be subsequently discussed. This issue is also discussed by Little (1995: 79).
5 Edwards (1985) provides a very clear discussion of Emmanuel's theory.
6 Wallerstein (1980b: 168) provides a further discussion of this issue.
7 Note though that this is not an analysis that Marx uses in his examination of the crisis of capitalism. Marx argued that there was a tendency for the rate of profit to fall, brought about by an increase in the organic composition of capital.
8 The issue of crisis is discussed elsewhere (Wallerstein 1991b: 262). However, note that an earlier definition of crisis is less apocalyptic. In this instance the inability of this system to cope with accumulated contradictions requires 'a major restructuring of the economy' (Wallerstein 1980a: 7).
9 Further elaboration on this point can be found elsewhere (Wallerstein 1974: 67; 1980b: 169).
10 This point is developed elsewhere (Wallerstein 1991b: 131).
11 A parallel can be drawn here with Skocpol's work on social revolutions. One impact of revolution, she argues, has been a rationalisation of the state, allowing it to compete more effectively internationally. See Chapter 4.
12 This view of Europe in the late middle ages as a Christian civilisation is similar to that of Mann. See Chapter 6.
13 Though note that elsewhere it has been argued that during the medieval period Europe comprised a peripheral area to a world-economy centred on the Middle East (Abu-Lughod 1989).
14 Worsley (1980: 305) makes a similar argument.
15 Kearns (1988: 286) and Sen (1985: 100) pursue similar arguments.
16 Interestingly, Wallerstein's view was treated with some scorn in a review by Mann (1986c).

8 HISTORICAL SOCIOLOGY AND INTERNATIONAL RELATIONS

1 See Chapter 7 for a fuller critique of Wallerstein's view of the international system.
2 That adding extra elements to the structure of Neorealism can result in a reduction in its parsimony is a point made by Wheeler (1993) about the work of Buzan, Little and Jones.

201

3 Halliday's contribution to the discussion of Historical Sociology within International Relations is discussed in greater depth in Hobson 1997: 14; 1998.
4 Hobson's discussion of the weaknesses in neorealist and Marxist approaches to International Relations was discussed in Chapter 1.

BIBLIOGRAPHY

Abbott, A. (1991) 'History and sociology: the lost synthesis', *Social Science History*, 15, 2: 201–38.

Abrams, P. (1982) *Historical Sociology*, Shepton Mallet: Open Books.

Abu-Lughod, J. L. (1989) *Before European Hegemony: The World System AD 1250–1350*, Oxford: Oxford University Press.

Agnew, J. (1994) 'The territorial trap: the geographical assumptions of international relations theory', *Review of International Political Economy*, 1, 1: 53–80.

Anderson, P. (1986) 'Those in authority: review of Mann's *The Sources of Social Power, Volume I*', *Times Literary Supplement*, 4367: 1405–6.

Arrighi, G., Hopkins, T. K. and Wallerstein, I. (1989) *Antisystemic Movements*, London: Verso.

Ashley, R. K. (1986) 'The poverty of neorealism', in R. O. Keohane (ed.) *Neorealism and its Critics*, New York: Columbia University Press.

Atkinson, R. F. (1978) *Knowledge and Explanation in History*, London: Macmillan.

Bachrach, P. and Baratz, M. S. (1963) 'Decisions and nondecisions: an analytical framework', *American Political Science Review*, 57, 3: 632–42.

Badie, B. (1992) 'Comparative analysis and historical sociology', *International Social Science Journal*, 44, 3: 319–27.

Banks, J. A. (1989) 'From universal history to Historical Sociology', *British Journal of Sociology*, 40, 4: 521–43.

Baran, P. (1957) *The Political Economy of Growth*, New York: Monthly Review Press.

Barkdull, J. (1995) 'Waltz, Durkheim and international relations: the international system as an abnormal form', *American Political Science Review*, 89, 3: 669–80.

Beard, C. A. (1934) 'Written history as an act of faith', *The American Historical Review*, 39, 2: 219–29.

Bierstedt, R. (1959) 'Toynbee and sociology', *British Journal of Sociology*, 10, 2: 95–104.

Blackburn, R. M. and Mann, M. (1979) *The Working Class in the Labour Market*, London: Macmillan.

Blomstrom, M. and Hettne, B. (1984) *Development Theory in Transition*, London: Zed Books.

Booth, K. (1996) '75 years on: rewriting the subject's past: reinventing its future' in S. Smith, K. Booth and M. Zalewski (eds) *International Theory: Positivism and Beyond*, Cambridge: Cambridge University Press.

Bosworth, R. J. B. (1993) *Explaining Auschwitz and Hiroshima: History Writing and the Second World War, 1945–1990*, London: Routledge.

Braudel, F. (1975) *The Mediterranean and the Mediterranean World in the Age of Phillip II*, trans. S. Reynolds, two vols, London: Fontana.

——(1980) *On History*, trans. S. Matthews, London: Weidenfeld and Nicholson.

Brenner, R. (1977) 'The origins of capitalist development: a critique of neo-Smithian Marxism', *New Left Review*, 104: 25–92.

Bryant, J. M. (1994) 'Evidence and explanation in history and sociology', *British Journal of Sociology*, 45, 1: 3–19.

Bryant, J. M., Goldthorpe, J. H., Hart, N., Mann, M. and Mouzelis, N. (1994) ' "The uses of history in sociology": a debate', *British Journal of Sociology*, 45, 1: 1–77.

Bull, H. (1966) 'The case for a classical approach', *World Politics*, 18, 3: 361–77.

——(1977) *The Anarchical Society: A Study of Order in World Politics*, London: Macmillan.

Burke, P. (1980) *Sociology and History*, London: Allen and Unwin.

Buzan, B. (1996) 'The timeless wisdom of realism?', in S. Smith, K. Booth and M. Zalewski (eds) *International Theory: Positivism and Beyond*, Cambridge: Cambridge University Press.

Buzan, B., Jones, C. and Little, R. (1993) *The Logic of Anarchy: Neorealism to Structural Realism*, New York: Columbia University Press.

Buzan, B. and Little, R. (1994) 'The idea of "international system": theory meets history', *International Political Science Review*, 15, 3: 231–55.

Carr, E. H. (1964) *What is History?*, Harmondsworth: Pelican.

Chirot, D. (1982) 'Review of Wallerstein's *The Modern World-System Volume II*', *Journal of Social History*, 15, 3: 561–65.

Claessen, H. J. M. (1992) 'Review of Tilly's *Coercion, Capital and Class*', *International Review of Social History*, 37, 1: 99–102.

Clegg, S. R. (1989) *Frameworks of Power*, London: Sage.

Collingwood, R. G. (1961) *The Idea of History*, Oxford: Oxford University Press.

Cox, R. W. (1986) 'Social forces, states and world orders: beyond international relations theory', in R. O. Keohane (ed.) *Neorealism and its Critics*, New York: Columbia University Press.

Davidheiser, E. B. (1992) 'Strong states, weak states: the role of the state in revolution', *Comparative Politics*, 24, 4: 463–75.

Dessler, D. (1989) 'What's at stake in the agent-structure debate?', *International Organisation*, 43, 3: 383–92.

Driver, F. (1991) 'Political geography and state formation: disputed territory', *Progress in Human Geography*, 15, 3: 268–80.

DuPlessis, R. S. (1987) 'The partial transition to world-system analysis in early modern European history', *Radical History Review*, 39: 11–27.

Durkheim, E., Bohannon, P., Coser, L. A., Duncan, H. D., Hinkle, R. C. Jnr, Honigsheim, P., Kurauchi, K., Neyer, J., Parsons, T., Peyre, H., Pierce, A., Richter, M. and Salomon, A. (1964) *Essays on Sociology and Philosophy*, ed. K. H. Wolff, New York: Harper and Row.

Easton, D. (1990) 'Specialization and integration', *American Behavioural Scientist*, 33, 6: 646–61.

Edwards, C. (1985) *The Fragmented World*, London: Methuen.

Elton, G. R. (1969) *The Practice of History*, Glasgow: Fontana.

Emmanuel, A. (1972) *Unequal exchange: A study of the Imperialism of Trade*, London: New Left Books.

Erikson, K. (1966) *Wayward Puritans*, New York: Wiley.

Evans, P. B., Rueschemeyer, D. and Skocpol, T. (eds) (1985) *Bringing the State Back In*, Cambridge: Cambridge University Press.

Evans, P. B. and Stephens, J. D. (1988) 'Studying development since the sixties: the emergence of a new comparative political economy', *Theory and Society*, 17, 5: 713–45.

Ferguson, Y. H. and Mansbach, R. W. (1989) *The State, Conceptual Chaos, and the Future of International Relations Theory*, Boulder CO: Lynne Reinner.

——(1996) *Polities: Authority, Identities, and Change*, Columbia SC: University of South Carolina Press.

Frank, A. G. (1969) *Capitalism and Underdevelopment in Latin America*, New York: Monthly Review Press.

Friedmann, H. (1983) 'Is there a world capitalist system?', *Queen's Quarterly*, 90, 2: 497–508.

Gellner, E. (1988) 'Review of Mann's *The Sources of Social Power, Volume I*', *Man*, 23, 1: 206–7.

George, J. (1994) *Discourses of Global Politics: A Critical (Re)Introduction to International Relations*, Boulder CO: Lynne Rienner.

Giddens, A. (1985) 'Review of Skocpol's *Vision and Method in Historical Sociology*', *Sociological Review*, 33, 4: 816.

——(1994) 'Rough and tough: review of Mann's *The Sources of Social Power, Volume II*', *New Statesman and Society*, 7 January 1994, 37–8.

Goldstone, J. A. (1991) 'States making war making states making war', *Contemporary Sociology*, 20, 2: 176–8.

Goldthorpe, J. H. (1991) 'The uses of history in sociology: reflections on some recent tendencies', *British Journal of Sociology*, 42, 2: 211–30.

Goodwin, J. and Skocpol, T. (1989) 'Explaining revolutions in the contemporary third world', *Politics and Society*, 17, 4: 489–509.

Gorin, Z. (1985) 'Socialist societies and world system theory: a critical survey', *Science and Society*, 49, 3: 332–66.

Griffin, L. J. (1995) 'How is sociology informed by history', *Social Forces*, 73, 4: 1245–54.

Haimson, L. and Tilly, C. (1989) *Strikes, War and Revolutions in an International Perspective*, Cambridge: Cambridge University Press.

Haldon, J. (1993) *The State and the Tributary Mode of Production*, London: Verso.

Hall, J. A. (1989) 'They do things differently there, or, the contribution of British historical sociology', *British Journal of Sociology*, 40, 4: 544–64.

Halliday, F. (1987) 'State and society in international relations: a second agenda', *Millennium*, 16, 2: 215–30.

——(1994) *Rethinking International Relations*, Basingstoke: Macmillan.

Harvey, D. (1987) 'The world systems theory trap', *Studies in Comparative International Development*, 22, 1: 42–7.

Helmes-Hayes, R. C. (1992) ' "From universal history to historical sociology" by J. A. Banks – a critical comment', *British Journal of Sociology*, 43, 3: 333–44.

Himmelstein, J. L. and Kimmel, M. S. (1981) 'States and revolutions: the implications and limits of Skocpol's structural model', *American Journal of Sociology*, 86, 5: 1145–54.

Hobson, J. M. (1994) 'The poverty of Marxism and Neorealism: bringing Historical Sociology back in to international relations', La Trobe Politics Working Paper no. 2, Melbourne: La Trobe University, School of Politics.

——(1997) *The Wealth of States: A Comparative Sociology of International Economic and Political Change*, Cambridge: Cambridge University Press.

——(1998) 'The historical sociology of the state and the state of historical sociology in international relations', *Review of International Political Economy*, 5, 2.

Hollis, M. (1994) *The Philosophy of Social Science*, Cambridge: Cambridge University Press.

Hollis, M. and Smith, S. (1990) *Explaining and Understanding International Relations*, Oxford: Clarendon Press.

——(1991) 'Beware of gurus: structure and action in international relations', *Review of International Studies*, 17, 4: 393–410.

——(1992) 'Structure and action: further comment', *Review of International Studies*, 18, 2: 187–8.

——(1994) 'Two stories about structure and agency', *Review of International Studies*, 20, 3: 241–51.

——(1996) 'A response: why epistemology matters in international theory', *Review of International Studies*, 22, 1: 111–16.

Hollist, W. L. and Rosenau, J. N. (1981) 'Editors introduction to world systems debates – special edition', *International Studies Quarterly*, 25, 1: 5–17.

Hunt, L. (1984) 'Charles Tilly's collective action', in T. Skocpol (ed.) *Vision and Method in Historical Sociology*, Cambridge: Cambridge University Press.

Jackson, S. (1992) 'Towards a historical sociology of housework – a materialist feminist analysis', *Women's Studies International Forum*, 15, 2: 153–72.

James, A. (1993) 'System or society?', *Review of International Studies*, 19, 3: 269–88.

James, P. (1995) 'Structural realism and the causes of war', *Mershon International Studies Review*, 39, 2: 181–208.

Jarvis, A. (1989) 'Societies, states and geopolitics: challenges from historical sociology', *Review of International Studies*, 15, 3: 281–93.

Kant, I. (1988) 'Idea for a universal history from a cosmopolitan point of view', in L. W. Beck (ed.) *Kant: Selections*, New York: Macmillan.

Kaplan, M. A. (1957) *System and Process in International Politics*, New York: Wiley.

——(1966) 'The new great debate: traditionalism vs. science in international relations', *World Politics*, 19, 1: 1–20.

——(1979) *Towards Professionalism in International Theory: Macrosystem Analysis*, New York: Free Press.

Kasza, G. J. (1996) 'War and competitive politics', *Comparative Politics*, 28, 3: 355–73.

Kearns, G. (1988) 'History, geography and world-systems theory', *Journal of Historical Geography*, 14, 3: 281–92.

Keohane, R. O. (1986) 'Theory of world politics: structural realism and beyond', in R. O. Keohane (ed.) *Neorealism and its Critics*, New York: Columbia University Press.

Kimmel, M. S. (1990) *Revolution: A Sociological Interpretation*, Oxford: Polity Press.

Klink, F. F. (1990) 'Rationalizing core-periphery relations: the analytical foundations of structural inequality in world politics', *International Studies Quarterly*, 34, 2: 183–209.

Knorr, K. (1956) *The War Potential of Nations*, Princeton NJ: Princeton University Press.

Kratochwil, F. (1993) 'The embarrassment of changes: neo-realism as the science of realpolitik without politics', *Review of International Studies*, 19, 1: 63–80.

LaCapra, D. (1972) *Emile Durkheim: Sociologist and Philosopher*, Ithaca NY: Cornell University Press.

Lehmann, D. (1980) 'Revolutions and the imperatives of state power', *Political Studies*, 28, 4: 622–5.

Linklater, A. (1990) *Beyond Realism and Marxism: Critical Theory and International Relations*, Basingstoke: Macmillan.

Little, R. (1978) 'A systems approach', in T. Taylor (ed.) *Approaches and Theory in International Relations*, London: Longman.

——(1985) 'Structuralism and neo-realism', in M. Light and and A. J. R. Groom (eds) *International Relations: A Handbook of Current Theory*, London: Pinter.

——(1994) 'International relations and large scale historical change', in A. J. R. Groom and M. Light (eds) *Contemporary International Relations: A Guide to Theory*, London: Pinter.

——(1995) 'International relations and the triumph of capitalism', in K. Booth and S. Smith (eds) *International Relations Theory Today*, Cambridge: Polity Press.

Lukes, S. (1974) *Power: A Radical View*, Basingstoke: Macmillan.

——(1975) *Emile Durkheim: His Life and Work*, Harmondsworth: Penguin.

McCormick, T. J. (1990) 'World systems', *Journal of American History*, 77, 1: 125–32.

MacKenzie, D. (1991) *Inventing Accuracy – A Historical Sociology of Nuclear Missile Guidance*, London: MIT Press.

McNeill, W. H. (1992) 'Review of Tilly's *Coercion, Capital and European States*', *Journal of Modern History*, 64, 3: 583–4.

Mann, M. (1973a) *Workers on the Move: The Sociology of Relocation*, Cambridge: Cambridge University Press.

——(1973b) *Consciousness and Action Among the Western Working Class*, London: Macmillan.

——(1981) 'Socio-logic', *Sociology*, 15, 4: 544–50.

——(1986a) *The Sources of Social Power, Volume I: A History of Power from the Beginning to AD 1760*, Cambridge: Cambridge University Press.

——(1986b) 'A crisis in stratification theory?', in R. Crompton and M. Mann (eds) *Gender and Stratification*, Cambridge: Polity Press.

——(1986c) 'Review of Wallerstein's *Politics of the World Economy*', *British Journal of Sociology*, 37, 1: 146–8.

——(1988) *States, War and Capitalism*, Oxford: Blackwell.

——(1991) 'Review of Tilly's *Coercion Capital and European States*', *American Journal of Sociology*, 96, 5: 1260–1.

——(1993a) *The Sources of Social Power, Volume II: The Rise of Classes and Nation States, 1760–1914*, Cambridge: Cambridge University Press.

——(1993b) 'Nation-states in Europe and other continents: diversifying, developing, not dying', *Daedalus*, 122, 3: 115–40.

——(1994) 'In praise of macro-sociology: a reply to Goldthorpe', *British Journal of Sociology*, 45, 1: 37–51.

——(1995) 'Review of Rosenberg's *The Empire of Civil Society*', *British Journal of Sociology*, 46, 3: 554–5.

——(1996) 'Authoritarian and liberal militarism: a contribution from comparative and historical sociology' in S. Smith, K. Booth and M. Zalewski (eds) *International Theory: Positivism and Beyond*, Cambridge: Cambridge University Press.

——(1997) 'Has globalization ended the rise and rise of the nation-state?', *Review of International Political Economy*, 4, 3: 472–96.

Marx, K. and Engels, F. (1977) *Manifesto of the Communist Party*, 2nd edn, Moscow: Progress Publishers.

Mokyr, J. (1991) 'Review of Wallerstein's *Modern World-System, Volume III*', *Theory and Society*, 20, 6: 895–9.

Moore, B. Jnr (1967) *Social Origins of Dictatorship and Democracy: Lord and Peasant in the Making of the Modern World*, Harmondsworth: Penguin.

——(1988) 'Review of Mann's *The Sources of Social Power, Volume I*', *History and Theory*, 27, 2: 169–77.

Morgenthau, H. J. (1960) *Politics Among Nations: The Struggle for Power and Peace*, 3rd edn, New York: Knopf.

——(1978) *Politics Among Nations: The Struggle for Power and Peace*, Fifth Edition, New York: Alfred A Knopf.

Motyl, A. (1992) 'Concepts and Skocpol: ambiguity and vagueness in the study of revolution', *Journal of Theoretical Politics*, 4, 1: 93–112.

Munz, P. (1991) 'How the west was won: miracle or natural event?', *Philosophy of the Social Sciences*, 21, 2: 253–76.

Navari, C. (1991) 'Introduction: the state as a contested concept in international relations', in C. Navari (ed.) *The Condition of States: A Study in International Political Theory*, Milton Keynes: Open University Press.

Northedge, F. S. (1976) *The International Political System*, London: Faber.

O'Brien, P. (1984) 'Europe in the world economy', in H. Bull and A. Watson (eds) *The Expansion of International Society*, Oxford: Clarendon Press.

Orloff, A. S. and Skocpol, T. (1984) 'Why not equal protection? Explaining the politics of public social spending in Britain, 1900–1911, and the United States, 1880–1920', *American Sociological Review*, 49, 6: 726–50.

Parsons, T. (1966) *Societies: Evolutionary and Comparative Perspectives*, Englewood Cliffs NJ: Prentice-Hall.

——(1971) *The System of Modern Societies*, Englewood Cliffs NJ: Prentice-Hall.

Pieterse, J. N. (1988) 'A critique of world-system theory', *International Sociology*, 3, 3: 251–66.

Puchala, D. J. (1995) 'The pragmatics of international history', *Mershon International Studies Review*, 39, 1: 1–18.

Ragin, C. and Chirot, D. (1984) 'The world-system of Immanuel Wallerstein: sociology and politics as history', in T. Skocpol (ed.) *Vision and Methodology in Historical Sociology*, Cambridge: Cambridge University Press.

Rasler, K. A. and Thompson, W. R. (1989) *War and State Making: The Shaping of the Global Powers*, Boston MA: Unwin Hyman.

Rengger, N. (1995) 'Review of Mann's *The Sources of Social Power, Volume II*', *Millennium*, 24, 1: 167–8.

Rosecrance, R. N. (1963) *Action and Reaction in World Politics: International Systems in Perspective*, Boston MA: Little, Brown.

Rosenau, J. N. (1970) *The Adaptation of National Societies: A Theory of Political System Behaviour and Transformation*, New York: McCaleb-Seiler.

Rosenberg, J. (1990) 'What's the matter with realism?', *Review of International Studies*, 16, 4: 285–303.

——(1994a) *The Empire of Civil Society: A Critique of the Realist Theory of International Relations*, London: Verso.

——(1994b) 'The international imagination: IR theory and "classic social analysis"', *Millennium*, 23, 1: 85–108.

Roth, G. (1976) 'History and sociology in the work of Max Weber', *British Journal of Sociology*, 27, 3: 306–18.

Roth, P. A. (1991) 'Truth in interpretation: the case of psychoanalysis', *Philosophy of the Social Sciences*, 21, 2: 175–95.

Ruggie, J. G. (1986) 'Continuity and transformation in the world polity: toward a neorealist synthesis', in R. O. Keohane (ed.) *Neorealism and its Critics*, New York: Columbia University Press.

Ryan, A. (1970) *The Philosophy of the Social Sciences*, Basingstoke: Macmillan.

Sanderson, S. K. (1988) 'The neo-Weberian revolution: a theoretical balance sheet', *Sociological Forum*, 3, 2: 307–14.

Scholte, J. A. (1993a) 'From power politics to social change: an alternative focus for international studies', *Review of International Studies*, 19, 1: 3–21.

——(1993b) *International Relations of Social Change*, Milton Keynes: Open University Press.

Schroeder, P. (1994) 'Historical reality vs. neo-realist theory', *International Security*, 19, 1: 108–48.

Sen, G. (1985) 'Review of Wallerstein's *The Politics of the World-Economy*', *Millennium*, 14, 1: 99–102.

Sewell, W. H. Jnr (1985) 'Ideologies and social revolutions: reflections on the French case', *Journal of Modern History*, 57, 1: 57–85.

Shimko, K. L. (1993) 'Realism, neorealism, and American liberalism', *Review of Politics*, 54, 2: 281–301.

Skocpol, T. (1973) 'A critical review of Barrington Moore's *Social Origins of Dictatorship and Democracy*', *Politics and Society*, 4, 1: 1–34.

——(1977) 'Wallerstein's *World Capitalist System*: a theoretical and historical critique', *American Journal of Sociology*, 82, 5: 1075–90.

——(1979) *States and Social Revolutions: A Comparative Analysis of France, Russia and China*, Cambridge: Cambridge University Press.

——(1982) 'Rentier state and Shi'a Islam in the Iranian Revolution', *Theory and Society*, 11, 3: 265–83.

——(1984) 'Sociology's historical imagination' in T. Skocpol (ed.) *Vision and Method in Historical Sociology*, Cambridge: Cambridge University Press.

——(1985) 'Cultural idioms and political ideologies in the revolutionary reconstruction of state power', *Journal of Modern History*, 57, 1: 86–96.

——(1987) 'Social history and historical sociology: contrasts and complementarities', *Social Science History Association*, 11, 1: 17–30.

——(1988a) 'An "uppity generation" and the revitalisation of macroscopic sociology', *Theory and Society*, 17, 5: 627–43.

——(1988b) 'Social revolutions and mass military mobilization', *World Politics*, 40, 2: 147–68.

——(1989) 'Reconsidering the French Revolution in world-historical perspective', *Social Research*, 56, 1: 53–70.

——(1992a) *Protecting Soldiers and Mothers: The Political Origins of Social Policy in the United States*, Cambridge MA: Belknap Press.

——(1992b) 'State formation and social policy in the United States', *American Behavioral Scientist*, 35, 4–5: 559–84.

——(1994a) 'Explaining social revolutions: first and further thoughts', in T. Skocpol (ed.) *Social Revolutions in the Modern World*, Cambridge: Cambridge University Press.

——(1994b) 'Reflections on recent scholarship about social revolutions and how to study them', in T. Skocpol (ed.) *Social Revolutions in the Modern World*, Cambridge: Cambridge University Press.

Smith, D. (1991) *The Rise of Historical Sociology*, Cambridge: Polity Press.

Smith, S. (1992) 'The forty years detour: the resurgence of normative theory in international relations', *Millennium*, 21, 3: 489–506.

Spruyt, H. (1994a) *The Sovereign State and its Competitors: An Analysis of Systems Change*, Princeton NJ: Princeton University Press.

——(1994b) 'Institutional selection in international relations: state anarchy as order', *International Organisation*, 48, 4: 527–57.

Stillman, P. G. (1987) 'Review of Mann's *The Sources of Social Power, Volume I*', *The International History Review*, 9, 2: 308–11.

Stinchcombe, A. L. (1982) 'Review of Wallerstein's *The Modern World System, Volume II*', *American Journal of Sociology*, 87, 6: 1389–95.

Strange, S. (1985) 'Review of Wallerstein's *The Politics of the World-Economy*', *International Affairs*, 61, 3: 497.

Taylor, P. J. (1994) 'Review of Tilly's *European Revolutions, 1492–1992*', *Journal of Historical Geography*, 20, 1: 87–113.

Thompson, K. (1982) *Emile Durkheim*, London: Tavistock.

Thompson, W. R. (1988) *On Global War: Historical Structural Approaches to World Politics*, Columbia SC: University of South Carolina Press.

Thomson, J. E. (1994) *Mercenaries, Pirates, and Sovereigns*, Princeton NJ: Princeton University Press.

——(1995) 'State sovereignty in international relations: bridging the gap between theory and empirical research', *International Studies Quarterly*, 39, 2: 213–33.

Tilly, C. (1964) *The Vendée*, London: Edward Arnold.

——(1975a) 'Reflections on the history of European state making', in C. Tilly (ed.) *The Formation of Nation States in Western Europe*, Princeton NJ: Princeton University Press.

——(1975b) 'Western state making and theories of political transformation', in C. Tilly (ed.) *The Formation of Nation States in Western Europe*, Princeton NJ: Princeton University Press.

——(1978) *From Mobilization to Revolution*, New York: McGraw Hill.

——(1981) *As Sociology Meets History*, New York: Academic Press.

——(1984) *Big Structures, Large Processes, Huge Comparisons*, New York: Russell Sage Foundation.

——(1985) 'War making and state making as organised crime', in P. Evans *et al.* (eds) *Bringing the State Back In*, Cambridge: Cambridge University Press.

——(1986) *The Contentious French*, Cambridge MA: Belknap Press.

——(1990) 'How (and what) are historians doing?', *American Behavioural Scientist*, 33, 6: 685–711.

——(1992a) *Coercion, Capital and European States, AD 990–1992*, revised paperback edn, Oxford: Blackwell.

——(1992b) 'Futures of European states', *Social Research*, 59, 4: 705–17.

——(1992c) 'War in history', *Sociological Forum*, 7, 1: 187–95.

——(1992d) 'Prisoners of the state', *International Social Science Journal*, 44, 3: 329–42.

——(1993) *European Revolutions 1492–1992*, Oxford: Blackwell.

——(1994) 'Entanglements of European cities and states', in C. Tilly and W. P. Blockmans (eds) *Cities and the Rise of States in Europe, AD 1000 to 1800*, Boulder CO: Westview.

Tooze, R. (1986) 'Review of Wallerstein's *The Politics of the World-Economy*', *Political Studies*, 34, 1: 175–6.

Vaughan, M. (1987) 'Historical leaps and sociological regularities: review of Mann's *The Sources of Social Power, Volume I*', *British Journal of Sociology*, 38, 3: 421–33.

Wallerstein, I. (1961) *Africa: The Politics of Independence*, New York: Vintage Books.

——(1964) *The Road to Independence: Ghana and the Ivory Coast*, The Hague: Mouton.

——(1966) *Social Change: The Colonial Situation*, New York: Wiley.

——(1967) *Africa: The Politics of Unity: An Analysis of a Contemporary Social Movement*, New York: Random House.

——(1974) *The Modern World-System, Volume I: Capitalist Agriculture and the Origins of the European World-Economy in the Sixteenth Century*, San Diego CA: Academic Press.

——(1979) *The Capitalist World-Economy*, Cambridge: Cambridge University Press.

——(1980a) *The Modern World-System, Volume II: Mercantilism and the Consolidation of the European World-Economy, 1600–1750*, San Diego CA: Academic Press.

——(1980b) 'The Future of the world-economy', in T. K. Hopkins and I. Wallerstein (eds) *Processes of the World-System*, Beverly Hills CA: Sage.

——(1980c) 'Friends as foes', *Foreign Policy*, 40: 119–31.

——(1984) *The Politics of the World-Economy: The States, the Movements, and the Civilisations*, Cambridge: Cambridge University Press.

——(1989) *The Modern World-System, Volume III: The Second Era of Great Expansion of the Capitalist World-Economy*, San Diego CA: Academic Press.

——(1991a) *Geopolitics and Geoculture: Essays on the Changing World-System*, Cambridge: Cambridge University Press.

——(1991b) *Unthinking Social Science: The Limits of Nineteenth-Century Paradigms*, Cambridge: Polity Press.

——(1992) 'The collapse of liberalism', in R. Miliband and L. Panitch (eds) *Socialist Register*, London: Merlin Press.

——(1993) 'The world-system after the Cold War', *Journal of Peace Research*, 30, 1: 1–6.

——(1996) 'The inter-state structure of the modern world-system', in S. Smith, K. Booth and M. Zalewski (eds) *International Theory: Positivism and Beyond*, Cambridge: Cambridge University Press.

Waltz, K. N. (1959) *Man, the State, and War: A Theoretical Analysis*, New York: Columbia University Press.

——(1979) *Theory of International Politics*, New York: Random House.

——(1986) 'Reflections on *Theory of International Politics*: a response to my critics', in R. O. Keohane (ed.) *Neorealism and its Critics*, New York: Columbia University Press.

——(1991) 'Realist thought and neorealist theory', in R. L. Rothstein (ed.) *The Evolution of Theory in International Relations: Essays in Honour of William T. R. Fox*, Columbia SC: University of South Carolina Press.

——(1993) 'The emerging structure of international politics', *International Security*, 18, 2: 44–79.

Washbrook, D. (1990) 'South Asia, the world system and world capitalism', *Journal of Asian Studies*, 49, 3: 479–508.

Watson, A. (1992) *The Evolution of International Society*, London: Routledge.

Weber, M. (1968) *Economy and Society: An Outline of Interpretive Sociology*, New York: Bedminster Press.

——(1976) *The Protestant Ethic and the Spirit of Capitalism*, London: Allen and Unwin.

Weltman, J. J. (1973) *Systems Theory in International Relations: A Study in Metaphoric Hypertrophy*, Lexington MA: Lexington Books.

Weiss, L. and Hobson, J. M. (1995) *States and Economic Development*, Cambridge: Polity Press.

Wendt, A. (1989) 'The agent-structure problem in international relations theory', *International Organization*, 43, 3: 335–70.

——(1991) 'Bridging the theory/meta-theory gap in international relations', *Review of International Studies*, 17, 4: 383–92.

Wheeler, N. (1993) 'Review of Buzan, Jones and Little's *The Logic of Anarchy*', *International Affairs*, 69, 4: 743–4.

Wickham, C. (1988) 'Historical materialism, historical sociology', *New Left Review*, 171: 63–78.

Worsley, P. (1980) 'One world or three? A critique of the world-system theory of Immanuel Wallerstein', *Socialist Register*, London: Merlin Press, 298–338.

Zolberg, A. R. (1981) 'Origins of the modern world-system: a missing link', *World Politics*, 33, 2: 253–81.

INDEX

Abbott, A. 25, 35–6
Abrams, P. 21, 22, 25, 28
Africa 142, 143, 160
agent–structure debate 60–3, 64, 76–7, 96–7, 157–8
Agnew, J. 7–8
Akkadia 123, 124
The Anarchical Society 44
anarchy 44, 47, 48–9, 54, 55, 58–9, 111, 113, 132, 134, 180
Anderson, P. 35, 109, 127, 129
Annales school 30, 32; influence on Wallerstein 144
L'Année Sociologique 23, 30
anthropology 32
anti-systemic movements 149, 151
archives 32
Ashley, R. K. 64–5
Austria 85, 126
autarky 144
authoritative power 119, 121, 129, 133

Badie, B. 77
balance of power 39, 137; Kaplan and 42; Morgenthau and 40; Rosecrance and 43; Wallerstein and 150, 161
Banks, J. A. 21
Baran, P. 143, 146
Bhaskar, R. 61
bipolar system 10, 35, 43, 54, 63, 65, 66–7, 180, 195
Bloch, M. 30, 31, 144
Booth, K. 2
borders *see* boundaries
bottom-up *see* individualistic accounts
boundaries: 'breaking down' 186, 187, 196; disciplinary 30, 32, 196; social

power and 120–1; state 4, 20, 67, 112, 120, 191
Braudel, F. 23, 24, 30, 31, 36, 186; influence on Wallerstein 144, 148; *la longue durée* 32; *The Mediterranean* 32–3
Brenner, R. 157
Britain: development of Historical Sociology in 25; example of capitalised coercion state 102; in inter-core rivalry 154; and opium war 85; state form 126, 192
Bryant, J. M. 24
Bull, H. 44–7, 108, 111, 113
Burke, P. 26
Buzan, B. 9, 11, 176, 177
Buzan, B., Jones, C. and Little, R. 66, 69, 84, 193–4; *The Logic of Anarchy* 58–60
Buzan, B. and Little, R. 11, 193

capital-intensive/coercion-sparse states 102, 105
capitalised-coercion state 102, 113
Cardoso, H. F. and Faletto, E. 35
Carr, E. H. 22
centre 143–4, 146, 147, 151; *see also* core
change: Cox and 63–4; Hegel and 27–8; in international system 10, 12, 19, 39, 41–3, 54, 56, 66, 67, 113, 118, 127, 140, 147–50, 164, 179, 190; Kant and 26–7; large-scale social 2, 3, 10, 11, 19, 21–2, 80–1; Mann and 121–2, 171; Marx and 29; Neorealism and 10, 12, 19, 39, 54, 56–9, 66–8, 164, 179, 190, 196; in

213

185, 195–6; Thomson and 190, 193;
Tilly and 13, 94–5, 97–8, 101,
106–16, 117, 170–1, 173–8, 185,
195–6; Wallerstein and 161–6,
172–3, 186, 196; Waltz and 6,
10–12, 47–57, 60–9, 179–85,
194–5; Watson and 45–6, 192–3
'interstitial emergence' 122, 128, 133,
187, 195
Iranian Revolution 75–6
Islam 75–6, 120
Italian city-states 102

James, P. 68
Japan 86, 87, 107, 155, 156; absence of
revolution 88, 89; rise of dictatorship
34
Jarvis, A. 5–6, 7

Kant, I. 26–7, 36
Kaplan, M. A. 12, 53; analysis of
international system 40–2, 46–7
Kasza, G. J. 103
Kennedy, P. 109
Keohane, R. O. 55–6, 58, 65
Kimmel, M. S. 158
Klink, F. F. 158
Knorr, K. 175
Kondratieff waves 148, 155
Kratochwil, F. 67

Latin America 35, 143, 160
Lehmann, D. 76
Lenin, V. I. 53, 143
Le Roy Ladurie, E. 144
Linklater, A. 2
Little, R. 2, 39; on Wallerstein 142,
161
The Logic of Anarchy 58–60; *see also*
Buzan, B., Jones, C. and Little, R.

McCormick, T. J. 144
McNeill, W. H. 103
macroscopic sociology 36
Malinowski, B. 32
Manifesto of the Communist Party 29
Mann, M. 8, 103, 117–41, 189, 191,
193; critics of 127–30; international
system and 13, 117–18, 130–41,
171–2, 173–8, 185, 187, 195–6;
origins of World War I 126; *The*

Sources of Social Power 118–27; state
and 118, 124, 125–6, 140, 171
Man, the State, and War 48–50, 66
marcher lords 123
Marshall, T. H. 34
Marx, K. 6, 25, 28–9, 35, 119, 122,
143
Marxism 1, 6–7, 9, 11, 48, 77, 82, 118,
146, 148; definition of capitalism
156–7; reductionism 53, 182; state
73, 92, 93, 125
medieval system 46, 56, 58–9, 113, 124
Mesopotamia 135–6
methodology 16; converging in History
and Sociology 23; Skocpol 70–1, 74,
78; Tilly 95; Wallerstein 143–4,
162; Weber 30–1
'metropolis-satellite' relationship 144
'military-fiscal extraction' 135
military power 121, 123, 129, 133, 171
Mill, J. S.: system of logic 71
modernisation theories 82, 143
modern world-system 146–56; anti-
systemic movements in 149, 151;
contradictions in 148–9, 152, 155,
157, 164; core of 144, 146–7, 151,
152, 153, 154, 161, 166, 172; crisis
of 148, 149–50, 151, 155, 156, 172;
cyclical rhythms in 148;
determinism of 150, 152, 158;
'geoculture' of 151–2; hegemony in
150–1, 153–4, 161; and interstate
system 150; periphery of 143–4,
146–7, 151, 160, 166, 172; secular
trends in 148; semiperiphery of 146,
147, 152, 154, 155, 161, 172;
socialist states and 155–6, 160–1;
spatial dimensions of 146–7;
temporal dimensions of 147–50;
unequal exchange in 147, 160
The Modern World-System 145–56
Mokyr, J. 142
Montesquieu, C. 25
Moore, B. Jnr 33–4, 74; criticisms of
Mann 128, 129; criticised by
Skocpol 80–1; influence on Skocpol
34, 71
Morgenthau, H. J. 12, 39–40, 48, 175
Motyl, A. 77
Mozambique 75
multipolar system 10, 43, 54, 66, 180
multi-power-actor civilisation 123,

INDEX

United Nations Economic Commission
for Latin America (UNECLA) 143–4
United States 156; development of
Historical Sociology in 25;
hegemony 154; social policy 79–80;
structural power 161; War of
Independence 85–6, 154, 169
universal history 36
urbanisation 94, 95–6

Vaughan, M. 127
The Vendée 95–6
verstehen 16
Vietnam 161

Wallerstein, I. 13, 84, 108, 109, 130,
142–66; compared with Waltz
163–5; critics of 156–61; influences
on 143–5; international system
161–6, 172–6, 186, 196; *The Modern
World-System* 145–56; criticised by
Skocpol 81; state and 150 154, 158,
164–5, 166, 173, 177, 178
Waltz, K. 8, 11–12, 47–54, 60–9, 84,
109, 111, 134, 175; compared with
Wallerstein 163–5; critics of 55–7,
60–5; international system 6, 10–12,
47–57, 60–9, 179–85, 194–5; *Man,
the State, and War* 48–50;
reductionism and 47, 50, 52–3, 66,
182; role of theory 50–2; state and
10, 12, 38–9, 48, 54, 64 65–9, 182;
Theory of International Politics 50–5,
194–5
war: focus on in Historical Sociology 9;

linked to state formation 12,
98–102, 110, 115, 124; Mann and
124, 135; Skocpol and 12, 71, 73,
88–93, 169–70, 175–6, 190–1; Tilly
and 98–102, 170–1, 110–16; Waltz
and 48–50
Washbrook, D. 160, 161
Watson, A. 45–6, 47, 192–3
Weber, M. 25 30–1, 119; state and 2, 8,
125, 190; *The Protestant Ethic and the
Spirit of Capitalism* 30; *verstehen* 16
Wendt, A. 62–3, 163
Wickham, C. 127, 129
world-economy 83, 145, 164, 172;
distinction from world-empire
145–6; modern world-system as
example of 146–56; *see also* modern
world-system
world-empire 145, 150, 172, 178;
distinction from world-economy
145–6
world-historical time 73, 83, 84, 85,
89, 132, 169
world-system 143, 148–52, 161–6;
defined 145; modern 146–7, 152–6
world-system theory: compared to
dependency theory 144; critics of
156–61; determinism of 158, 166,
185, 195
World War I 86, 88, 192; analysis of
origins 126
Worsley, P. 157, 160

Zolberg, A. R. 159